Date Due

Dryden's Criticism

Dryden's Criticism

ROBERT D. HUME
CORNELL UNIVERSITY

Cornell University Press / ITHACA AND LONDON

First published 1970

International Standard Book Number 0-8014-0585-8

Library of Congress Catalog Card Number 70-124725

PRINTED IN THE UNITED STATES OF AMERICA
BY VAIL-BALLOU PRESS, INC.

For Maurice Johnson

Preface

As an important figure in the history of English criticism, Dryden deserves more scrutiny than he has received. A few of his works have been studied closely —notably *Of Dramatic Poesy*—but no full-scale account of his criticism has yet appeared. My object is to fill this need. Rather than offering a descriptive-chronological treatment of Dryden's rather scrappy critical corpus, I have preferred to focus on some problems which transcend the tangles and inconsistencies of his specific judgments. Chapters 1 through 3 assess Dryden's critical aims and methods; chapters 4 and 5 place them in the context of his age; chapter 6 is a demonstration of the essential stability of his principles.

Dryden presents the scholar with many difficulties. To generalize blurs vital distinctions; to focus closely on single works leaves one floundering in a welter of apparently contradictory details. Certainly Dryden needs to be viewed in his intellectual context, but all too often (especially in literary histories) such considerations rest on vague assumptions about "neoclassical" orthodoxy and revolt against it. At their best, general discussions of Dryden can be helpful. James Sutherland's recent volume of the Oxford History is refreshingly sane, and T. S. Eliot's famous essay, though sketchy and impressionistic, is a charming appreciation. But no brief account can begin to do justice to the complexities of the subject.[1] Probably the most useful studies have been those which concentrate on single works or problems. John M. Aden, Dean T. Mace, John C. Sherwood, and Hoyt Trowbridge have all made important contributions; Frank Livingstone Huntley's *On Dryden's Essay of Dramatic Poesy* (1951) is a landmark in the explicative mode; recent attention to Dryden's critical vocabulary is welcome.[2] Inevitably though, all these studies reflect their authors' limited purposes and perspectives: an overview has long been in order.

Dryden's frequent borrowings and adaptations are a major problem.[3] George Watson comments glumly that

1. James Sutherland, *English Literature of the Late Seventeenth Century* (Oxford, 1969), chap. 11; T. S. Eliot, *John Dryden: The Poet, the Dramatist, the Critic* (New York, 1932). Perhaps the best such study is Arthur C. Kirsch's brief Introduction to his selection, *Literary Criticism of John Dryden* (Lincoln, Nebraska, 1966).

2. See especially Barbara M. H. Strang, "Dryden's Innovations in Critical Vocabulary," *DUJ*, n.s. 20 (1959), 114–123; H. James Jensen, *A Glossary of John Dryden's Critical Terms* (Minneapolis, 1969); and articles by Aden and Thale discussed in more detail later. Special attention should be called to a crisply readable monograph by Max Nänny, *John Drydens rhetorische Poetik* (Bern, 1959).

3. See particularly John M. Aden, "Dryden and Boileau: The Question of Critical Influence," *SP*, 50 (1953), 491–509, "Dryden and Saint Evremond," *CL*, 6 (1954), 232–239, "Dryden, Corneille, and the *Essay of Dramatic Poesy*," *RES*, n.s. 6 (1955), 147–156;

"there are moments when one feels as if every major English critic has some Continental skeleton in his cupboard" [4]—and certainly a literary archeologist can find enough such bones in Dryden's criticism to furnish out a fair-sized museum. But Dryden's pilfering is generally creative, and we would be foolish to expect of a Restoration writer what we find in later ages. Dryden's ideas and vocabulary are for the most part far from original, as any casual browser through contemporary English and French criticism can easily see. For my purposes though, what matters is not where Dryden found his material, but what he managed to do with it. And to accept resemblance as proof of borrowing or influence is risky. Aden's articles are a salutary lesson: we need to assess the use to which apparently borrowed material is put and consider differences as well as resemblances before we leap to conclusions.

In any case, my questions concern what Dryden was trying to do rather than the particulars of what he said. [5] By themselves, Dryden's critical opinions have little more than historical and curiosity value, for rightly or not we

John C. Sherwood, "The Sources of John Dryden's Critical Essays," unpubl. diss. (Yale, 1944), "Dryden and the Critical Theories of Tasso," CL, 18 (1966), 351–359; Pierre Legouis, "Corneille and Dryden as Dramatic Critics," in *Seventeenth-Century Studies Presented to Sir Herbert Grierson* (Oxford, 1938), pp. 269–291; Marvin T. Herrick, *The Poetics of Aristotle in England* (New Haven, 1930); A. F. B. Clark, *Boileau and the French Classical Critics in England* (Paris, 1925).

4. *The Literary Critics* (Baltimore, 1962), p. 16.

5. In this approach I am obviously indebted to the position sketched out by R. S. Crane in "On Writing the History of Criticism in England, 1650–1800," UTQ, 22 (1953), 376–391, reprinted in *The Idea of the Humanities*, 2 vols. (Chicago, 1967), II, 157–175.

[ix]

believe that we understand his subjects better than he did. Consequently we tend to allow him some patronizing praise for anticipating—far more than Rymer, say—some of our judgments. But Dryden's opinions make sense and are worth serious consideration only when they are treated as part of a coherent and sophisticated view of literature. I hope to increase our understanding of this outlook by analyzing Dryden's critical concerns and assumptions, seeking the terms in which we can best discuss them.

An earlier form of the first section of chapter 4 appeared in *The Review of English Studies*, n.s. 19 (1968), and is reprinted, with some modifications, by permission of the Clarendon Press.

My thanks are due Arthur H. Scouten and James L. Rosier for useful criticism and advice.

A NOTE ON TEXTS AND DATES

The most comprehensive edition of Dryden's criticism (which also has the merit of being available) is that of George Watson, *Of Dramatic Poesy and Other Critical Essays*, 2 vols. (London, 1962). Watson has supplanted W. P. Ker's long-standard *Essays of John Dryden*, 2 vols. (Oxford, 1900; reprinted 1926), now out of print. Both Watson and Ker modernize their texts. Samuel Holt Monk's *Of Dramatic Poesy and Other Prose Writings* (vol. 17 of the "California" edition of Dryden) should be available soon and will presumably become the definitive text for the works it contains.

Quotations from Dryden are from Watson's edition, identified by volume number and page, normally in parentheses in the text. Quotations from contemporary critics (except Rymer and Dennis) are when possible from J. E.

[x]

Spingarn's convenient, unmodernized collection, *Critical Essays of the Seventeenth Century*, 3 vols. (Oxford, 1908–1909). Quotations from Rymer are from the excellent, unmodernized edition by Curt A. Zimansky, *The Critical Works of Thomas Rymer* (New Haven, 1956). Quotations from Dennis are from *The Critical Works of John Dennis*, ed. Edward Niles Hooker, 2 vols. (Baltimore, 1939, 1943), which is likewise unmodernized.

Dates given for the critical essays (including prefaces and dedications) are those of first publication unless otherwise indicated. The dates given for plays (when no critical material is involved) are those of first performance.

ROBERT D. HUME

Cornell University
September 1970

Contents

A Chronological List of Dryden's Major Critical Essays

Dedication of *The Rival Ladies* (1664)
An Essay of Dramatic Poesy (written 1665–1666? pub. 1668)
Preface to *Annus Mirabilis* (1667)
A Defence of *An Essay of Dramatic Poesy* (1668)
Preface to *The Tempest* (1670)
Preface to *Tyrannic Love* (1670)
Preface to *An Evening's Love* (1671)
An Essay of Heroic Plays (1672)
Defence of the Epilogue to *The Conquest of Granada*, Part II (1672)
Notes and Observations on The Empress of Morocco (1674; probably a collaboration with Shadwell and John Crowne; authorship disputed)
Dedication of *Aureng-Zebe* (1676)
The Author's Apology for Heroic Poetry and Poetic Licence, prefaced to *The State of Innocence* (1677)
Heads of an Answer to Rymer (marginalia, pub. 1711; probably written in late 1677)
Preface to *All for Love* (1678)
Preface to *Troilus and Cressida*   } (published together
The Grounds of Criticism in Tragedy   } in 1679)

Preface to *Ovid's Epistles* (1680)
Dedication of *The Spanish Friar* (1681)
The Vindication of the Duke of Guise (1683)
The Life of Plutarch (1683)
Preface to *Sylvæ* (1685)
Preface to *Albion and Albanius* (1685)
Preface to *Don Sebastian* (1690)
Dedication of *Eleonora* (1692; "To the Earl of Abingdon")
The Character of Polybius (1693)
A Discourse Concerning the Original and Progress of Satire (1693)
Dedication of the *Examen poeticum* (1693)
A Parallel of Poetry and Painting (1695)
The Life of Lucian (written c. 1696; pub. 1711)
Dedication of the *Aeneis* (1697)
Preface to *Fables Ancient and Modern* (1700)

Detailed references to Dryden's opinions and terms can be found in John M. Aden, *The Critical Opinions of John Dryden: A Dictionary* (Nashville, Tenn., 1963); H. James Jensen, *A Glossary of John Dryden's Critical Terms* (Minneapolis, 1969); and the index of Watson's edition.

Abbreviations

CL   Comparative Literature
DUJ   Durham University Journal
ECS   Eighteenth-Century Studies
ELH   A Journal of English Literary History
JEGP   Journal of English and Germanic Philology
JWCI   Journal of the Warburg and Courtauld Institute
MLN   Modern Language Notes
MP   Modern Philology
N&Q   Notes and Queries
OED   The Oxford English Dictionary
PLL   Papers on Language and Literature
PMLA   Publications of the Modern Language Association
PQ   Philological Quarterly
RES   The Review of English Studies
RLV   Revue des Langues Vivantes
SEL   Studies in English Literature (Rice University)
ShS   Shakespeare Survey
SP   Studies in Philology
SR   Sewanee Review
UTQ   University of Toronto Quarterly

Dryden's Criticism

CHAPTER 1

Dryden's Critical Endeavor

What does Dryden set out to accomplish in his criticism? Many studies have been made of what Dryden said and the sources he drew on, but little consideration has been given to the *sort* of criticism he produced. His essays do not easily fit the critical kinds to which we are now accustomed: assessing his work we find that the father of English criticism did not practice the art as we know it. Any undergraduate ought to be able to produce a better examen than Dryden's on *The Silent Woman*, and even by mid-eighteenth-century standards his grasp of literary history, psychology, and critical biography is rudimentary— but it is hard not to agree, reading through his criticism, that he is astonishingly good at something.

Dryden has often been praised as a great appreciator, and correctly so, for he was able to enjoy a wide variety of literature and discuss it in a delightfully readable style. This led some older critics to claim that Dryden was an intuitive reader and a rebel against "rules." [1] But Samuel

1. For example, George Saintsbury, *A History of Criticism and Literary Taste in Europe*, 3 vols. (London, 1900–1904), II, 372–

Johnson could say that it was Dryden who first taught the English to criticize by rule,[2] and such modern critics as Trowbridge and Sherwood have demonstrated that Dryden did indeed work comfortably within a framework of "rules," or objective, rational standards.[3] Nonetheless, very little of Dryden's criticism is "prescriptive"; he is no procrustean believer in absolute standards. So we can agree happily with Sherwood that Dryden is not the prisoner of the rules, but rather uses them for his own ends—but we may well want to enquire what these may be. The particular ends of the major essays have been analyzed and argued over, but no one, to my knowledge, has seriously considered what sort of enterprise is involved. Actually, his various critical efforts are quite disparate in kind. By no means are Dryden's aims and methods identical throughout; hence by paying attention to the variety of his purposes, we can make his apparent inconsistencies far more comprehensible.

I

Dryden's criticism (excepting *Of Dramatic Poesy*) is occasional and reflects the quarrels and concerns of the

---

373; E. M. W. Tillyard, "A Note on Dryden's Criticism," in R. F. Jones and others, *The Seventeenth Century: Studies in the History of English Thought and Literature from Bacon to Pope* [Jones Festschrift] (Stanford, 1951), pp. 330–338.
 2. *Lives of the Poets*, ed. G. B. Hill (Oxford, 1905), I, 410–411.
 3. Hoyt Trowbridge, "The Place of Rules in Dryden's Criticism," *MP*, 44 (1946), 84–96; John C. Sherwood, "Dryden and the Rules: The Preface to *Troilus and Cressida*," *CL*, 2 (1950), 73–83, "Dryden and the Rules: The Preface to the *Fables*," *JEGP*, 52 (1953), 13–26, "Precept and Practice in Dryden's Criticism," *JEGP*, 68 (1969), 432–440.

[2]

moment. It is more commercial work than a labor of love: Dryden defends the plays and translations by which he helped support himself, and he lends his name to help his publisher Tonson sell the work of others. His indifference to a subject is sometimes plain, as in his brief and slapdash "Character of St. Evremond" (1692), in which he spends much of his time criticizing St. Evremond's views on Virgil. But in general Dryden's prefatory essays, dedications, prologues, and the like record his responses to the literary practice and problems of his age.

Dryden's sincerity (or honesty) is difficult to judge. George Watson sees Dryden as timid and conformist, afraid to say outright what he really felt.[4] Certainly Dryden is usually cautious about provoking critical quarrels,[5] and his fulsome dedications to a variety of patrons do not strike us as heartfelt, except in their appeal for funds. One cannot imagine Dryden writing a letter of proud refusal to Lord Chesterfield. He took what he could get, late or not, and was glad of it. We doubt that Dryden thought Anne Killigrew a great poetess, and the modern reader may wince at the "Panegyrical Poem" on the late Countess of Abingdon (1692), especially when Dryden mentions that he found the commission harder because he had never known or seen the lady (II, 61), but Donne carried out

4. *The Literary Critics* (Baltimore, 1962); *Of Dramatic Poesy and Other Critical Essays*, 2 vols. (New York, 1962), I, xiii–xiv. Quotations from the book *Of Dramatic Poesy and Other Critical Essays* by John Dryden, edited by George Watson, Everyman's Library, 1962, are reprinted by permission of E. P. Dutton & Co., Inc., and J. M. Dent & Sons Ltd.

5. Note though that he can be truculently disputatious in his controversial works, such as his "Defence of *An Essay*" (1668) or *The Vindication of the Duke of Guise* (1683).

[3]

commissions on similar terms, and his "sincerity" is seldom called in question. We simply have to accept the conditions and literary conventions of the age. Dryden's immediate purpose in much of his criticism is self-recommendation, and, as Kirsch notes of his writings on the heroic play, "he was inclined to emphasize his innovations and minimize his debts." [6] Nonetheless, we can find some stable convictions and interests reflected in Dryden's criticism; we should not mistake his lack of dogmatism and his readiness to appreciate many kinds of writing for lack of genuine convictions.

The break in literary, particularly dramatic, tradition imposed by the Commonwealth period was certainly one of the factors which encouraged the growth of literary criticism in the Restoration. Its rise suggests a self-consciousness about art that Renaissance writers did not feel to nearly the same degree. Dryden and his contemporaries have a conscious sense of making a new start and being able to explore a variety of options. Ben Jonson could cry up classical precedent, but he had to work within the limits of an established theater. Restoration writers were without the restrictions—and benefits—of such active tradition. Concerning his endeavor in the *Essay of Dramatic Poesy* Dryden said, long afterward:

I was drawing the outlines of an art without any living master to instruct me in it . . . before the use of the loadstone, or knowledge of the compass, I was sailing in a vast ocean, without other help than the pole-star of the Ancients, and the rules of the French stage amongst the Moderns, which are extremely different from ours, by reason of their opposite taste" [II, 73–74].

6. Arthur C. Kirsch, *Dryden's Heroic Drama* (Princeton, 1965), p. 4.

[4]

The profusion of new forms in both comedy and serious drama is evidence of the experimental and innovative nature of early Restoration writing. We must not, then, neglect the exploratory function of Restoration criticism.

Dryden's criticism in the 1660s and 1670s is largely a response to a practical problem: how should the English be writing plays? He is busy on the one hand asking what should be done (*Of Dramatic Poesy*, "Apology for Heroic Poetry," "Heads of an Answer to Rymer"), and on the other defending what he has in fact done (Preface to *An Evening's Love*, "An Essay of Heroic Plays"). To a considerable extent Dryden is feeling his way, creating and adopting standards as he goes along. He sees himself as part of a European tradition which stretches back to Greece and Rome, and quite naturally he looks to the Ancients and the French for help. But writing in a different tongue, age, and clime, Dryden feels that he cannot adopt the practices of the Ancients outright. Although he draws willingly on Tasso and the French, he always maintains that national differences are considerable. Dryden shares the widespread Restoration resistance to French influence on patriotic grounds: *Of Dramatic Poesy*, for instance, though it offers in Lisideius an effective proponent of the French, seems to be at least in part an attempt to vindicate the English stage against French strictures.[7] Dryden's admiration for his

7. George Williamson, in "The Occasion of *An Essay of Dramatic Poesy*," *MP*, 44 (1946), 1–9, says that Dryden is replying to Samuel Sorbière's *Relation d'un voyage en Angleterre* (1664), which attacked English drama for neglect of rime and the unities. Dryden, in his notice "To The Reader," says: "The drift of the ensuing discourse was chiefly to vindicate the honour of our English writers from the censure of those who unjustly prefer the French before them" (I, 17). But this is by no means a full or balanced assessment of his concerns in the essay.

Elizabethan predecessors is great, but his belief in the more refined nature of his age always makes him chary of following them too closely, even after he has come to rate their efforts above those of the Restoration. These attitudes, considered together, form what we find a peculiar blend of empiricism and authority. Dryden's liking for objective, rational standards—rules in the broadest sense of the term—is not easy for us to appreciate, and the specific issues which recur in his criticism are sometimes hard to take seriously. To us the great rime controversy appears farcical and the heroic plays which Dryden defends so passionately seem no more than historical curiosities. We find it easier to admire the later criticism (mostly 1680–1700), in which Dryden is less involved with the Restoration stage and more often concerned with the work of other writers.

To look for a tidy pattern in the development of Dryden's criticism is ultimately pointless. He never tried to work out a formal aesthetic, and his comments on the practice of criticism amount to no more than some scattered commonplaces. His critical work is incidental, an adjunct to other writings that are themselves directed by economic and political factors. (Dryden's increasing preoccupation with translation, for instance, reflects neither burning interest nor a poetic falling-off so much as economic necessity.) What we can most usefully do is to distinguish the different sorts of critical enterprises in which he engages.

I would like to suggest that Dryden's critical work can conveniently be placed in three categories: speculative (*Of Dramatic Poesy*, "Heads of an Answer to Rymer"); prescriptive ("The Grounds of Criticism in Tragedy," "A Parallel of Poetry and Painting"); and explanatory, covering the vast majority of his critical efforts. In the third category I would make a further distinction between Dryden's justifications of his own work and his analyses of the work of others. Such categories are far from absolute. The "Defence of *An Essay of Dramatic Poesy*" (1668), for instance, is a short-tempered justification of his work against Howard's criticisms, but it also clarifies and extends the *Essay*. And few pieces are without any self-recommendation or some literary theorizing. Nor need we downgrade the "justificatory" essays, for they contain some of Dryden's freshest ideas. But in discussing the criticism it is handy to be able to note, for example, that the "Heads of an Answer to Rymer" and "The Grounds of Criticism in Tragedy," which have often been called two versions of the same enterprise, actually have quite different aims and critical orientations.[8] Failure to make such distinctions can lead to serious misreadings of both essays. At this point I want to discuss each of Dryden's critical modes in some detail, trying to show just how different they are.

Only two pieces of Dryden's criticism are sufficiently removed from his other work to be called genuinely speculative. In them he enquires how a drama should be constructed. *Of Dramatic Poesy* was written at the outset of his dramatic career (1665–1666?) and represents his initial exploration of the field. The "Heads of an Answer to Rymer" is not formal criticism at all, but merely a series of notes written in a copy of Rymer's *The Tragedies of the Last Age*. Both works are exciting for their sense of exploration and freedom from rigid preconceptions. In them we see Dryden examining possibilities rather than proving points or trying to reach firm conclusions, though how literally we should take Dryden's disclaimers of legislative intent in

8. For a detailed discussion of this point, see chap. 4, sec. I.

Of Dramatic Poesy is arguable.[9] Certainly Neander is allowed the last word in the second and third exchanges, and the balance of the argument seems to lie on his side. But as David Nichol Smith says, Dryden "states contradictory views, and very fairly, as they are all tenable. If we suspect how his preferences lay, we note his freedom from the didactic manner which was common in earlier criticism.[10] Only the first of the three exchanges is explicitly judged: we are told that Eugenius "seemed to have the better of the argument" (I, 43). Dryden's support of the Moderns here is in line with one of his most stable convictions. Neander's position undoubtedly comes closest to representing Dryden's beliefs at this time, but in the positions of the others we can see fragments of opinions and ideas that he would later embrace. In the "Defence of *An Essay*" (also published in 1668) Dryden lays claim to what he calls "my definition of a play" (I, 122), which is presented by Lisideius in the *Essay* (I, 25).

What Dryden does in *Of Dramatic Poesy* is to sketch out some possible positions. Each one is coherent and reasonably self-contained, which makes the essay unique in Dryden's criticism. His concern is as always ultimately practical. But whereas normally his response is syncretic—

9. "I will give your Lordship the relation of a dispute betwixt some of our wits . . . neither do I take upon me to reconcile, but to relate them" (I, 16). "This I intimate, lest any should think me so exceeding vain as to teach others an art which they understand much better than myself" (I, 17). "My whole discourse was sceptical, according to that way of reasoning which was used by Socrates, Plato, and all the Academics of old. . . . It is a dialogue sustained by persons of several opinions, all of them left doubtful, to be determined by the readers in general" ("Defence of *An Essay*," I, 123).

10. *John Dryden* (Cambridge, England, 1950), p. 13.

[8]

he lumps together what seems best in the various positions —here he keeps the positions discrete. This separation is, I think, one of the best arguments for calling *Of Dramatic Poesy* exploratory rather than legislative in intent.

The "Heads of an Answer to Rymer," Dryden's other speculative work, consists of debater's notes, outlines of arguments: "He who undertakes to answer this excellent critique of Mr Rymer, in behalf of our English poets against the Greek, ought to do it in this manner" (I, 211). Again, Dryden is examining possibilities. First, Rymer's premises might be denied; next, his conclusions might be challenged in the light of theatrical experience; finally, it might be claimed that English and Greek writers emphasize different parts of drama. The subject is that of the *Essay:* how should English drama be constructed? Rymer had criticized "Fletcher's" practice; Dryden examines—and basically upholds—Rymer's premises while trying to mitigate the harshness of his censure.

Dryden's prescriptive criticism is strikingly different from his speculative work, and clearly does not show him at his best. Abstract problems seem to make him uncomfortable, and he generally prefers to deal with specific details of language, plot, character, and theatrical convention. Only twice (in "The Grounds of Criticism in Tragedy" and "A Parallel of Poetry and Painting") does he try to lay down general rules in formal, legislative criticism. Dryden's lack of ease in such work is made clear by the extent of his borrowings. He seldom borrows heavily except when he is passing on biographical or historical facts (e.g., "The Character of Polybius," and the Dedication of the *Aeneis*), or when he is in need of general principles. That Dryden turns immediately to the French for such principles seems

[9]

clear proof that, as he might put it, his genius is not for literary theory. This is not to say that his prescriptive works are bad, or that he did not believe what he said, but merely that critical legislation was not one of his principal interests and did not fully engage or display his critical powers.

"The Grounds of Criticism in Tragedy," prefacing his adaptation of Shakespeare's *Troilus and Cressida* (1679), is a response to a practical problem. Dryden wishes "to inquire how far we ought to imitate our own poets, Shakespeare and Fletcher" (I, 243). But here he undertakes to supply a formal, prescriptive answer, not a series of sceptical speculations. His procedure is to lay down Aristotelian precepts (mostly taken from Rapin and Le Bossu), and then to extract the more "classical" parts from Shakespeare and Fletcher, trying to preserve them as models. He concludes that "we ought to follow them so far only as they have copied the excellencies of those who invented and brought to perfection dramatic poetry," excepting those things altered by religion, laws, and "customs of countries" (I, 246).

To see what this rather vague prescription means one can read Dryden's dismemberment of *Troilus and Cressida* (of which "The Grounds" is in part a justification), or better, *All for Love*, which attempts to "follow" Shakespeare while improving on him, and probably comes closest, among all of Dryden's plays, to embodying the dramatic theory of his maturity.[11] He said much later that "I never writ anything for myself but *Anthony and Cleopatra*"

11. See Ruth Wallerstein, "Dryden and the Analysis of Shakespeare's Techniques," *RES*, 19 (1943), 165–185.

(meaning *All for Love;* see "A Parallel of Poetry and Painting," II, 207). The play certainly displays in practice the syncretic methodology of "The Grounds of Criticism in Tragedy," as Dryden makes plain in his preface: "I have endeavoured in this play to follow the practice of the Ancients, who, as Mr Rymer has judiciously observed, are and ought to be our masters. . . . Yet, though their models are regular, they are too little for English tragedy, which requires to be built in a larger compass." In "style" Dryden has "professed to imitate the divine Shakespeare" (I, 230–231), but he has kept an eye on French notions of decorum and unity: "The fabric of the play is regular enough . . . and the unities of time, place, and action more exactly observed than, perhaps, the English theatre requires" (I, 222). In practice as in theory Dryden is trying to have the best of all worlds.

In "The Grounds of Criticism in Tragedy" Dryden uses French theory to assess the worth of Shakespeare and Fletcher. The result, interestingly, is not denigration of the English poets, but praise for them. As Sherwood says, Shakespeare "emerges as a poet endowed with a multitude of neoclassical virtues; his manners are 'apparent' and appropriate, his thoughts are natural, his characters distinguished, he can move terror, and he can 'prepare' a passion." [12] Dryden finds Shakespeare's language dated and unrefined and his plots defective, but can admire his thoughts and characters. The prescriptive theory of the essay is not original with Dryden and therefore has little interest for us; nonetheless we should note that it in no way diminishes his appreciation of Shakespeare. A French critic

12. Sherwood, *CL*, p. 82.

would probably not have come out with the same conclusions in assessing Shakespeare, but Dryden gets what he wants from French, Ancients, and Elizabethans.

"A Parallel of Poetry and Painting" (1695) is a piece of hastily executed hack work. Dryden pads it with long quotations from Bellori (c. 1615–1696; an Italian critic), and his borrowings from French critics are frequent. The interest of the essay lies in its explicit elaboration of the case for "ideal" imitation in art. This idea, which can be traced back in Dryden's work to *Of Dramatic Poesy*, is central to his theory of heroic drama as outlined in "Of Heroic Plays" (1672) and the "Apology for Heroic Poetry" (1677). But here he undertakes to justify rules, classical precedent, and ideal imitation in a formal way. Although Dryden certainly believed in what he had to say, the essay remains a slightly laborious compilation of commonplaces. It is important for what it tells us about his later thoughts on imitation, though as a piece of criticism it is no great success. Even in this essay Dryden is not primarily concerned with abstract principles; he puts them together tidily enough, but he does little more with them than did the critics from whom he has borrowed.

In his speculative work Dryden examines possibilities; in his prescriptive essays he tries to lay down general rules. In the bulk of his criticism, however, Dryden is more specifically pragmatic, concentrating on particular works, types, or authors. I call this explanatory criticism because its primary function is to help the reader understand the subject. Dryden's attention is still directed to the craft of the writing, but his explanations seem meant for the reader, not for himself or other writers. In such works as the Preface to *Tyrannic Love*, "Of Heroic Plays," and the Preface to *All for Love*, he explains what he has done and why and justifies his practice, usually against fairly specific (rather than theoretical) standards. In the later criticism, which is less often related to his own creations (e.g., the Preface to *Ovid's Epistles*, "The Life of Plutarch," the "Discourse on Satire," the Dedication of the *Aeneis*, the Preface to *Fables*) his purposes become even more purely analytic and explanatory: he is sharing his skill in reading with his audience.

Dryden's perspective in this sort of criticism is of particular interest. Earlier English critics look at the utility of literature (Sidney, Bacon, Henry Reynolds) or more usually the ways of writing it (Wilson, Puttenham, Jonson, Davenant). To Dryden belongs the credit of initiating in England the move toward the appreciative criticism which would later find its first systematic expression in the affective theories of Addison.[13] Dryden is still talking about what writers do, rather than how the audience responds, but unlike his predecessors, he is no longer explaining how to write.

Presumably Dryden's practice in justifying his own work was his training for explaining the productions of others. Certainly his method carries over. Dryden's aim in his earlier criticism is almost always the recommendation or defense of a play, but the relative amounts of general explanation and specific justification vary. The Preface to *An Evening's Love* (1671) contains a typical mingling of these elements. Dryden starts by noting the difference of Renaissance and Restoration in refinement—for he plans to

13. See Clarence D. Thorpe, "Addison's Contribution to Criticism," in R. F. Jones and others, *The Seventeenth Century*, pp. 316–329.

praise Ben Jonson, but justify departures from his practice. The bulk of the essay falls into three sections, plus a conclusion. First, Dryden differentiates comedy from farce, using Hobbesian psychological distinctions to back up his value judgments. Then he praises Ben Jonson, but with the qualification that heightened imitation is preferable to "the natural imitation of folly." Third, Dryden defends (with reference to Jonson and the Ancients) his own preference for ridiculing rather than punishing vice. In conclusion, he explains his belief that the actions, passions, and language are of greater import than the mere story. This last point has a dual purpose: it helps excuse Dryden for borrowing his plots, and it reinforces his emphasis on heightened imitation as the principal business of the author. Dryden's concerns here are practical and concrete. His appeals are to example, psychology, and to utilitarian definition of what different types of drama are to *do*. Thus his reference to "the rules of tragedy and comedy" is pragmatic, not theoretical in origin.

A similar organization can be found in "Of Heroic Plays" (1672). Again, Dryden discusses the genre (here with reference to Davenant), arguing for imitation of the "highest pattern of human life" rather than "a bare representation of what is true, or exceeding probable" (I, 161–162). Defending a new form, Dryden appeals, perhaps misleadingly, to an epic parallel, invoking among others the names of Petronius, Davenant, Horace, Homer, Virgil, Statius, Ariosto, Tasso, Spenser, Hobbes, and Cowley. Finally Dryden defends Almanzor, out of his own *Conquest of Granada*, as a pattern of heroic virtue by comparing him with Achilles.

Dryden's method in this sort of criticism is to explain

what he has tried to do, using as a standard of reference some basic assumptions, stated or implied, about the kind of work he is writing. These assumptions concern the rules "for imitating nature rightly" (I, 122); the point of the imitation is to rouse the desired effect in the reader or audience. The elements present in these essays normally include such a general premise, a statement of aims, and a refutation of criticisms. Some essays stress one, some another. Thus "Of Heroic Plays" and the "Apology for Heroic Poetry" emphasize the nature of a form; the Preface to *All for Love* concentrates on Dryden's particular aims in the most carefully constructed of his plays; the "Defence of *An Essay*" and "Defence of the Epilogue" (to *The Conquest of Granada*) are rebuttals of his critics.

To draw a sharp distinction between the essays of the 1670s and those of the 1680s and 1690s can be misleading, but clearly we can see a shift in the nature of Dryden's critical practice. His principles do not change markedly; his opinions alter more in detail than in substance, and he continues to defend and recommend his own work. Nonetheless the focus of his critical attention shifts. In the 1670s Dryden's primary concern is literary *form*—the "rules" of comedy, tragedy, and heroic drama. By the 1690s the particular "powers" of individual poets have become the focal point of his criticism. The change is obviously related to Dryden's turning from his own work to that of others, but it goes beyond the dictates of the new subject matter. Thus in the "Discourse on Satire" (1693) Dryden is describing the history of a form, but his attention is largely taken up with the achievement and characteristics of a few writers, not with the form or its rules.

The "Discourse on Satire" and the Dedication of the

Aeneis are somewhat overstuffed with borrowed learning, as we might expect in a historical survey from Dryden. Particularly in the Dedication, the theory consists of commonplaces taken from the French. On satire his ideas are fresher—as Watson puts it (II, 71), "Dryden never wrote an epic, but he knows what it is to write a satire"—and he offers some brilliant comments on how effective satire can be produced.[14] Dryden's dislike of more abstract theory is again plain: he grumpily grants that " 'Tis but necessary that after so much has been said of satire, some definition of it should be given" (II, 143)—so he quotes one from Heinsius, criticizes it as "obscure and perplexed," and promptly wanders off into a discussion of style. The bulk of the essay is devoted to assessing the powers of individual writers.

This development reaches its fullest extent in the Preface to *Fables* (1700). Comparing Chaucer with Ovid and Boccaccio, Dryden tries to characterize their work as a display of their "natural inclinations," rather than discussing their performance in the literary "kinds." [15] M. H. Abrams says

14. Particularly interesting as a gloss on Dryden's own "indirect" and burlesque methods in satire is this oft-quoted passage: "The nicest and most delicate touches of satire consist in fine raillery. . . . How easy is it to call rogue and villain, and that wittily! But how hard to make a man appear a fool, a blockhead, or a knave, without using any of those opprobrious terms! To spare the grossness of the names, and to do the thing yet more severely. . . . This is the mystery of that noble trade, which yet no master can teach to his apprentice: he may give the rules, but the scholar is never the nearer in his practice. . . . There is still a vast difference betwixt the slovenly butchering of a man, and the fineness of a stroke that separates the head from the body, and leaves it standing in its place" (II, 136–137).

15. Consider, for instance, Dryden's statement that of Chaucer's works he prefers *"Palamon and Arcite,* which is of the epic kind,

that the Preface goes "just about as far in this direction as any critic was to go for almost a hundred years." [16] Certainly he is correct in adding that Dryden, far more than Samuel Johnson (despite his biographical approach), sees literary works as the product of the author's character. Actually Dryden was not being boldly original or revolutionary. His contrast of the "manners and natural inclinations" displayed in the writings of Homer and Virgil (II, 274–275) can be found in Blackmore's Preface to *King Arthur* (1697). And this mode of critical discussion, though not common in England till the eighteenth century, has respectable precedent in French and classical critics, as R. S. Crane points out.[17] The unrevolutionary nature of the enterprise does not detract, though, from Dryden's achievement in the form.

What he tries to explain in this later criticism is the particular qualities of great writers, for increasingly he is coming to regard literature as the product of the individual, and he derives the "character" of the author from his writings. Comparing Chaucer and Ovid he says that "both of them were well-bred, well-natured, amorous, and libertine, at least in their writings, it may be also in their lives" (II, 277). Dryden did not have much biographical detail at his disposal, living as he did in the infancy of English literary

---

and perhaps not much inferior to the *Ilias* or the *Aeneis*" (II, 290). This opinion is thrown out in passing; it seems hard to believe that twenty years earlier Dryden would not have tried to demonstrate his point in some detail, for the epic-heroic mode was always his favorite.

16. *The Mirror and the Lamp* (New York, 1953), p. 232.

17. "On Writing the History of Criticism in England 1650–1800," *UTQ*, 22 (1953), reprinted in *The Idea of the Humanities*, 2 vols. (Chicago, 1967), II. 171–172.

scholarship, but he probably would have found little use for it in any case.[18] Rather, he is concerned with the writer's way of looking at things. In these late appreciations we find a sense of his own personal identification: "I found I had a soul congenial to his," Dryden says in explaining his work on Chaucer (II, 287). Of Homer and Virgil he says in a famous passage:

The Grecian is more according to my genius than the Latin poet. In the works of the two authors we may read their manners and natural inclinations, which are wholly different. Virgil was of a quiet, sedate temper: Homer was violent, impetuous, and full of fire. The chief talent of Virgil was propriety of thoughts, and ornament of words: Homer was rapid in his thoughts, and took all the liberties, both of numbers and of expressions, which his language, and the age in which he lived, allowed him. Homer's invention was more copious, Virgil's more confined [II, 274].

Comparisons of this sort can be traced back in Dryden's criticism to the distinctions among Shakespeare, Fletcher, and Ben Jonson in *Of Dramatic Poesy* thirty-five years earlier. What has changed is the prominence Dryden accords them.

When we survey Dryden's criticism in its entirety we see various sorts of enterprises. We find Dryden searching for standards, occasionally trying to formulate them, and most often working from or with reference to a single text or author. His rhetorical heritage is plain, but he is moving away from it and the prescriptive, composition-oriented

18. This statement seems borne out by the somewhat sketchy evidence available in "The Life of Plutarch" (1683), "The Character of Polybius" (1693), and "The Life of Lucian" (written 1696?).

criticism it implies, toward the sort of descriptive and analytic criticism that we practice today.

II

Dryden is often put in a line of poet-critics which includes Samuel Johnson, Coleridge, Matthew Arnold, and T. S. Eliot. Sidney and Ben Jonson are generally excluded on the grounds that they did not practice criticism as we understand the art: the *Apologie for Poetrie* (pub. 1595) is a defense of the utility of literature; *Timber* (pub. 1641) is a lively but derivative miscellany of observations on the art of writing. From this point of view, Dryden is both the father of our critical tradition and the first in a series of great poet-critics. There are some intriguing parallels to be found here, but they are, I think, as often misleading as helpful.

The notion that the critic should be a man skilled in the art he discusses is a venerable one. Each of these writers derives a prestige from his creative writing which adds to the authority of his critical pronouncements, both for us and for the contemporary audience. Each man speaks with something of the authority of the sage (Dryden less than the others), and all five, interestingly, have or grow into a conservative religious outlook which can extend even to Catholic or Anglo-Catholic belief. Other parallels can be multiplied: Dryden, Johnson, and Coleridge are major critics of Shakespeare; Dryden and Coleridge stand accused of unacknowledged Continental appropriations; Dryden, Arnold and Eliot are deeply concerned with a European rather than merely an English literary tradition. Yet a look at the differences makes the connections seem tenuous indeed.

[19]

To begin with, of this group of poet-critics only Eliot produced major criticism while still fully active as a poet and only Dryden practiced both arts throughout his life— the others dried up as poets. Perhaps this helps explain both why Dryden is by far the most concerned with his own work in his criticism, and why he, more than the others, emphasizes the craft of writing rather than the pleasures of reading. Johnson assesses a writer's performance; Coleridge, despite his liking for aesthetic-psychological speculation, tends to analyze specific works from the perspective of the audience. Dryden, even when writing an "appreciation" for the audience's benefit, works from the point of view of the practicing writer. We find in Dryden few of Johnson's magisterial pronouncements, little of Coleridge's psychological analysis of author or character, almost nothing of Arnold's cultural-religious concern. Dryden's view of literature is radically different. To put it bluntly, he does not insist on judging art by life [19] and does not treat literature as a surrogate for religion.[20] Eliot remarked in 1929 that it is the great virtue of seventeenth- and eighteenth-century English writers that they treat literature as no more than itself.[21] For Dryden this is true. He found in the Horatian doctrine of pleasant instruction more than the platitude

19. See W. R. Keast, "The Theoretical Foundations of Johnson's Criticism," in *Critics and Criticism*, ed. R. S. Crane (Chicago, 1952), p. 404; René Wellek, *A History of Modern Criticism 1750–1950*, vol. I (New Haven, 1955), p. 79.

20. See D. G. James, *Scepticism and Poetry* (London, 1937), and *Matthew Arnold and the Decline of English Romanticism* (Oxford, 1961), particularly p. 21.

21. In his essay "Experiment in Criticism," in *Tradition and Experiment in Present-Day Literature* [Addresses Delivered at the City Literary Institute (London) by divers persons] (Oxford, 1929), pp. 198–215.

that we do, but he felt no need to justify literature on utilitarian grounds or to claim for it an exalted metaphysical "truth" or cultural purpose. Dryden considers literature justified in its own terms, and so he considers it as art, no more and no less. Some of Eliot's essays (such as those on Dryden) come closest to Dryden's work, particularly his appreciative efforts. In both cases the style of enquiry is informal, the analysis untechnical and undetailed, the object more explanatory than legislative. But even in their "appreciative" criticism the differences between the two are great. Eliot seems further removed from his subjects; he delves into the past, trying to bring it to life. For Dryden, it is alive. Eliot is almost excruciatingly conscious of the Western Literary Tradition, and he strives to find roots and a place in it. Dryden accepts his place in the tradition without considering any other possibility.

This sort of easy differentiation tells us only the obvious—that in the sort of criticism they practice, we can find few ties among these men. To discuss their differences more systematically, or even simply to define Dryden's practice meaningfully, we need to use the frameworks provided by some theories of critical "orientation." I say "some" because there are a multitude of ways to analyze criticism into types. Any division is made for our convenience; no such distinct categories exist independently in the material on which we work—a point too easily forgotten in the fever of critical creation. Thus such critics as Abrams, Watson, Marsh, and Crane work with systems of their own, and each seems valid in light of its author's aims: different presuppositions breed different sets of categories, all of which may be useful if properly understood.

Generally, one can consider what M. H. Abrams calls

the "major orientation" of a critical theory. Thus theories may be distinguished by their varying emphasis on different "elements" in the "total situation of a work of art"— the work itself, the artist who creates it, the universe which is its subject, and the audience to whom it is addressed. Granting that "any reasonably adequate theory takes some account of all four elements," Abrams insists that "almost all theories . . . exhibit a discernible orientation toward one only." By "orientation" he means that "a critic tends to derive from one of these terms his principal categories for defining, classifying, and analyzing a work of art, as well as the major criteria by which he judges its value." [22]

According to this scheme, Coleridge emphasizes the mind of the artist, Dryden and Johnson the demands of the audience. Johnson insists that art must mirror life and instruct in doing so, but his primary aesthetic criterion is that a poem must please its audience—otherwise it will have no effect. Dryden can be said to believe much the same thing. It is the communicative, not the expressive function of literature in which these two believe. "If the first end of a

22. Abrams, pp. 6–7. Abrams seems to assume that literature is to be studied for its own sake, and does not make sufficient allowance for the importation of extrinsic moral or religious standards, which is probably why his scheme fits Arnold and Eliot less well than it does the others. For critics in the "neoclassical" period Robert Marsh's distinctions according to "method" may form a more useful system of classification. Marsh suggests that in this period the basic standards of reference can be: (1) a theory of the general nature of literature; (2) rhetorical assumptions; (3) "causal" theories, which explain literature in terms of human nature; (4) "dialectical" theories, which invoke transcendental values and essences as a standard of judgment. He places Hobbes, Dryden, Addison, and Hartley in these categories respectively. See Robert Marsh, *Four Dialectical Theories of Poetry* (Chicago, 1965), chap. 1.

[22]

writer be to be understood, then, as his language grows obsolete, his thoughts must grow obscure," says Dryden in justifying his modernizations of Chaucer (Preface to *Fables*, II, 288). We may guess that he would not have liked, understood, or approved of either "Kubla Khan" or the essentially evocative poetry of "Ossian." That Dryden's major orientation is pragmatic, or "rhetorical" as other critics put it, is quite undeniable. Dryden's primary assumption is that the author must try to communicate with his audience.[23]

To define a writer's most general orientation does not, however, tell us much about the actual criticism he produces. A critic with pragmatic assumptions can, after all, talk about either the work or the audience which it is designed to affect. Dryden does the former; Addison begins to do the latter, yet many of their assumptions are not greatly different. The aim of the criticism may vary greatly: to lay down rules for composition and to explain the import and beauties of the result are plainly not the same endeavor, though both can be carried out by a "rhetorically" oriented critic.

Plainly then a subsidiary orientation must be taken into account in defining a critic's perspective. It is a function of the subject and the purpose of his criticism. A critic may be concerned with *construction* (how to make a work) or *appreciation* (how to understand or enjoy it). Frequently the best way to understand a work is to analyze the way it

23. Dryden's pragmatic orientation and rhetorical critical vocabulary and assumptions are well analyzed by Max Nänny, in *John Drydens rhetorische Poetik* (Bern, 1959), especially pp. 18ff. Nänny does a fine job of describing Dryden's rhetorical stance; I am concerned with a broader definition of Dryden's critical *kind*.

[23]

is put together, but the critic's purpose here is still to make the work comprehensible to the audience. Discussion of aesthetics or the psychology of creation (which is outside this framework) normally shares the explanatory purposes of appreciative criticism.

An excellent set of distinctions related to the purposes of criticism has been proposed by George Watson.[24] First, "legislative" criticism is addressed to writers and offers rules and principles for writing (Gascoigne, Puttenham, and others); second, literary aesthetics (which Watson calls "theoretical criticism"), concerns the nature of literature or its creation (Hobbes, Coleridge); third, "descriptive" criticism is the analysis of specific works or authors.

Dryden is not easy to pigeonhole. By my reckoning he produces all three sorts of criticism,[25] though theoretical aesthetics (mostly in the psychological tradition of Hobbes) appears only infrequently in his work, and then in a subsidiary role.[26] What I call Dryden's speculative and prescriptive essays are not all legislative in a literal sense, but they are concerned with the problems a writer faces. In his explanatory criticism, as we have seen, Dryden moves from the author's problems to the comprehension of his results, and in doing so begins to practice something like descriptive criticism as we know it. Dryden is, I believe, the key figure in a transition from composition-oriented to ap-

24. *The Literary Critics*, chap. 1.
25. Watson argues at length that Dryden is the first "descriptive" critic in England. This is true, though I feel that he underemphasizes the transitional nature of Dryden's work.
26. For a discussion of Dryden which emphasizes the Hobbesian and psychological approach in his work, see Clarence D. Thorpe, *The Aesthetic Theory of Thomas Hobbes* (Ann Arbor, 1940), chap. 7.

[24]

preciation-oriented criticism. His work is a rather confusing mixture of the two, the more so because he always retains his feeling for the author's viewpoint.

Comparison with Rymer is instructive here. Rymer works in what is basically the descriptive mode, but he writes with the frank intention of reforming the stage. (He does not prescribe rules so much as demolish particular plays.) *The Tragedies of the Last Age* (1677) in particular is clearly addressed to writers. But *Edgar* notwithstanding, Rymer was no playwright. He sees with the eyes of the audience, asking: "Does the play make sense to the man who is watching it?" Dryden, even when writing explanatory criticism, sees his subject in terms of the writer's aim and craft. He asks not "how does this strike one?" but "what is the author up to and how is he doing it?" Even in his appreciative criticism Dryden remains distinctly composition-oriented in his subjects and perspective. In major orientation Dryden is essentially rhetorical, but his poet-critic status makes his perspective that of the author, and his subject remains the aims and construction of the work, though his purposes become increasingly explanatory.

Another way of looking at the critical engagements of Dryden's time is offered by R. S. Crane's theory of critical modes based upon the "types of questions" posed.[27] The first mode, rules/genre criticism, is followed by enquiry into the qualities of individual writers, and finally by historical criticism, the study of the relation of the literary work to the particular conditions of its production. Each of these,

27. "On Writing the History of Criticism," pp. 169–173. This is a simplification of his six-part scheme in "English Neoclassical Criticism," in Shipley's *Dictionary of World Literature* (New York, 1943); reprinted in *Critics and Criticism*, pp. 372–388.

Crane says, is a respectable "neoclassical" critical endeavor, justified by a decent antiquity. That these are not mutually exclusive categories is obvious. Dryden manages to combine the first two more completely than most critics (in the "Discourse on Satire," for example), though many critics produce work in both modes.[28] Historical criticism comes to maturity only with Thomas Warton, but the assumptions which make it possible are already clearly present in Dryden's frequent comments on the temper of various ages and the varying demands of English, French, and Greek audiences. Dryden's speculative and prescriptive criticism clearly draws on the assumptions of rules and genres, as do most of his early justifications. Only in the later explanatory criticism does Dryden move decisively toward definition of the qualities of individual writers.

We should realize, though, that the abandonment of strict generic distinctions is implicit in Dryden's work as early as *Of Dramatic Poesy*. Lisideius' definition of a play, claimed by Dryden as his own, is "a just and lively image of human nature, representing its passions and humours, and the changes of fortune to which it is subject, for the delight and instruction of mankind" (I, 25). This definition is accepted and used, "though Crites raised a logical objection against it, that it was only *a genere et fine*"—that is, it included other literary forms. That this vagueness is utterly deliberate is made clear near the end of the essay, when Neander says that there is a "great affinity" between tragedy and epic, "as may easily be discovered in that definition of a play which Lisideius gave us. The genus of them is the same, a just and lively image of human nature, in its actions, passions, and traverses of fortune: so

28. For example, Dennis, Johnson, Addison, Blair.

is the end, namely for the delight and benefit of mankind" (I, 87).

In Dryden's own works he often breaks the bounds of traditional genres—in his heroic plays and in his heroically-inclined satires. He wrote a number of tragicomedies, as a concession to English tradition and audience taste, though he had doubts about the effectiveness of the form. Probably Dryden's obsessive concern with the heroic, as Swedenberg calls it, is largely responsible for his conflating genres. What matters though is that from the beginning Dryden is primarily interested in creating an effective work, and the rules of genres are merely means toward that end; in themselves they possess no mysterious virtues for him. Thus in the "Heads of an Answer to Rymer" he argues that, rules or no rules, "Fletcher" must be good since his plays "have moved both those passions [pity and terror] in a high degree upon the stage" (I, 213). Dryden later grants that the "faults" Rymer "found in their designs" may reduce the plays' effectiveness, but he insists that if they are effective on the stage, they must be fundamentally good.

The critical standards that Dryden uses are ultimately empirical, resting on the particulars of style, "thought," and characterization which experience has proved effective. Yet he does not, like Johnson, appeal to the taste of audience or readers as the final critical standard. Although he consistently maintains that the business of an author is to please his age, he grows increasingly distrustful of audience taste.[29] Dryden's final critical appeal is to that fuzziest of

29. Thus as early as the "Defence of *An Essay*" (1668) he says: "To please the people ought to be the poet's aim, because plays are made for their delight; but it does not follow that they are

notions, the "imitation of nature," a concept which he uses in a confusing variety of ways.[30] He does not, like Rymer, ask for a literal but decorous representation of the probable. Nor does he, like Johnson, treat art as a judiciously generalized slice of life. Rather, what Dryden most frequently seems to want in art is "nature wrought up to an higher pitch" (I, 87), made more stimulating and hence more effective. Inevitably then, Dryden tends to see the "imitation" as a demonstration of the creative powers of the artist. John M. Aden has shown how advanced Dryden was in the significance he attached to such terms as "imagination," "wit," and "fancy." [31] These usages are clearly a result of a conception of imitation which requires not merely selection but active improvement.

Dryden hedges his claims for individual creativity by insisting that its products must be checked by judgment, but in essay after essay he finds imagination (or fancy) the vital creative power.[32] Dryden never has much use for

---

always pleased with good plays, or that the plays which please them are always good" (I, 120). In the Dedication of the *Examen poeticum* (1693), Dryden remarks: "I dare establish it for a rule of practice on the stage, that we are bound to please those whom we pretend to entertain; and that at any price, religion and good manners only excepted" (II, 162). Yet as early as the Dedication of *The Spanish Friar* (1681) he could say of his plays: "I knew they were bad enough to please, even when I writ them" (I, 276). In the Dedication of the *Aeneis* Dryden borrows Segrais' distinction among readers "according to their capacity of judging," and his condemnation of popular taste is scathing (II, 243–244).

30. This point is discussed in detail in chapter 6.

31. "Dryden and the Imagination: The First Phase," *PMLA*, 74 (1959), 28–40. For a reconsideration and continuation of Aden's study, see my essay, "Dryden on Creation: 'Imagination' in the Later Criticism," forthcoming in *RES*.

32. See such works as the Dedication of *The Rival Ladies, Of Dramatic Poesy* (I, 91–92), Preface to *Annus Mirabilis*, "Defence

"natural imitation" (I, 148), even in comedy. Consequently, he attaches great importance to the free imaging-power of the mind, and it is impossible for him to reduce art to life, as Johnson does. Dryden's attention is mostly fixed on the skill with which the work is wrought, since his dislike of the abstract keeps him from speculating about the author's motives. Nonetheless, Dryden clearly conceives of art as a *doing* on the part of the artist, a creative heightening of nature to increase its impact on the audience, and he judges a work according to the power with which its author has invested it. "Natural" is a term of praise for Dryden (e.g., I, 220), but it means "unexaggerated," not "realistic." [33]

In sum, Dryden is a transitional figure in whose works the traits of both legislative and descriptive criticism are clearly discernible. We find in his criticism change (increasing emphasis on the powers of individual artists) and some distinct modes—speculative, prescriptive, and explanatory, as I call them. In critical theory as in literary practice Dryden is a syncretist, trying to reconcile and use what he finds best in the English, French, and Classical traditions. I cannot agree with Ker's famous judgment that Dryden "is sceptical, tentative, disengaged, where most of his con-

---

of *An Essay*," Preface to *Tyrannic Love*, "Of Heroic Plays," Preface to *Ovid's Epistles*, "To the Earl of Abingdon." A greater reliance on judgment is plain by the time of the Dedication of the *Aeneis* (II, 244).

33. Dryden would, I think, have understood and approved of Horace Walpole's claim for *The Castle of Otranto*: "Allow the possibility of the facts, and all the actors comport themselves as persons would do in their situations" ("Preface to the First Edition"). Dryden could even have approved Walpole's marvels, for he always maintains that "poets may be allowed the . . . liberty for describing things which really exist not, if they are founded on popular belief. . . . For 'tis still an imitation, though of other men's fancies . . ." ("Apology for Heroic Poetry," I, 204).

[29]

temporaries, and most of his successors for a hundred years, are pledged to certain dogmas and principles." [34] Dryden is refreshingly undogmatic and unprescriptive, but in neither kind nor principles is his criticism greatly different from that of his contemporaries. He is indeed a great appreciator, but his reactions are not intuitive; rather, he judges and explains works by practical standards expressed in the rhetorical vocabulary of the rules. Dryden's excellence as a critic follows not from the lack of principles which romantically-oriented scholars have wished on him, but from his ability to use his principles creatively to explain the effectiveness of the works and authors he considered.

34. Ker, I, xv.

CHAPTER 2

Critical Methods

Having discussed what Dryden tries to do in his criticism, I am ready to consider in more detail how he goes about it. Two questions seem paramount: how does Dryden attempt to solve the problems he sets himself, and how does he attempt to put across his answers? The latter point plainly will bear investigation, since Dryden's rhetorical structures and devices are strikingly different from ours. For the former, we must note that Dryden's procedures vary greatly with the mode in which he is working: he adopts new tactics as he tries to do different things. The analytic method of the later essays is of special interest; Dryden was a pioneer in such descriptive criticism and his method in it seems to lie near the heart of his special skill at explaining the effectiveness of other men's writing.

I

Since, always excepting *Of Dramatic Poesy*, Dryden's critical works are prefaces and dedications doubling as prefaces, his critical essays are couched in the terms he considered appropriate to such ventures in self-recommendation. Dryden is very seldom as much concerned with proving anything as he is with selling his work and keeping himself solvent. Pope is often said to have been the first writer who managed to support himself entirely by letters, without recourse to patrons (theatrical work not counting as letters in those days); we need to remember this and treat Dryden's pleas for funds seriously. Reference to Ward's *Life of John Dryden* tells us that he was always struggling to keep afloat financially. During the late 1660s and the 1670s Dryden's part in the Theatre Royal gave him some income, but his earnings as Poet Laureate and Historiographer Royal were almost never paid in full— and sometimes it was only through his brother-in-law Howard's intercession that they were paid at all. Dryden seems at times to have been well off, but only precariously so. After 1688 he was, of course, thrown back entirely on the theater, book sales, and patronage; the extant letters to Tonson demonstrate clearly his preoccupation with financial detail. But at no point are Dryden's appeals to patrons merely *pro forma*.

Dryden's tone in these appeals does vary according to his relationship to the patron [1] and, one suspects, his need. His earlier dedications, particularly the ones after those in *The Rival Ladies* (1664) and *Of Dramatic Poesy*, are not at all fulsome by the standards of the day.[2] During the

1. On this point see Irène Simon, "Dryden's Prose Style," *RLV*, 31 (1965), 506–530.
2. Dryden's praise of Orrery's *The General* in the former is clearly extravagant ("your Lordship's soul is an entire globe of light, breaking out on every side"), and his compliment to Buckhurst is certainly not stinted: "It was an honour which seemed

1670s and 1680s the dedications seem more explanatory than merely complimentary. In such late works as the "Discourse on Satire" (addressed to Dorset, 1693) Dryden does seem extravagant.

There is not an English writer this day living who is not perfectly convinced that your Lordship excels all others in all the several parts of poetry which you have undertaken to adorn. . . . I will not attempt, in this place, to say any thing particular of your lyric poems, though they are the delight and wonder of this age, and will be the envy of the next. . . . Donne alone, of all our countrymen, had your talent; but was not happy enough to arrive at your versification; and were he translated into numbers, and English, he would yet be wanting in the dignity of expression. That which is the prime virtue, and chief ornament of Virgil, which distinguishes him from the rest of writers, is so conspicuous in your verses, that it casts a shadow on all your contemporaries; we cannot be seen, or but obscurely, while you are present. You equal Donne in the variety, multiplicity, and choice of thoughts; you excel him in the manner and the words. . . . For my own part, I must avow it freely to the world that I never attempted anything in satire wherein I have not studied your writings as the most perfect model. I have continually laid them before me; and the greatest commendation which my own partiality can give to my productions is that they are copies, and no farther to be allowed than as they have something more or less of the original. Some few touches of your Lordship, some secret graces which I have endeavoured to express after your manner, have made whole poems of mine to pass with approbation; but take

---

to wait for you to lead out a new colony of writers from the mother nation. . . . I am almost of opinion that we should force you to accept of the command" (I, 13-15). But by contemporary standards such praise was not overdone.

your verses altogether, and they are inimitable. If therefore I have not written better, 'tis because you have not written more. You have not set me sufficient copy to transcribe; and I cannot add one letter of my own invention, of which I have not the example there [II, 74–76].

Here it seems highly probable that Dryden is shoveling out compliments with more of an eye to his exchequer than to his conscience. We cannot be certain of this: by our standards Dryden's taste was quite reliable in the classics, but less so in the work of his contemporaries.[3] In the early 1690s his urgent need of money led him to return, most unwillingly, to the theater and to writing panegyrical poems. He was able to say in a prefatory note to the Earl of Abingdon, who gave him such a commission: "I could not answer it to the world, nor to my conscience, if I gave not your Lordship my testimony of being the best husband now living"—though he admits shortly afterwards that " 'tis not my happiness to know you" (II, 62–64). Putting " 'tis no flattery" before a fulsome compliment, however neat rhetorically, breeds little confidence in the writer's sincerity. Of course the sincerity of such compliments has little to do with these essays as critical ventures—in judging them we must merely make allowance for what may politely be called extrinsic considerations.

More important for our purposes are the pains Dryden takes to avoid any imputation of formality and rigor: he

3. For example, he says in a letter to Dennis (*c.* March 1694): "Your own poetry is a more powerful example to prove that the modern writers may enter into comparison with the Ancients than any which Perrault could produce in France" (II, 177), and similarly his praise of William Walsh seems out of all proportion (e.g., II, 173).

[34]

adopts the pose of a gentleman writing to his fellows, sometimes giving a sneer at hoi polloi.[4] *Of Dramatic Poesy*
is clearly his most carefully written essay, and in 1684 he
even took the trouble (unusual for him) of revising it
stylistically.[5] Nonetheless he begins his Dedication to Buckhurst with the preposterous statement: "As I was lately
reviewing my loose papers, amongst the rest I found this
Essay, the writing which, in this rude and indigested manner wherein your Lordship now sees it, served as an amuse-
ment to me in the country, when the violence of the last
plague had driven me from the town" (I, 12–13). Such
gentility is practically overwhelming.

A corollary to this gentlemanly pose is the deliberate
digressiveness of the essays. In his last essay Dryden excuses his meandering progress with the statement that "the
nature of a preface is rambling, never wholly out of the
way, nor in it. This I have learned from the practice of
honest Montaigne, and return at my pleasure to Ovid and
Chaucer, of whom I have little more to say" (Preface to
Fables, II, 278). Particularly in his longest essays, the "Discourse on Satire" and the Dedication of the *Aeneis*, Dryden
is rather self-conscious about his leisurely progress, and
makes some apologetically self-deprecating jokes about it.

4. See, for example, the Dedication to Sedley of *The Assignation*
(I, 184–189), and the famous condemnation of popular taste
adapted from Segrais in the Dedication of the *Aeneis* (II, 243–
244).

5. On these revisions see Irène Simon, "Dryden's Revision of
the *Essay of Dramatic Poesy*," *RES*, n.s. 14 (1963), 132–141;
Janet M. Bately, "Dryden's Revisions in the *Essay of Dramatic
Poesy*: The Preposition at the end of the Sentence and the Expression of the Relative," *RES*, n.s. 15 (1964), 268–282, "Dryden
and Branded Words," *N&Q*, n.s. 12 (1965), 134–139.

By this time, my Lord, I doubt not but that you wonder why I have run off from my bias so long together, and made so tedious a digression. . . . But if you will not excuse it by the tatling quality of age . . . yet I hope the usefulness of what I have to say on this subject will qualify the remoteness of it ["Discourse," II, 85].

But I have already wearied myself, and doubt not but I have tired your Lordship's patience, with this long, rambling, and, I fear, trivial discourse [II, 139].

I am still speaking to you, my Lord, though in all probability you are already out of hearing. Nothing which my meanness can produce is worthy of this long attention. But I am come to the last petition of Abraham: if there be ten righteous lines in this vast preface, spare it for their sake; and also spare the next city, because it is but a little one [II, 152].

I have detained your Lordship longer than I intended in this dispute of preference betwixt the epic poem and the drama. . . . In this address to your Lordship, *I design not a Treatise* of Heroic Poetry, but write in a loose, epistolary way, somewhat tending to that subject after the example of Horace. . . . I have taken up, laid down, and resumed as often as I pleased, the same subject; and this loose proceeding I shall use thro' all this prefatory Dedication. Yet all this while I have been sailing with some side-wind or other toward the point I proposed in the beginning: the greatness and excellency of an heroic poem ["Dedication," II, 231–232; italics added].

I am now drawing towards a conclusion, and suspect your Lordship is very glad of it [II, 253].

A disgressive approach—and apologies for it—are of course characteristic of Restoration criticism.[6]

6. Compare, for example: "I would only have you before hand advertiz'd, that you will find me ty'd to no certain *stile*, nor

Nonetheless, Dryden's essays are for the most part carefully put together. He knows very well what he wants to get across, and he does it quite efficiently. Dryden can go to some pains to give an impression of a casualness which does not exist. For instance, late in the "Discourse on Satire" he brings up Butler and says, "I ought to have mentioned him before, when I spoke of Donne; but by a slip of an old man's memory he was forgotten" (II, 147). This creates the rather charming impression that he is discoursing casually—the writer of a formal treatise could, after all, have gone back to interpolate what he had missed. Actually, Dryden is dissembling, for Butler is in his proper place.

Consider the structure of the "Discourse." After some initial compliments to Dorset (in which Donne does figure), Dryden, with apologies to the reader, makes a lengthy excursion into matters mostly connected with the epic (pp. 82–95). There follows a long discussion of the origin of satire and its growth in Rome—Dryden's main subject here (pp. 95–135). Having completed the history, Dryden assesses and ranks the three principal Roman satirists (pp.

---

laying my reasons together in *form* and *method*. . . . This variety made the travel more easy. And you know I am not cut out for writing a *Treatise*, nor have a *genius* to *pen* any thing *exactly;* so long as I am *true* to the *main sense* before me, you will pardon me in the rest" (Thomas Rymer, *The Tragedies of the Last Age,* in *Critical Works,* ed. Curt A. Zimansky [New Haven, 1956], pp. 20–21). "But I feel, Sir, that I am falling into the dangerous Fit of a hot Writer; for in stead of performing the promise which begins this Preface, and doth oblige me, after I had given you the judgement of some upon others, to present my self to your censure, I am wandering after new thoughts; but I shall ask your pardon, and return to my undertaking"; "Now, Sir, I again ask you pardon, for I have again digressed, my immediate business being . . ." (Sir William Davenant, Preface to *Gondibert,* Spingarn, II, 9, 16).

[37]

135–143). The remainder of the essay is taken up with two related points: the nature and kinds of satire, and the style appropriate for it, particularly in translation. Dryden starts by quoting Heinsius' definition of satire, and then, not really liking such theoretical rigidities, departs from it to consider the worth of farrago versus satire of unified design. He compares the latter, quite aptly, to Copernican astronomy and to English tragicomedy in which "there is to be but one main design; and tho' there be an under-plot, or second walk of comical characters and adventures, yet they are subservient to the chief fable, carried along under it, and helping to it" (II, 145). Having explained his preference for unity of design and social utility, Dryden says that he "will proceed to the versification." In this context of the "dignity of style," Butler is then discussed as a writer who lowers the subject (II, 147), and Tassone, Boileau, and particularly Virgil are praised and preferred for raising it. "Virgil . . . perpetually raises the lowness of his subject by the loftiness of his words. . . . This, I think, my Lord, to be the most beautiful and most noble kind of satire" (II, 149). Dryden concludes with a discussion of sublimity in English verse and a word of recommendation for his "paraphrased" translation.

Was Butler really forgotten and pushed in at random when recollected? Scarcely. Near the outset of the essay Dryden permits himself to range away from his subject as literally defined. But for all the essay's wealth of detail, he moves cogently from point to point. What we miss is not organization—it is there—but focus. Dryden strengthens the illusion of discourse by not troubling to heighten his main points and subordinate his lesser; all are delivered with the same pitch and emphasis. Little attention is called to the

[38]

transitions, and Dryden rouses no structural expectations in his reader. The net result is the illusion of a casualness which he felt was appropriate to a critical essay.

Of course the would-be-aristocratic amateurishness of Restoration writing did not always go unchallenged, and Dryden himself can betray sensitivity on the point. "A Parallel of Poetry and Painting" (1695) is a rather slovenly production—as Dryden hints when he says that "it was not of my own choice that I undertook this work" (II, 182). Toward the end of the essay he drops further hints of real or feigned impatience: "I have not leisure to run through the whole comparison"; and "In as much haste as I am, I cannot forbear giving one example" (II, 204, 205). He concludes by apologizing for the essay on grounds of haste and then neatly deprecates such an excuse.

The things which are behind are too nice a consideration for an essay begun and ended in twelve mornings, and perhaps the judges of painting and poetry, when I tell them how short a time it cost me, may make me the same answer which my late Lord Rochester made to one who, to commend a tragedy, said it was written in three weeks: 'How the devil could he be so long about it?' For that poem was infamously bad; and I doubt this Parallel is little better; and then the shortness of the time is so far from being a commendation, that it is scarcely an excuse [II, 207–208].

Thus Dryden makes his apology—honest or not—without leaving himself open to the obvious rejoinder.

All of Dryden's critical essays are tidily constructed, despite their apparent casualness; they do, however, vary considerably in tone. Very broadly, a distinction can be drawn between the slight edginess of the self-justifying works and the greater ease and flow of the later, more

[39]

purely explanatory essays, which seem akin in this respect to *Of Dramatic Poesy*. Clearly different, however, are a few works in which Dryden is engaged not merely in self-recommendation but in public controversy. The principal examples are the "Defence of *An Essay*" (1668), and *The Vindication of the Duke of Guise* (1683); the "Defence of the Epilogue" (1672) seems less specifically directed against opponents, and the authorship of *Notes and Observations on The Empress of Morocco* (1674), allegedly by Dryden, Crowne, and Shadwell, is a matter of some dispute.[7]

As a controversialist, Dryden is high-pitched and nasty, and he tends to hide behind authority. Consider the "Defence of *An Essay*." In the Preface to *The Duke of Lerma* (1668) Sir Robert Howard had, in about four pages, criticized some of Dryden's points in *Of Dramatic Poesy*. Howard argues that "a Play will still be supposed to be a Composition of several Persons speaking *ex tempore*"; hence rime is less natural than blank verse and, further, the unities of place and time do not hold up, since

if strictly and duely weigh'd, 'tis as impossible for one stage to present two Houses or two Roomes truely as two Countreys

7. Charles E. Ward, in *The Life of John Dryden* (Chapel Hill, 1961), pp. 328–329 (Appendix D), denies that Dryden was likely to have been involved in this controversy or in the writing of the *Notes and Observations*. Anne Doyle, in "Dryden's Authorship of *Notes and Observations on The Empress of Morocco* (1674)," *SEL*, 6 (1966), 421–445, has argued the contrary case; her view is largely supported by Maximillian E. Novak in his Introduction to *The Empress of Morocco and Its Critics*, Augustan Reprint Society Special Series (Los Angeles, 1968), pp. ix–x. Because the issue still seems clouded, I prefer not to base much discussion on this work, though I certainly agree with Novak that Dryden appears to have written the preface.

or Kingdomes, and as impossible that five houres, or four and twenty houres should be two houres and a halfe as that a thousand houres or yeares should be less then what they are . . . Impossibilities are all equal [Spingarn, II, 109].

What Howard says seems to me generous, just and reasonable, and he concludes by remarking that he is "extreamly well pleas'd with most of the *Propositions* which are ingeniously laid down in that *Essay*."

Dryden's angry, twenty-page reply seems out of all proportion to what Howard said. (Of course we do not know what family causes may have been involved in this disagreement between brothers-in-law.) Dryden announces that Howard is "combating the received opinions of the best ancient and modern authors," and that he will "defend the right of Aristotle and Horace" (I, 111). Later he says that Howard

attacks not me, but all the Ancients and Moderns; and undermines, as he thinks, the very foundations on which dramatic poesy is built. . . . He must pardon me if I have that veneration for Aristotle, Horace, Ben Jonson, and Corneille, that I dare not serve him in such a cause, and against such heroes, but rather fight under their protection [I, 121].

Dryden mixes personal sneers into the argument: he implies that Howard was guilty of plagiarism in *The Duke of Lerma* (I, 112), and ridicules him for including an errata sheet and claiming that his sense was distorted by the printer (I, 117). The bulk of the essay does make it plain that Dryden is both the better rhetorician and the shrewder man. Given the assumptions of the day, we may say that Dryden comes out ahead—particularly as Howard seems to have thought the *Essay* far more magisterial than it was.

[41]

But Dryden is forced toward a much more explicitly anti-naturalistic position than he had originally admitted to (I, 125–128). And he is so angrily argumentative, even allowing for his final compliment to Howard, that his controversial force is considerably subverted.[8]

The importance of the occasional circumstances of Dryden's criticism can scarcely be overemphasized. Not only were his essays occasioned by his other writings, but they were produced in the midst of a kind of literary warfare whose ferocity we have trouble comprehending. Restoration writers expressed themselves with remarkable freedom, and particularly after 1680 Dryden was the object of some extraordinary attacks. To a surprising extent he refrained from replying directly: possibly he had learned something from the row with Howard. In part, his careful cultivation of a pose—the "professional gentleman of letters"—masks his response to the vituperation to which he was subjected. Unlike Dennis, Dryden was neither pretentious nor arrogantly combative, but by no means was he humble. He tries to be cool and aloof and above the fray (see for example the Dedication to Sedley of *The Assignation*, 1673). But when his temper gives way, he can be both

8. Critics have generally been scornful of Howard's showing in this controversy. Charles E. Ward, for example, suggests that Dryden is able "to annihilate his antagonist"—see *The Life of John Dryden*, p. 66. This seems to me a distinctly biased reading. The fairest account of the quarrel is probably H. J. Oliver's, in *Sir Robert Howard* (Durham, N.C., 1963), chap. 6. Oliver skilfully disentangles references to extraneous and personal issues, notes contemporary reactions to the quarrel, and concludes with an obvious but usually neglected point: despite his rhetorical overkill, within a decade Dryden was tacitly to admit that on the issue of the appropriateness of rime in drama, it was Howard who was closer to right.

unpleasant and longwinded, as in *The Vindication of the Duke of Guise*. Many critics have suggested that Dryden was an expert controversialist. A good satirist yes, but nowhere I think do we find a Johnsonian skill in argumentation: he tends to seize on the trivial and the irrelevant. In consequence, none of his specifically controversial works ranks with his best. Nonetheless, although Dryden has the reputation of being a bit of a twister, we can say in his favor that his critical principles seem remarkably little influenced by controversy. Though Dryden is obviously stung by criticism, his response to it seldom takes the form of direct critical reply; most often (as in "Of Heroic Plays") he responds with a justification of his own practice or principles, but without direct counterargument. And it is surely noteworthy that he continues to cite Rymer as an authority throughout the 1680s and 1690s, despite their fierce personal and political quarrels. Dryden figures in much controversy, but these broils are less central to his critical practice than one might expect—largely, I suspect, because in the image he tries to project, as in his prose, he works hard to give the impression of gentlemanly indifference and ease.

In considering Dryden's prose style we must distinguish between what is intended as easy, informal discourse, and a genuinely conversational style. The two are occasionally confounded, particularly when the subject is *Of Dramatic Poesy*. Thus David Nichol Smith says that "the Essay has the vivacity of a good conversation in which the speakers pass easily from one point to another, and lighten the main discussion with remarks now and again on other matters." [9] Granting the discursiveness, I think that George

9. *John Dryden* (Cambridge, England, 1950), p. 21.

Watson is correct in pointing out (I, 12; headnote) that even the *Essay* consists not of conversation but of set speeches, though undeniably Dryden is more Senecan than Ciceronian.[10] I believe that Irène Simon has come closest to characterizing Dryden's style: comparing his work with epistolary passages from Burton, Browne, and Milton, she argues that Dryden is attempting to *suggest* a slightly formalized conversational style. Dryden's own scattered prescriptions seem to confirm this: he wants style to be easy and natural, correct—for he is always fussy about grammar —but not pedantic. (See, for example, the letter to Walsh [early 1691?], II, 53.)

Most of Dryden's critical essays contain no more of the first person singular than do those of his contemporaries. But in the essays of the 1690s there is a marked strain of personal complaint and outspoken self-pity for the ravages of age and fortune, and the significance of these personal references requires consideration. They begin after the revolution of 1688, when Dryden, as a Catholic and a nonsupporter of William, was in financial straits, and characteristically they appear in his appeals for funds. Thus, writing to Dorset, Dryden says of his failure to write an epic:

my little salary ill paid . . . I was then discouraged in the beginning of my attempt; and now age has overtaken me; and

10. To what extent his style was influenced by Restoration science is still a matter of debate. See (among others) R. F. Jones, "Science and English Prose Style in the Third Quarter of the Seventeenth Century," *PMLA*, 45 (1930), 977–1009; Claude Lloyd, "Dryden and the Royal Society," *PMLA*, 45 (1930), 967–976; George Watson, "Dryden and the Scientific Image," *Notes and Records of the Royal Society of London*, 18 (1963), 25–35. Watson argues convincingly that the influence is much less than has been supposed.

want, a more insufferable evil. . . . Since this revolution, . . . I have patiently suffered the ruin of my small fortune, and the loss of that poor subsistence which I had from two kings, whom I had served more faithfully than profitably to myself [II, 92].

Appealing to Lord Clifford, he says in dedicating his translations of Virgil's *Pastorals:* "What I now offer to your Lordship is the wretched remainder of a sickly age, worn out with study and oppressed by fortune: without other support than the constancy and patience of a Christian" (II, 217). And when Dryden says "I will neither plead my age nor sickness in excuse of the faults which I have made" (II, 236), he is in effect doing precisely that.

It is natural to wonder whether Dryden is simply indulging in extravagant self-pity. I think not. For one thing, these laments about age, illness, poverty, and neglect sound a distinctly formulaic note. For another, all of the instances of such lamentation occur in public writing; there is almost no hint of them in Dryden's letters, which, if anything, give quite an opposite picture. As far as we can tell from the letters known to us, Dryden remained vigorous and cheerful to the end of his life—age did not sour him or notably reduce his intellectual vigor and productivity, as he himself says in the Preface to *Fables* (II, 272–273). And Dryden well knew that he could help repair his fortunes by forsaking his Catholic and Stuart allegiances. His refusal to do so is firm, even noble, and without ostentation.

I remember the Counsell you give me in your letter: but dissembling, though lawfull in some Cases, is not my talent: yet for your sake I will struggle, with the plain openness of my nature, & keep in my just resentments against that degenerate Order. In the mean time, I flatter not my self with any manner

[45]

of hopes. But do my duty & suffer for God's sake, being assurd before hand, never to be rewarded, though the times shoud alter. . . . My Virgil succeeds in the World beyond its desert or my Expectation. You know the profits might have been more, but neither my conscience nor honour wou'd suffer me to take them: but I never can repent of my Constancy; since I am thoroughly perswaded of the justice of the laws, for which I suffer [Letter to his sons; Ward, no. 47].[11]

I can never go an Inch beyond my Conscience & my Honour. If they will consider me as a Man, who have done my best to improve the Language, & Especially the Poetry, & will be content with my acquiescence under the present Government, & forbearing satire on it, that I can promise, because I can perform it: but I can neither take the Oaths, nor forsake my Religion, because I know not what Church to go to, if I leave the Catholique. . . . May God be pleasd to open your Eyes, as he has opend mine: Truth is but one [Letter to Mrs. Steward; Ward, no. 67].

We are left to conclude, I believe, that Dryden's personal lamentations are a deliberate rhetorical device, for they do not seem to reflect his real feelings about his situation, and they appear in his pleas for patronage. Thus in the "Postscript to the Reader" appended to the *Aeneid* translation he starts out: "What Virgil wrote in the vigour of his age, in plenty and at ease, I have undertaken to translate in my declining years; struggling with wants, oppressed with sickness, curbed in my genius, liable to be misconstrued in all I write" (II, 258). He goes on to thank a variety of patrons for their gifts, and implies clearly enough that more would be welcome. We can only suppose

11. See *The Letters of John Dryden*, ed. Charles E. Ward (Durham, N.C., 1942).

[46]

that he was deliberately painting himself in the colors which he thought might best attract patronage.

To sum up this discussion of his rhetorical structures and devices: the air of casualness and informality with which Dryden invests his essays makes them seem attractive and readable—particularly when they are compared to ponderous modern academic criticism. Dryden's lack of formal divisions and his easy if uncolloquial style add to the illusion of nonprofessionalism, despite the rather careful construction of most of the essays. The stance which Dryden generally adopts is that of author speaking directly to patron or reader; the impression conveyed, and certainly intended, is more of casual discourse than of treatise.

II

In the first chapter of this study I distinguished speculative, prescriptive, and explanatory modes in Dryden's criticism; here I want to contrast his procedures in them. It must be noted at once that there are no neat distinctions to be made. Dryden did not have a formal methodology in the modern academic sense; his work does not break down into portions which are biographical, textual, historical, and so forth. As a generalization we can say only that his speculative work is characterized by debate form, his prescriptive essays by heavy reliance on authority, his later explanatory work by contrasts of different writers.

Of Dramatic Poesy (1668) is a formal debate on dramatic practice. After the scene is established and a definition of drama accepted, it consists of six set speeches arranged in three pairs. Crites upholds the Ancients, Eugenius the Moderns; Lisideius cries up the French method, Neander the English; Crites argues for blank verse, Neander for rime. In the first exchange Eugenius is said "to have the better of the argument" (I, 43);[12] in the others the issues are left to the reader's judgment. What is striking here is the way in which Dryden keeps the different positions discrete. Examining the merits of the various systems he forgoes his usual syncretic method.[13] He makes no attempt to argue the issues out, see where the positions overlap, or arrive at compromises. Such reconciliation is precluded by the fixed format of set statement and reply. George Watson is absolutely right in saying that Dryden fails to provide the cut-and-thrust of a "Socratic inquisition";[14] he has none of Plato's forward motion toward a solution. Cer-

12. If Eugenius is indeed (as is generally thought) meant to represent Buckhurst, to whom the *Essay* is dedicated, then this is presumably thrown in as an extra compliment. Of course Dryden, a believer in progress, was in substantial agreement with Eugenius' position.

13. This point is debatable. Did Dryden forgo his syncretic method or had he not yet developed it? John C. Sherwood, in "Dryden and the Rules: The Preface to *Troilus and Cressida*," *CL*, 2 (1950), 73–83, says that Dryden is guilty of "some sort of evasion or escape into critical dualism" in *Of Dramatic Poesy* (p. 82); Sherwood praises "The Grounds of Criticism in Tragedy" for "reconciling the plays of Shakespeare with the rules of Corneille." I would argue that Sherwood fails to take into account the very different nature of Dryden's purposes in the two essays. Dryden does respect all of the positions advanced in *Of Dramatic Poesy*, and though Neander is clearly closest to his beliefs in the 1660s, there is much in the thought of the others which, even this early, he can claim as his own—such as Lisideius' very French definition of a play. I find it hard to believe that Dryden was incapable of pulling these positions together in the mid-1660s; it seems far more probable to me that he was deliberately keeping them apart for speculative, comparative purposes.

14. *The Literary Critics* (Baltimore, 1962), p. 40.

tainly Dryden is not using dialogue form to argue forcefully for a position of his own—as Dennis does in *The Impartial Critick* (1693). Instead he sketches out each position and goes on, content to have clarified the issues by contrast. He does have a stake in the arguments, and with the benefit of hindsight we can easily deduce his feelings, but to a surprising degree the issues are, as he says in his "Defence," "left doubtful, to be determined by the readers in general" (I, 123).

Dryden's other speculative work, the "Heads of an Answer to Rymer" (1677) is quite literally a set of debater's notes.[15] Taking the criticisms of English tragedy in *The Tragedies of the Last Age* and with them Dryden's notes toward a reply, we have something like one of the exchanges in *Of Dramatic Poesy*. And I, at least, am prepared to argue that in the "Heads" as well as in *Of Dramatic Poesy* Dryden is working out and examining a position, rather than making a statement of firm personal conviction.

There have been many critical squabbles about what is often called Dryden's "sceptical" temperament, and there is no point in continuing them. Harth is certainly right in denying Dryden's alleged Pyrrhonism,[16] but nonetheless Dryden's is essentially an enquiring, exploratory mind. His freedom from rigid preconceptions makes possible his receptiveness to very different kinds of literature. A corollary of this openmindedness is his unease in prescribing rules. Dryden's speculative works rely relatively little on

15. For a detailed account of the "Heads of an Answer to Rymer," see chap. 4.

16. See Phillip Harth, *Contexts of Dryden's Thought* (Chicago, 1968), chap. 1. Cf. Louis I. Bredvold, *The Intellectual Milieu of John Dryden* (Ann Arbor, 1934).

other critics,[17] but his prescriptive essays rely heavily on the importation of authorities.

"The Grounds of Criticism in Tragedy" (1679) is a good example. Dryden undertakes to answer a set problem: to what extent should Shakespeare and Fletcher serve as models for imitation? His procedure on all matters of theory involved is to pose the problem and quote an answer from Rapin or Bossu.

After all, if any one will ask me whether a tragedy cannot be made upon any other grounds than those of exciting pity and terror in us, Bossu, the best of modern critics, answers thus in general: that all excellent arts, and particularly that of poetry, have been invented and brought to perfection by men of a transcendent genius; and that therefore they who practise afterwards the same arts are obliged to tread in their footsteps. . . . Rapin writes more particularly thus: that no passions in a story are so proper to move our concernment as fear and pity [I, 246].

The whole essay is laden with such phrases as: "Rapin, a judicious critic, has observed"; "The first rule which Bossu prescribes"; "Bossu shall answer this question for me"; "Longinus, whom I have hitherto followed"; "Longinus thinks"; "I will conclude with the words of Rapin." Nonetheless, John Sherwood shows that "it is only through

17. This has been a disputed point: *Of Dramatic Poesy* has often been called derivative, and Dryden himself says it is "for the most part borrowed from the observations of others" ("Defence of *An Essay*," I, 112)—though we must remember that in this passage Dryden is concerned to establish his orthodoxy. And I refer the reader to an excellent article by John M. Aden, "Dryden, Corneille, and the *Essay of Dramatic Poesy*," *RES*, n.s. 6 (1955), 147–156. Aden points out many apparent borrowings, but argues that there is not much *significant* influence, since there is a great deal more in Corneille that Dryden did *not* use.

painstaking investigation that we come to realize how extensive the borrowing is and how small a proportion of it is acknowledged.[18] Dryden's application of this French theory to Shakespeare and Fletcher is his own, but the principles on which he works are borrowed wholesale. Why? We may guess that Dryden cites Aristotle, Horace, Longinus, and the French critics partly for the weight their authority confers. Further, he certainly believes that general truth (which he undertakes to supply here) must have been long and widely held, and consequently he looks to his predecessors for confirmation of truth.

Dryden's earlier explanatory criticism—justifying his own work—is quite different. Usually it is based on his concept of the potentiality of a literary form. I have already discussed this briefly in the first chapter. Dryden's later, more analytic explanatory essays proceed quite differently. His endeavor there is to explain the powers of various authors. He may discuss a writer's exploitation of a form (for example, Virgil's of the epic), but his concern is more with the writer's skills and predilections than with genre. His aims seem implicit in a passing compliment to St. Evremond as critic· "He generally dives into the very bottom of his authors, searches into the inmost recesses of their souls, and brings up with him those hidden treasures which had escaped the diligence of others" (II, 59).

Dryden's aim then is to display the beauties and characteristics of the authors he analyzes. His method is usually to contrast the work of two or more writers. We meet this procedure as early as the comparison of Shakespeare, Jonson, and Fletcher in *Of Dramatic Poesy,* and it reappears in snatches for the next dozen years—as in the famous com-

18. Sherwood, *CL,* p. 75.

ment that "Shakespeare generally moves more terror, and Fletcher more compassion" (I, 247). Dryden's first use of extended analytic contrast, a brilliant one, occurs in "The Life of Plutarch" (1683).

But the likeness of Seneca is so little that, except the one's being tutor to Nero, and the other to Trajan, both of them strangers to Rome yet raised to the highest dignities in that city, and both philosophers tho' of several sects (for Seneca was a Stoic, Plutarch a Platonician, at least an Academic, that is, half Platonist half Sceptic); besides some such faint resemblances as these, Seneca and Plutarch seem to have as little relation to one another as their native countries, Spain and Greece. If we consider them in their inclinations or humours, Plutarch was sociable and pleasant, Seneca morose and melancholy; Plutarch a lover of conversation and sober feasts, Seneca reserved, uneasy to himself when alone, to others when in company. Compare them in their manners: Plutarch everywhere appears candid, Seneca often is censorious. Plutarch, out of his natural humanity, is frequent in commending what he can; Seneca, out of the sourness of his temper, is prone to satire, and still searching for some occasion to vent his gall. Plutarch is pleased with an opportunity of praising virtue; and Seneca (to speak the best of him) is glad of a pretence to reprehend vice. Plutarch endeavours to teach others, but refuses not to be taught himself, for he is always doubtful and inquisitive: Seneca is altogether for teaching others, but so teaches them that he imposes his opinions; for he was of a sect too imperious and dogmatical either to be taught or contradicted. And yet Plutarch writes like a man of a confirmed probity, Seneca like one of a weak and staggering virtue. Plutarch seems to have vanquished vice, and to have triumphed over it: Seneca seems only to be combating and resisting, and that too but in his own defence. Therefore Plutarch is easy in his discourse, as one who has overcome the difficulty: Seneca is painful, as he who still labours under it. Plutarch's virtue is humbled and civilized: Seneca's haughty and ill-bred. Plutarch allures you, Seneca commands you. One would make virtue your companion, the other your tyrant. The style of Plutarch is easy and flowing, that of Seneca precipitous and harsh. The first is even, the second broken. The arguments of the Grecian, drawn from reason, work themselves into your understanding, and make a deep and lasting impression in your mind: those of the Roman, drawn from wit, flash immediately on your imagination, but leave no durable effect. So this tickles you by starts with his arguteness, that pleases you for continuance with his propriety. The course of their fortunes seems also to have partaken of their styles; for Plutarch's was equal, smooth, and of the same tenor: Seneca's was turbid, unconstant and full of revolutions [II, 11–13].

The notion of the comparison Dryden has taken from essays by Montaigne and St. Evremond, and part of his point is to show that Montaigne "has done too great an honour to Seneca by ranking him with our philosopher and historian." But the primary aim of the passage is surely to characterize Plutarch—personally, morally, literarily, and stylistically—as sharply as possible, and Dryden is trying to clarify his picture by adding an extra dimension to his perspective.

This method appears frequently during the late 1680s and the early 1690s, as in the comparison of Theocritus to Ovid, Horace, and Pindar (Preface to *Sylvæ*), Polybius to Tacitus ("Life of Polybius"), and most prominently in the "Discourse on Satire" where Persius, Horace, and Juvenal are elaborately contrasted and compared. Here and elsewhere Dryden takes pains to give "to each his proper due"

[53]

(II, 117). He does rank the Roman satirists in order of merit ("Let Juvenal ride first in triumph"),[19] but is at pains not to undervalue the lesser satirists, or to ignore the lessons they offer. Thus he condemns Juvenal's preference for farrago, saying: "Will you please but to observe that Persius, the least in dignity of all the three, has notwithstanding been the first who has discovered to us this important secret in the designing of a perfect satire: that it ought only to treat of one subject" (II, 144–145). In this three-way comparison Dryden not only explores the aesthetic and moral possibilities of satire as a form, but he manages to give a sympathetic account of each of its practitioners.

Dryden's most famous critical comparison comes in the Preface to *Fables*, in which he sets Chaucer against Ovid and Boccaccio. Here there are no generic considerations, and the method is used solely for the light it sheds on the three authors. In purely technical terms, Dryden's advance over his earlier comparisons is remarkable. The tone is relaxed and the organization gives the impression of casual

19. In setting Juvenal above Horace (II, 127, 141–142) Dryden explicitly reverses his opinion in the Preface to *Sylvæ* (1685), where he says that Horace's satires "are incomparably beyond Juvenal's, if to laugh and rally is to be preferred to railing and declaiming" (II, 31). Watson suggests that "loss of Court favour" may be responsible for this change (II, 127n). But since Dryden still prefers "fine raillery" (II, 136–137), we cannot say that loss of favor gave him a taste for fulmination. "The manner of Juvenal is confessed to be inferior" to Horace's (II, 138). Dryden's new preference seems to be based on the opinion that Juvenal's subjects are more fitted for satire (II, 132), and the delight that he took in Juvenal's "more vigorous and masculine wit" (II, 130). This enjoyment of fire and vigor appears again in Dryden's praise of Homer's "fiery way of writing which, as it is liable to more faults, so it is capable of more beauties than the exactness and sobriety of Virgil" (Letter, to Charles Montague? Oct. 1699? II, 266).

[54]

discourse. The structure of the essay actually follows roughly the description Dryden gives of the way he wrote the *Fables:* he started with Homer, went on to Ovid's account of the Trojan war, and then "it came into my mind that our old English poet, Chaucer, in many things resembled him" (Ovid); from here he was led to think (since "thoughts, according to Mr Hobbes, have always some connection") of Boccaccio, who was not only Chaucer's contemporary, "but also pursued the same studies; wrote novels in prose, and many works in verse," and was similarly a refiner of his language (II, 270–271).

The terms of these comparisons include character, morals, "invention," style, and what may be termed historical position. To take the last first: Dryden says that "with Ovid ended the golden age of the Roman tongue: from Chaucer the purity of the English tongue began" (II, 277); similarly he comments that "Dante had begun to file their language, at least in verse, before the time of Boccace, who likewise received no little help from his master Petrarch. . . . [But] Chaucer (as you have formerly been told by our learned Mr Rymer) first adorned and amplified our barren tongue" (II, 271–272).

Looking at his authors Dryden views their productions as somehow characterizing them, and so he can lump together character, morals, and "invention."

The manners of the poets [Ovid and Chaucer] were not unlike: both of them were well-bred, well-natured, amorous, and libertine, at least in their writings, it may be also in their lives. Their studies were the same, philosophy and philology. Both of them were knowing in astronomy, of which Ovid's books of the *Roman Feasts,* and Chaucer's *Treatise of the Astrolabe,* are sufficient witnesses. But Chaucer was likewise an astrologer,

[55]

as were Virgil, Horace, Persius, and Manilius. Both writ with wonderful facility and clearness; neither were great inventors: for Ovid only copied the Grecian fables, and most of Chaucer's stories were taken from his Italian contemporaries, or their predecessors [II, 277].

Dryden goes on to praise both men for their imitation of nature—by which he means skillful and effective "descriptions of persons, and their very habits."

For an example, I see Baucis and Philemon as perfectly before me, as if some ancient painter had drawn them; and all the Pilgrims in the *Canterbury Tales*, their humours, their features, and the very dress, as distinctly as if I had supped with them at the Tabard in Southwark. Yet even there, too, the figures of Chaucer are much more lively, and set in a better light [II, 278].

Coming to "thoughts and words" Dryden starts "by owning that Ovid lived when the Roman tongue was in its meridian; Chaucer, in the dawning of our language: therefore that part of the comparison stands not on an equal foot." Dryden then balances Ovid's unique "wit" against Chaucer's "simplicity." [20]

This whole comparison, plainly enough, is based on the

20. Dryden's comparison elicited at least one amusing fantasy from a contemporary, Mr. Thomas Brown of Shifnal (d. 1704). The following dialogue between Dryden and Chaucer is said to take place in one of the coffeehouses of hell. "Sir, cries he [Chaucer], you have done me a wonderful Honour to Furbish up some of my old musty Tales, and bestow modern Garniture upon them, and I look upon myself much oblig'd to you for so undeserv'd a favour; however, Sir, I must take the Freedom to tell you that you overstrain'd Matters a little, when you liken'd me to *Ovid*, as to our Wit and manner of Versification. Why, Sir, says Mr. *Dryden*, I maintain it, and who then dares be so sawcy as to oppose me? But under favour, Sir, cries the other, I think I should know *Ovid* pretty well, having now conversed with him almost three

works of the two writers. Dryden extrapolates from text to character, but neither here nor elsewhere does he make a practice of employing biographical information in his criticism. In the Preface to *Ovid's Epistles* (1680), he does discuss briefly the enigmas of Ovid's life, basing his account on the "Life" written by George Sandys as a preface to his *Metamorphosis Englished* (1626). Dryden's purpose here is to mitigate charges of immorality—that is, his purpose is more moral than literary. Similarly, in "The Character of Polybius" (1693) Dryden makes use of biographical information to raise our estimate of a writer's character, for he does see a close connection between the writer's morals and his writings. Nonetheless his *modus operandi* is almost always to deduce the character from the writings, and it is with rhetorical effectiveness that he is mostly concerned.

Although Dryden's focus is on the work rather than on the author, his procedure is very much less textual than, say, Rymer's. Apart from the examen in *Of Dramatic Poesy* and perhaps the Dedication of the *Aeneis*, Dryden

---

hundred Years, and the Devil's in it if I don't know my own Talent, and therefore tho' you past a mighty compliment upon me in drawing this parallel between us, yet I tell you there's no more resemblance between us as to our manner of Writing, than there is between a Jolly well complexion'd *Englishman* and a black-hair'd thin-gutted *Italian*. Lord, Sir, says *Dryden* to him, I tell you that you're mistaken, and your two Stiles are as like one another as two Exchequer Tallies. But I, who should know it better, says *Chaucer*, tell you the contrary." "Letters from the Dead to the Living: The third and last letter of News from Signior Giuseppe Hanesio, high German Doctor in Brandipolis, to his Friends at Will's Coffee-house . . ." in *The Works of Mr. Thomas Brown*, ed. James Drake (London, 1707), vol. II, part 3, pp. 206–207. (I owe thanks to Professor Richard L. Hoffman of Queens College for bringing this passage to my attention.)

never comes close to making a systematic analysis of a single work. Nor is he in the habit of quoting passages for illustrative purposes, except in the cases of classical tags and occasional stylistic illustration (e.g., II, 149). By way of contrast we may note that Rymer's *The Tragedies of the Last Age* (1677) consists of blow-by-blow dismemberments of three "Fletcher" tragedies. In each case Rymer starts with a summary account of the "Fable," and then runs through the play, quoting dozens of passages long and short, analyzing and often objecting to them.

We must make a distinction of perspective. Dryden is writing appreciative criticism, Rymer something more (in intention) like legislative criticism. But though Dryden is writing for the audience, he views his subject from the writer's standpoint. Rymer, who addresses himself to writers for their improvement, has the outlook of the spectator. Both men have rhetorical assumptions, but Dryden looks at the work to see how it is contrived, Rymer considers how it will strike an audience.

This distinction raises another point: in his criticism Dryden appears almost startlingly devoid of the theatrical sense we would expect of a professional playwright. "Spectacle" is the one part of drama isolated and discussed by Aristotle that Dryden ignores, although it played, of course, an important part in the staging of his operatic and musical-comedy productions. Dryden does not seem to visualize a play in the way that Rymer does. He grants that seeing an action represented makes it more immediate than merely reading about it,[21] but even in his plays Dryden is writing, as he occasionally says, to be read.

21. "In a playhouse, everything contributes to impose upon the judgment: the lights, the scenes, the habits, and, above all, the

But as 'tis my interest to please my audience, so 'tis my ambition to be read: that I am sure is the more lasting and the nobler design: for the propriety of *thoughts and words,* which are the hidden beauties of a play, are but confusedly judged in the vehemence of action [Dedication of *The Spanish Friar;* I, 278; italics added].

"Thoughts and words"—Dryden returns to these again and again, for they are the center of a literary outlook which is far more rhetorical than generic. The procedure which he brings to any work or author amounts to a systematic evaluation of effectiveness by categories—invention, fable, character, manners, thoughts, words. Dryden varies his emphasis on these criteria somewhat in different essays,[22] but on the whole they constitute his scheme for approaching

---

grace of action, which is commonly the best where there is the most need of it, surprise the audience, and cast a mist upon their understandings; not unlike the cunning of a juggler, who is always staring us in the face, and overwhelming us with gibberish, only that he may gain the opportunity of making the cleaner conveyance of his trick. But these false beauties of the stage are no more lasting than a rainbow; when the actor ceases to shine upon them, when he gilds them no longer with his reflection, they vanish in a twinkling" (Dedication of *The Spanish Friar;* I, 275). "I know not of any one advantage which tragedy can boast above heroic poetry, but that it is represented to the view as well as read. . . . This is an uncontended excellence and a chief branch of its prerogative; yet . . . herein the actors share the poet's praise. Your Lordship knows some modern tragedies which are beautiful on the stage, and yet I am confident you would not read them" (Dedication of the *Aeneis,* II, 229).
    22. Compare "Heads of an Answer to Rymer," "The Grounds of Criticism in Tragedy," "A Parallel of Poetry and Painting," and Preface to *Fables.* "Invention" is Dryden's term for an author's ability to produce "fable"; similarly "character" is sometimes construed as the implicit personality of the author, particularly in nondramatic works.

[59]

any work. Of course this method—like the categories—is simply part of the Aristotelian tradition to which he was heir.

But Dryden's use of these analytic categories is by no means Aristotelian, for he severely downgrades fable and invention.

Rapin attributes more to the *dictio*, that is, to the words and discourses of a tragedy, than Aristotle had done, who places them in the last rank of beauties; perhaps only last in order, because they are the last product of the design, of the disposition or connection of its parts; of the characters, of the manners of those characters, and of the thoughts proceeding from those manners. Rapin's words are remarkable: " 'Tis not the admirable intrigue, the surprising events, the extraordinary incidents that make the beauty of a tragedy; 'tis the discourses when they are natural and passionate" ["Heads of an Answer to Rymer," I, 219–220].

Thus he suggests that the "thoughts" and "words" are ultimately responsible for a work's effectiveness. Rymer, more traditional in this respect, says that "there is no talking of Beauties when there wants Essentials. . . . [Therefore] I have chiefly consider'd the *Fable* or *Plot*, which all conclude to be the *Soul* of a *Tragedy*." [23] Note that Dryden does not attempt to defend the Elizabethan playwrights against Rymer's strictures on their plots—rather, he upholds the beauty and effectiveness of their expression. Dryden has only contempt for the plot and structure of *Troilus and Cressida*, but he admires Shakespeare's characters and the "many excellent thoughts" which "lay wholly buried" in what he bluntly called "a heap of rubbish."

23. *The Tragedies of the Last Age*, in *Critical Works*, p. 18.

To take a specific example of Dryden's categorical critical procedure, consider again the Preface to *Fables*. When
he deals with the work of Ovid and Chaucer, nondramatic
writers, Dryden considers under "character" not the par-
ticipants in an action but the implicit personality of the
author. After a comment on the two of them ("well-bred,
well-natured, amorous, and libertine"), Dryden notes that
neither was strong on "invention" ("Both of them built on
the inventions of other men")—no great deficiency in the
eyes of a man who cheerfully borrowed all his plots. He
then goes on to discuss the "manners" they imitate and the
skill with which they represent them, and finally he says,
"The thoughts and words remain to be considered." Each
point is taken up in order and a judgment rendered on the
respective merits of the two poets.

Quite probably it is Dryden's experience as a writer that
makes him so sensitive to nicety of expression. Certainly
he expends a good deal of his critical attention on "thoughts
and words." Whether David Nichol Smith is correct in
thinking that Dryden gives us "the first deliberate examination in English of an author's prose style" [24] I cannot say.
The passage in question, part of "The Life of Plutarch"
(1683), is an example of skilful characterization (largely
through comparison) without quotation.

This last reflection leads me naturally to say somewhat in
general of his style, tho' after having justly praised him for
copiousness of learning, integrity, perspicuity, and more than
all this for a certain air of goodness which appears through all
his writings, it were unreasonable to be critical on his elocution.
As on a tree which bears excellent fruit, we consider not the
beauty of the blossoms, for if they are not pleasant to the eye,

24. D. N. Smith, p. 84.

or delightful to the scent, we know at the same time that they are not the prime intention of nature, but are thrust out in order to their product; so in Plutarch, whose business was not to please the ear but to charm and to instruct the mind, we may easily forgive the cadences of words and the roughness of expression. Yet for manliness of eloquence, if it abounded not in our author, it was not wanting in him: he neither studied the sublime style, nor affected the flowery. The choice of words, the numbers of periods, the turns of sentences, and those other ornaments of speech, he neither sought nor shunned. But the depth of sense, the accuracy of judgment, the disposition of the parts and contexture of the whole in so admirable and vast a field of matter, and lastly the copiousness and variety of words, appear shining in our author. 'Tis indeed observed of him that he keeps not always to the style of prose, but if a poetical word which carries in it more of emphasis or signification offer itself at any time, he refuses it not because Homer or Euripides have used it. But if this be a fault, I know not how Xenophon will stand excused. Yet neither do I compare our author with him or with Herodotus in the sweetness and graces of his style, nor with Thucydides in the solidity and closeness of expression. For Herodotus is acknowledged the prince of the Ionic, the other two of the Attic eloquence. As for Plutarch, his style is so particular that there is none of the Ancients to whom we can properly resemble him. And the reason of this is obvious; for being conversant in so great a variety of authors, and collecting from all of them what he thought most excellent, out of the confusion or rather mixture of all their styles he formed his own, which partaking of each was yet none of them, but a compound of them all, like the Corinthian metal, which had in it gold, and brass, and silver, and yet was a species by its self [II, 10–11].

This not only stands as an example of Dryden's deft comparisons, but serves to illustrate his sensitivity to an author's style of expression and its suitability to his subject.[25] I think it safe to say that in almost every essay Dryden discusses style or stylistic problems—they are his most abiding concern.

Dryden's critical essays have, I wish to emphasize, a dual purpose: they express both his observations on literature and his appeals for funds. In assessing the content and rhetoric of the essays we must simply accept the fact that the two aims have little to do with each other. About all that can be said for the combination is that it is less inappropriate than it would be in more formal works—just as Edmund Wilson's personal digressions would be far more jarring if they appeared in academic criticism. In most of these essays (excluding "The Grounds of Criticism in Tragedy," for instance), Dryden makes a studied attempt to produce what sounds like casual discourse. This may be part of the reason he avoids a more textual approach; long quotations would not fit this intent. Rymer, who does use quotations, is similarly informal, and actually more colloquial, but he is more explicitly concerned with critical *problems*, although like Dryden he does disavow any intention of producing a formal "Treatise."

Dryden is seldom concerned with set problems, except in his speculative and prescriptive essays. Still more rarely does he worry about the meaning of a work—he makes the uniformitarian assumption that any rational man can understand it. Generally Dryden examines what he calls

The parts of a poem, tragic or heroic, [which] are:
I. The fable itself.

25. For an account of the stylistic pains Dryden took in translating Ovid to retain "his native sweetness, easiness, and smoothness," see the Dedication of the *Examen poeticum* (II, 164-165).

II. The order or manner of its contrivance in relation of the parts to the whole.

III. The manners or decency of the characters in speaking or acting what is proper for them, and proper to be shewn by the poet.

IV. The thoughts which express the manners.

V. The words which express those thoughts ["Heads of an Answer to Rymer," I, 217].

In his explanatory criticism Dryden assesses these parts in order to arrive at an estimate of the effectiveness of a work and the authorial powers which it displays. Thus his procedure is rhetorical in its assumptions and almost exclusively work-oriented in its practice.

Dryden does adopt a special approach for each critical mode, and the prescriptive essays with their authoritative rulings follow a markedly different pattern from the others. There Dryden must assert a single truth—and he goes to other men to find it. But in both the speculative and the later explanatory work he attempts merely to offer clarification by contrast, and even when he makes explicit value judgments they are tentative and comparative, never absolute. Dryden is by no means incapable of making an extended analysis of a single author—his assessments of Virgil and Chaucer show otherwise. But his natural habit of mind is exploratory and comparative, and this bent appears clearly in his characteristic critical methods.

CHAPTER 3

Sense of History

Dryden lived during the infancy of what we regard as literary history, a discipline which came to maturity in England only with Thomas Warton's *History of English Poetry* (1774–1781). His attempts at writing the history of literary forms in the "Discourse on Satire" and the Dedication of the *Aeneis* are both derivative and not notably successful, for his concept of evolution is clearly elementary, both there and elsewhere. Consequently Dryden's historical perspective has received rather cursory attention. René Wellek treats Dryden and his contemporaries briefly as the possessors of an incipiently historical outlook —which makes their work merely a step toward something else.[1] The most usual approach is typified by David Nichol Smith, who praises Dryden's statement that "Milton was the poetical son of Spenser, and Mr Waller of Fairfax; for

1. René Wellek, *The Rise of English Literary History* (Chapel Hill, 1941), chap. 2. On the parallel rise of English historical scholarship during the Restoration see David C. Douglas, *English Scholars* (London, 1939).

we have our lineal descents and clans as well as other families" (Preface to *Fables*, II, 270). Smith sees in this an intuitive reaching for a developmental concept of literary history, and like George Watson, he is politely regretful that Dryden did not carry his idea further.[2]

But this view misses the point. Except in such a venture as Wellek's, there is little object in looking for hints of later developments. We can use Dryden's historical observations to help understand his own literary perspective and should not think them unimportant merely because they seem rudimentary to us. On the contrary they play, I believe, a major role in determining his view of literature, and therefore it seems useful both to define Dryden's opinions on progress and history more thoroughly and to assess their influence on his critical stance.

I

Wellek observes that advanced concepts of "*individuality*" and *development*" are a prerequisite for writers of "genuine literary history."[3] By "individuality" he means a sense of the uniqueness of each artist's vision and creations; by "development" he means the assumption that there is an organic evolution of literary forms in time. Our immediate object must be to determine to what extent Dryden possesses these concepts.

Two general observations should be made at once. First, Dryden believes in progress; he most certainly does not

2. *John Dryden* (Cambridge, England, 1950), p. 84; Watson, II, 270n. G. M. Miller, in *The Historical Point of View in English Literary Criticism from 1570 to 1770* (Heidelberg, 1913), pp. 94–100, concludes only that Dryden was of little importance in the rise of historical criticism.

3. Wellek, p. 25.

[66]

subscribe to what Lovejoy calls "a negative philosophy of history." [4] Second, Dryden displays, from the beginning of his career, a strong sense of cultural relativity. For him each age and country, and even each writer, appears distinct. Wellek correctly observes that "before the seventeenth century, with a few exceptions, Greece and Rome were considered as being on the same plane as contemporary England. Virgil and Ovid, Homer and Pindar, were discussed as almost contemporary writers." [5] Dryden, in acute contradistinction, sees the classical writers as far removed from his own age and as representative of very different periods of their own.[6]

Dryden's work as a commercial playwright undoubtedly sensitized him to the demands of his audience and helped make him aware of variations in taste from age to age and country to country. The structure for *Of Dramatic Poesy* makes it plain that already Dryden conceived the English dramatic form as, in some sense, distinct. The separate claims of English, French, and Ancient dramatic practice are argued—and kept separate. Crites denies that "the Moderns have acquired a new perfection in writing," but grants that "they have altered the mode of it" (I, 42). Neander wonders "why Lisideius and many others should cry up the barrenness of the French plots above the variety

4. A. O. Lovejoy, "The Parallel of Deism and Classicism," *MP*, 29 (1932), 281–299; reprinted in *Essays in the History of Ideas* (Baltimore, 1948), p. 88. Cf. Earl Miner, "Dryden and the Issue of Human Progress," *PQ*, 40 (1961), 120–129.

5. Wellek, p. 26.

6. Thus comparing Horace and Juvenal, Dryden gives the preference to the latter with the comment, "After all, Horace had the disadvantage of the times in which he lived; they were better for the man, but worse for the satirist. . . . Therefore Juvenal had a larger field than Horace" ("Discourse on Satire," II, 132).

and copiousness of the English" (I, 58–59). Without claiming outright that any is preferable, Dryden is clearly suggesting that there are three distinct traditions here.

Dryden's normal critical method is, as I have noted, syncretic—he borrows whatever seems best from all three traditions. He is able to do so because he sees much common ground among them and believes firmly in the essential uniformity of human nature. We must not, however, suppose that his qualifications of this doctrine are of little import. On the contrary, they are central to his theory and practice of literature.

Rymer says of Greek and English writing: "Certain it is, that *Nature* is the same, and *Man* is the same, he *loves, grieves, hates, envies,* has the same *affections* and *passions* in both places, and the same *springs* that give them *motion.* What mov'd pity there, will *here* also produce the same effect." [7] Dryden replies that "tho' nature, as he objects, is the same in all places, and reason too the same, yet the climate, the age, the dispositions of the people to whom a poet writes, may be so different that what pleased the Greeks would not satisfy an English audience" ("Heads of an Answer to Rymer," I, 214).

This qualified uniformitarianism of Dryden's appears clearly in "The Grounds of Criticism in Tragedy" (1679) when he concludes that

we ought to follow them [Shakespeare and Fletcher] so far only as they have copied the excellencies of those who invented and brought to perfection dramatic poetry: those things only excepted which *religion, customs of countries, idioms of languages,* etc., have altered in the *superstructures,* but not in the *foundation* of the design [I, 246; italics added].

7. *The Tragedies of the Last Age,* in *The Critical Works of Thomas Rymer,* ed. Curt A. Zimansky (New Haven, 1956), p. 19.

The exceptions here are more than pious platitudes to Dryden. To begin with, his concern about the effect of religious differences is obvious in his elaborate denial that Moderns cannot write great epics because, it is suggested, "Christianity is not capable of those embellishments which are afforded in the belief of those ancient heathens" ("Discourse on Satire," II, 85). He goes on to claim at length that Christianity can indeed supply the necessary "machinery" for an epic (II, 85–90).[8] Next, Dryden is always conscious of differences imposed by language. Thus the Dedication of the *Aeneis* (1697) contains a detailed assessment of the difficulties of rendering a Latin work effectively in English (II, 246–252), and in the Preface to *Albion and Albanius* (1685) Dryden discusses the suitability of different languages for opera.[9] Finally, by "custom of countries" (to judge from his other works) he has two things in mind. First, he is asking for historicity. Manners must "be suitable

8. Dryden leaves Milton out of account here because "his subject is not that of an heroic poem, properly so called. . . . His event is not prosperous, like that of all other epic works" (II, 84).
9. "Italian . . . is the softest, the sweetest, the most harmonious, not only of any modern tongue, but even beyond any of the learned. It seems indeed to have been invented for the sake of poetry and music; the vowels are so abounding in all words, especially in terminations of them. . . . The French, who now cast a longing eye to their country, are not less ambitious to possess their elegance in poetry and music: in both which they labour at impossibilities. 'Tis true, indeed, they have reformed their tongue. . . . But, after all, as nothing can be improved beyond its own species, or farther than its original nature will allow . . . so neither can the natural harshness of the French, or their perpetual ill accent, be ever refined into perfect harmony like the Italian. The English has yet more natural disadvantages than the French; our original Teutonic consisting most in monosyllables, and those encumbered with consonants, cannot possibly be freed from those inconveniences" (II, 37–38).

to the age, quality, *country*, dignity, etc., of the character." [10] Second, and more important, he is aware of the force of local tradition. This force is what he has in mind when he says that "the rules of the French stage . . . are extremely different from ours, by reason of their opposite taste" ("Discourse on Satire," II, 74). Dryden never feels bound by Elizabethan practices, but he recognizes their relation to English taste and tradition. Thus he can say

I have endeavoured in this play to follow the practice of the Ancients, who, as Mr Rymer has judiciously observed, are and ought to be our masters. . . . Yet, though their models are regular, they are too little for English tragedy, which requires to be built in a larger compass [Preface to *All for Love*, I, 230–231].

He further elucidates this difference in the Preface to *Oedipus* (1679), where he describes the Greek method and says, "The conduct of *our* stage is much more difficult.

10. "The Grounds of Criticism in Tragedy," I, 251; italics added. In the Preface to *Don Sebastian* (1690) Dryden apologizes for altering the character of Sebastian: " 'Tis true I have no right to blast his memory with such a crime: but declaring it to be fiction, I desire my audience to think it no longer true than while they are seeing it represented" (II, 48). Thus Dryden demands not only suitability, but what he calls "resemblance": "This is founded upon the particular characters of men, as we have them delivered to us by relation or history; that is, when a poet has the known character of this or that man before him, he is bound to represent him such, at least not contrary to that which fame has reported him to have been. Thus, it is not a poet's choice to make Ulysses choleric, or Achilles patient, because Homer has described 'em quite otherwise" ("Grounds," I, 249). We find little sense of even general historicity in Shakespeare's plays, and not much more in Jonson's. Dryden can sin against his own prescription, but nonetheless he insists that "in all things we are to imitate the customs and the times of those persons and things which we represent" ("A Parallel of Poetry and Painting," II, 195).

. . . *Custom* likewise has obtained that we must form an under-plot" (I, 234; italics added).[11]

Dryden believes firmly that neither the general end of writing nor its method can vary. ("The foundation of the design" does not change, as he puts it in the passage quoted above, I, 246.) [12] Nonetheless, the alterations in literary superstructures imposed by differences of age and nation assume considerable importance for him in the actual execution of the design. He consistently objects to Elizabethan irregularity of plot (e.g., "The Grounds of Criticism in Tragedy," I, 246–247), but he does recognize a basic difference between the English and French theatrical traditions in this respect: the English stress variety and liveliness, the French exactness and singleness of design.[13] Dryden's own practice between 1668 and 1680 did move toward

11. Dryden's sense of the differentness of his own time, country, and language appears clearly later in his discussions of translation. "Imitation," he says, is for the translator "to write, as he supposes that author would have done, had he lived in our age, and in our country" (Preface to *Ovid's Epistles*, I, 270). Here Dryden condemns this as a "libertine" way of writing. Later he alters his method to fall somewhere "betwixt a paraphrase and imitation. . . . We . . . have endeavoured to make him [Juvenal] speak that kind of English which he would have spoken had he lived in England, and had written to this age. If sometimes any of us (and 'tis but seldom) make him express the customs and manners of our native country rather than of Rome; 'tis either when there was some kind of analogy betwixt their customs and ours; or when, to make him more easy to vulgar understandings, we give him those manners which are familiar to us" ("Discourse on Satire," II, 152–155).

12. The general end of writing is of course to cause the appropriate response in the reader or audience; the method is imitation of nature.

13. This distinction is one of the basic conceptions behind *Of Dramatic Poesy* (e.g., I, 58–60), and it is maintained with minor variations throughout Dryden's career.

[71]

greater "regularity," and he did finally condemn tragi-comedy,[14] but it remained his conviction that "the genius of the English cannot bear too regular a play; we are given to variety, even to a debauchery of pleasure" (Preface to *Don Sebastian*, II, 49).

He realizes that national taste may change: "The opinion of the people may alter, and in another age, or perhaps in this, serious plays may be set up above comedies" ("Defence of *An Essay*," I, 120). Much later he comments that "if hereafter the audience will come to taste the confinement of the French (which I believe the English never will), then it will be easy for their poets to follow the strictness of the mechanic rules" (Letter to Walsh, 12 December 1693; II, 173). But even in later life Dryden can say, "I dare establish it for a rule of practice on the stage, that we are bound to please those whom we pretend to entertain; and that at any price, religion and good manners only excepted" (Dedication of the *Examen poeticum*, II, 162), and so he can defend the Elizabethans against Rymer's strictures by saying:

Shakespeare and Fletcher have written to the genius of the age and nation in which they lived. . . . And if they [the Greeks] proceeded upon a foundation of truer reason to please

14. Dryden's tragicomedies are a clear instance of his acceding to local custom. Early in his career he defends the form: "We have invented, increased, and perfected a more pleasant way of writing for the stage than was ever known to the ancients or moderns of any nation, which is tragi-comedy" (*Of Dramatic Poesy*, I, 58). In the "Parallel of Poetry and Painting" (1695) he condemns it as "wholly Gothic" and "an unnatural mingle" (II, 202). Perhaps this judgment is rendered excessively severe by the formal, prescriptive nature of the "Parallel." Only two years earlier Dryden speaks favorably of the form as "a play of the English fashion" ("Discourse on Satire," II, 145).

[72]

the Athenians than Shakespeare and Fletcher to please the English, it only shows that the Athenians were a more judicious people; but the poet's business is certainly to please the audience ["Heads of an Answer to Rymer," I, 214].

Uniformitarian though his assumptions are, Dryden objects to the importation of foreign standards which would lead to the "destruction of our poetical church and state" (Dedication of the *Examen poeticum*, II, 160); firmly and consistently he upholds the validity of changes in literary superstructures wrought by age and nation.

Just how Dryden conceives of change is a less clearcut matter. Indubitably he was a "Modern" and believed in progress. He says in the "Defence of the Epilogue" (1672), "I profess to have no other ambition in this essay than that poetry may not go backward, when all other arts and sciences are advancing" (I, 169). Admittedly his purpose here is to defend his criticims of the Elizabethans. And certainly his opinion of Restoration writers soon fell (see the Prologue to *Aureng-Zebe*, 1675). Nonetheless, even late in his career he could say

the Greek writers only gave us the rudiments of a stage which they never finished; . . . many of the tragedies in the former age amongst us were without comparison beyond those of Sophocles and Euripides. . . . For if we, or our greater fathers, have not yet brought the drama to an absolute perfection, yet at least we have carried it much farther than those ancient Greeks [Dedication of the *Examen poeticum*, II, 160–161].

This seems to be his considered opinion, for it is several times reiterated in different forms.[15]

15. The "Discourse on Satire" places the English above all others in tragedy and satire (II, 81). "To My Dear Friend Mr Congreve"

Granted then that Dryden believed progress possible, we are left to ask what sort of progress. The matter is complicated by his dual perspective. At times he looks at ancient and modern literatures as a single developing whole: "And thus I have given the history of satire, and derived it as far as from Ennius to your Lordship; that is, from its first rudiments of barbarity to its last polishing and perfection" ("Discourse on Satire," II, 142). More frequently, Dryden seems to think of literary progress in terms of national developments, as in the Preface to *Fables*, where he says of Chaucer: "We can only say that he lived in the infancy of our poetry, and that nothing is brought to perfection at the first" (II, 281).

Believing as he did that the Ancients had established the proper foundations of literature, Dryden had no option but to regard English writing as essentially an extension of Greek and Roman beginnings. Yet plainly the particularities of English language and taste had produced unique developments. One of his major problems was to be sure that English additions did not contravene the foundations laid down by the Ancients—hence his concern "to inquire how far we ought to imitate our own poets, Shakespeare and Fletcher" ("The Grounds of Criticism in Tragedy," I, 243). In general, as we have seen, Dryden does seem satisfied that the English had advanced what they received.

English developments are then generally regarded as ac-

(1694) asserts that the Restoration writers have finally surpassed their English predecessors (though admittedly the context renders the compliment suspect). In a letter to Dennis (*c.* March 1694) Dryden says: "I cannot but conclude with Mr Rym[er] that our English comedy is far beyond any thing of the Ancients. And notwithstanding our irregularities, so is our tragedy" (II, 178).

[74]

cretions to prior tradition. Dryden insists many times that "the first inventors of any art or science, provided they have brought it to perfection, are, in reason, to give laws to it; and according to their model, all after-undertakers are to build" (Preface to *Albion and Albanius*, II, 35).[16] Changes must be justified by religion, language, or local custom—as in the case of adapting epic "machinery" to Christianity. When Dryden tries to vindicate Elizabethan drama, he argues merely that "the English have added to their [Greek] beauties: as, for example, not only more plot, but also new passions; as namely, that of love" ("Heads of an Answer to Rymer," I, 212).

Dryden appears to assume that change is a matter of linear progress toward perfection through progressive refinement. He never really faces the cyclical nature of nations and their literatures, though such a view seems implicit in the biological metaphors he frequently employs. For example: "Dramatic poesy had time enough, reckoning from Thespis (who first invented it) to Aristophanes, to be born, to grow up, and to flourish in maturity" (*Of Dramatic Poesy*, I, 25–26). But Dryden largely ignores the ultimate decline and death of Greek and Roman literature and the implied lesson for the English; it is Temple who first elaborates in England what Wellek calls an "almost Spenglerian theory of closed cycles of culture." [17] Dryden's assumption, of course, is that whatever the fate of a single nation, its culture stands as part of a broader tradition. For each country, he assumes a parallel pattern of development from crudity to refinement.

16. Cf. "The Grounds of Criticism in Tragedy," I, 246; "A Parallel of Poetry and Painting," II, 191.
17. Wellek, p. 41. See Temple's *Of Poetry* (1690).

We must be children before we grow men. There was an Ennius, and in process of time a Lucilius, and a Lucretius, before Virgil and Horace; even after Chaucer there was a Spenser, a Harington, a Fairfax, before Waller and Denham were in being; and our numbers were in their nonage till these last appeared [Preface to *Fables*, II, 281].

Wellek caustically observes that the "biological" metaphor illustrates an utterly unjustifiable assumption of an exact parallel between English and Latin poetry. This assumption was no passing whim. In 1683 Dryden had advised Soame on the substitution of English names in a translation of Boileau's *L'Art poétique*, evidently supposing that the pattern of development must be identical, whatever the country or the individuals involved.[18]

Indeed, Dryden's sense of evolution is largely concerned with refinement of language and decorum. His objections to earlier English writers are generally either that they reflect the manners of a cruder age or that their language is imperfect. He does suppose that refinement will continue. Thus, justifying his revisions of Chaucer, he says: "Another poet, in another age, may take the same liberty with my writings; if at least they live long enough to deserve correction" (Preface to *Fables*, II, 287). Or as Pope put it: "As Chaucer is shall Dryden be." Dryden specifically objects here to "veneration" for "old language"; his notions of increasing correctness and refinement make such feeling impossible.

Dryden expects that the writers of each age will for the most part work in the forms established by their predecessors. He does recognize, very early, that "the genius of

18. See *The Poetical Works of Dryden*, ed. George R. Noyes (Cambridge, Mass., 1950), pp. 916–925.

every age is different" (*Of Dramatic Poesy*, I, 85), and that this genius will incline men to pursue certain forms and adopt varying conventions. Thus he remarks the suitability of Juvenal's age for satire, and acidly comments after what he considered a far from glorious revolution: "They say my talent is satire; if it be so, 'tis a fruitful age, and there is an extraordinary crop to gather" ("To the Earl of Abingdon," II, 63). But despite his recognition of such temporary predispositions, Dryden continues firmly to hold that modern literature builds on ancient foundations. Certainly he wants to believe that "we have wholly finished what they began" ("Heads of an Answer to Rymer," I, 218). And thoroughly though he believes in following the rules of the inventors of a form, he realizes that "few men have the happiness to begin and finish any new project" ("Of Heroic Plays," I, 158), and thus "no art or science is at once begun and perfected, but that it must pass first through many hands, and even through several ages" ("Discourse on Satire," II, 139).

Within established forms Dryden is chary of innovation, and so he can say, in discussing "how a modern satire should be made," that he "will not deviate in the least from the precepts and examples of the Ancients, who were always our best masters" ("Discourse," II, 144). But as he remarks elsewhere, "Imitation is a nice point, and there are few poets who deserve to be models in all they write" (Preface to *Sylvæ*, II, 32). Dryden finds fault with all three of the principal Roman satirists, and so he is prepared to select, correct, and amalgamate from their examples, as well as to make the changes appropriate to age and country. The result, he believed, was progress.

One might easily suppose that Dryden objected to innovation, for his criticism is liberally larded with admonitions to follow the Ancients, "always our best masters." Certainly too he has little sense of "originality" in the late eighteenth-century meaning of the term.[19] But he is never in favor of "too servile imitation of the Ancients" (letter to Walsh, 12 December 1693, II, 173), and he is consistently proud to draw attention to his own experiments—he is even inclined to exaggerate his innovations. He asks that the faults of his opera *Albion and Albanius* (1685) be excused, "because it has attempted a discovery beyond any former undertaker of our nation" (II, 38), remarking further that "the newness of the undertaking is all the hazard" (II, 42). Similarly, he gives Davenant high marks for giving "first light" on heroic drama ("Of Heroic Plays"), and comments that in the "Pindaric" what Cowley has started another age may bring to perfection (Preface to *Sylvæ*, II, 32–33).

19. Wellek says that "a book like Langbaine's lists of 'thefts' and 'plagiaries' shows how sharply the so-called unoriginality of an older period was suddenly felt" (p. 25). I think this needs qualification. Langbaine is not asking for "original composition" in Young's sense of the term; "imitation" has not yet become a term of reproach. But it is quite true that he is making greater demands on the poet's "invention," or selection of materials for elaboration. Langbaine's strictures are liberally applied to Dryden: see Spingarn, III, 110–147. Dryden's response to such charges (which Langbaine ridicules) is to appeal to the example of the Ancients, and to denigrate mere plot. " 'Tis true that, where ever I have liked any story in a romance, novel, or foreign play, I have made no difficulty, nor ever shall, to take the foundation of it, to build it up, and to make it proper for the English stage" (Preface to *An Evening's Love*, I, 153). This accords with Dryden's belief that it is the ornament and composition which make a work good: "The fable is not the greatest masterpiece of a tragedy, tho' it be the foundation of it" ("Heads of an Answer to Rymer," I, 211).

[78]

What we can conclude here is that Dryden conceives of each literary form as possessing inherently certain powers, beauties, and possibilities, all of which must be discovered, elaborated, and exploited before they are fully understood. Thus he says:

An heroic play ought to be an imitation, in little, of an heroic poem; and, consequently . . . Love and Valour ought to be the subject of it. Both these Sir William Davenant had begun to shadow; but it was so, as first discoverers draw their maps, with headlands, and promontories, and some few outlines of somewhat taken at a distance, and which the designer saw not clearly ["Of Heroic Plays," I, 158–159].

This passage suggests the essence of Dryden's conception of change and evolution: he sees them as a process of discovery of inherent potentialities in literary forms. Progress in any well-developed form will consist more of refinement than innovation. "To quit the beaten road of the Ancients, and take a path of his own choosing, he acknowledges to be a bold and ridiculous attempt if it succeed not" ("Life of Lucian," II, 212)—in other words, such a course may succeed, but probably won't. This is why Dryden warns against trying "to make new rules of the drama, as Lopez de Vega has attempted unsuccessfully to do" ("A Parallel of Poetry and Painting," II, 195). But where the possibilities are less fully charted, Dryden is ready enough to sanction experiment. He says of Pindaric form in a letter to John Dennis (c. March 1694):

You . . . know how far the boldness of a poet may lawfully extend. I could wish you would cultivate this kind of ode, and reduce it either to the same measures which Pindar used, or give new measures of your own. For, as it is, it looks like a vast tract of land newly discovered. The soil is wonderfully fruitful, but unmanured, overstocked with inhabitants, but almost all salvages, without laws, arts, arms, or policy [II,179].

To return to the problem posed at the start of this section: we find that Dryden's notions of individuality and development are quite different from ours. Change, for Dryden, is generally either the discovery of potentiality latent in literary forms, or the adaptation of forms to national circumstances. The differences between authors he conceives as either a matter of age and country (for a uniformitarian he has a strong sense of cultural relativity), or a matter of differing skills in composition.

This last point demands some explanation. Dryden can make sharp individual distinctions—among Elizabethan playwrights in *Of Dramatic Poesy*, or Roman satirists in the "Discourse on Satire," or "heroic" writers in the Dedication of the *Aeneis*. But he regards literature as a performance on the part of the writer, a display of powers, and so he tends to base his differentiations on rhetorical skills. "The difference between Shakespeare and Fletcher in their plotting seems to be this: that Shakespeare generally moves more terror, and Fletcher more compassion" ("The Grounds of Criticism in Tragedy," I, 247). Dryden comments on his own aptitude for satire, and lack of it for comedy, and he is excellent at explaining the effectiveness of Ovid's wit. What Dryden lacks, from our point of view, is a sense of an author's individual viewpoint. The writer is to express truth which holds good for all men in all ages, and the value of what he says rests on the accuracy of his imitation and the effectiveness with which he invests it, never on his individual insight or perspective.

[80]

Hazlitt could say in 1822 that "originality is the seeing of nature differently from others, and yet as it is in itself" (*OED*). Dryden would deny flatly that this is possible.

Dryden's uniformitarianism is then significantly qualified to allow for national differences and tradition, but it remains his essential assumption. Consequently, in his accounts of various literatures Dryden feels that he has to treat the work of Ancients and Moderns as a continuum founded upon immutable principles. Such an outlook makes Dryden's historical descriptions rather awkward. We should examine them, however, for the light that they shed on his understanding of change and his attitudes toward his predecessors.

II

Perhaps because literary criticism was for Dryden merely an adjunct to other work, not really a discipline in its own right, he seldom discusses its theory or practice, and not surprisingly he left no formal statement at all on literary history. We can, however, make some guess at his understanding of it by extrapolating from his discussion of history in "The Life of Plutarch" (1683). History, he says, "is principally divided into these three species: *commentaries* or *annals*; *history* properly so called; and *biographia*, or the lives of particular men" (II, 5). Annals are "naked history; or the plain relation of matter of fact, according to the succession of time, divested of all the other ornaments. The springs and motives of actions are not here sought, unless they offer themselves, and are open to every man's discernment." History proper seeks to explain these springs and motives of actions. Biography Dryden praises

[81]

as easier to make perfect and equal to the others in "pleasure and instruction," though inferior in "dignity."

If for "biography" we substitute "accounts of single authors," this scheme can readily be adapted to descriptive literary criticism. Dryden himself is excellent at giving appreciative accounts of other writers. In the other two forms he, like his contemporaries, is less successful. The mediocrity of Restoration "annals," particularly on English literature, can be set down to their writers' lack of adequate information. Systematic scholarship really begins only with Richard Bentley and others near the end of the century. Hence even chronological information was often sketchy. Seventeenth century failure at history proper is crisply documented by Wellek. But the story of literary history in the Restoration (and considerably beyond) is that of a struggle to move from annals to history. Increasingly writers do seek the springs and motives of change.

Mid-century literary chronicles at best fall into the category of annals. Davenant's Preface to *Gondibert* (1650) can serve as an example. Davenant is by no means in thrall to his predecessors; he explains at length his determination to seek new ground. We might think that he would justify this with reference to his age, country, language, and the special purposes and subjects they give him. But not so. Davenant starts with a chronological account of heroic writers from Homer and Virgil through Lucan, Statius, Tasso, and Spenser, and he is aware of the debts of later writers to earlier. But he assumes that the endeavor of all of them, himself included, is identical—to produce a certain kind of imitation of nature. He hopes to improve on others by avoiding mere imitation of them; nonetheless, he makes no allowance for differences in authorial purpose or culture. It is quite evident that Davenant believes that all works conform to a single standard of judgment.[20]

Richard Flecknoe's "A Short Discourse of the English Stage" (1664) represents "annals" at their most straightforward. Flecknoe is aware of a change between early and late century theatrical production:

Now, for the difference betwixt our Theaters and those of former times, they were but plain and simple, with no other Scenes nor Decorations of the Stage, but onely old Tapestry, and the Stage strew'd with Rushes, with their Habits accordingly, whereas ours now for cost and ornament are arriv'd to the heighth of Magnificence; but that which makes our Stage the better makes our Playes the worse perhaps, they striving now to make them more for sight then hearing [Spingarn, II, 95].

His concept of literary change is based on "refinement": "*Shakespear* was one of the first who invented the Dramatick Stile from dull History to quick Comedy, upon whom *Johnson* refin'd; as *Beaumont* and *Fletcher* first writ in the Heroick way, upon whom *Suckling* and others endeavoured to refine agen" (Spingarn, II, 92). He does grant that English plays ("excepting onely some few of *Johnsons*") tend to have "faults," but "if the French have fewer . . . 'tis because they confine themselves to narrower limits, and consequently have less liberty to erre." His differentiation among the Elizabethans is straightforward: Shakespeare is natural; Jonson artful and judicious; Fletcher witty but indecorous (in the Restoration sense of the term).

20. In a brief discussion of English heroic writing, Rymer shows far more awareness of national tradition, and criticizes Davenant sharply for not taking an English subject ("Preface to Rapin," *Critical Works*, pp. 5–6).

We may say that Flecknoe's work is pat, superficial, and rather ill-informed. But nonetheless—and regardless of any comment implicit in *Mac Flecknoe*—we must grant that Dryden's own assessments do not differ greatly from Flecknoe's. Both of them (perhaps influenced by patriotism) have a sense of national differences, and *Of Dramatic Poesy* (written 1665-1666?) shows Dryden particularly to have a grasp of cultural relativity which Davenant utterly lacks. But in the 1660s Dryden is no more advanced than the others in suggesting how change occurs or a literary form comes into being. Discussions of epic tend to start: in the beginning, there was Homer—which is not surprising. But that Shakespeare should head discussions of English drama *is* surprising. Dryden, in theory at least, knew all about "Queen Gorboduc" (Dedication of *The Rival Ladies*, 1664, I, 5). Even thirty years later Dryden shows no sign of possessing any real comprehension of the chronology of Elizabethan drama. Jonson and Fletcher are said to learn from Shakespeare, but beyond this Dryden never goes. In *Of Dramatic Poesy* we need not expect much of a historical survey, since that is outside Dryden's immediate purpose. Astonishingly, he never comments on the improvements Shakespeare wrought on his predecessors; nor does he consider the traditions on which Shakespeare might have drawn.

Not until the 1690s does Dryden attempt to write what we would call literary history. The "Discourse on Satire" (1693) and the Dedication of the *Aeneis* (1697) are, of course, more histories of literary forms than accounts of national literatures. Obviously Dryden continued to believe that writers worked by developing the potentialities of literary forms, not by trying to express the temper of an age. (He does, as we have seen, believe that an age may predispose its writers toward a single form.) Most of what Dryden has to say is derivative—he was after all not a scholar, and he had to get his material from somewhere—but nonetheless what he does, especially in the "Discourse on Satire," makes a new departure in English criticism.

He undertakes

to give you [the Earl of Dorset], from the best authors, the origin, the antiquity, the growth, the change, and the completement of satire among the Romans; to describe, if not define, the nature of that poem, with its several qualifications and virtues, together with the several sorts of it; to compare the excellencies of Horace, Persius, and Juvenal, and shew the particular manners of their satires ["Discourse," II, 95].

This critical endeavor, in its aims, at any rate, approaches history proper. Dryden does propose to investigate origins and describe change and growth. He will, further, assess the potentialities of the form and the particular powers of its greatest practitioners. He limits his subject to the Roman satirists, but since the "Discourse" is a preface to translations of Juvenal and Persius, this is understandable. We find Dryden's references to English satirists tantalizing, but he had no handy foreign commentators to give him all the facts on them, and so evidently he has to rely on his own rather sketchy acquaintance with the subject.

This work is easy to criticize, though I believe that Wellek is rather too harsh. Undeniably the "Discourse" is unoriginal; it stops with the Romans; and Dryden tends to see merely a uniform advance to something like perfection. More important, he did assemble all this material, enquire into origins, and attempt systematically to analyze the potentiality of the form. With great skill he shows what can

[85]

be done in it and how its greatest exponents have exploited the mode. And when he says "Thus I have treated, *in a new method*, the comparison betwixt Horace, Juvenal, and Persius" (II, 135; italics added), he is at least half correct, despite his heavy reliance on other critics. His comment on his method is interesting:

I am now almost gotten into my depth; at least, by the help of Dacier, I am swimming towards it. Not that I will promise always to follow him any more than he follows Casaubon; but to keep him in my eye, as my best and truest guide; and where I think he may possibly mislead me, there to have recourse to my own lights, as I expect that others should do by me" ["Discourse," II, 104].

Here in a nutshell we have Dryden's views on the utility of his critical predecessors.

The Dedication of the *Aeneis* suffers by comparison to the "Discourse," in part precisely because its orientation is less historical. Dryden intends merely to give an account of "the greatness and excellency of an heroic poem, with some of the difficulties which attend that work" (II, 232). His comments on Homer, Tasso, Spenser, and Milton are purely incidental and illustrative. But as in the earlier work he succeeds very well in explaining the potentiality of the epic form, and particularly in contrasting it with the dramatic mode (II, 226–232). The most historical considerations in the essay concern not literary form proper, but its relation to historical periods.[21] At some length Dryden

21. These are to be found in the central section of the essay, the analysis of Virgil, which Watson omits because it is mostly derivative. (I think his decision is unfortunate.) My references to this part of the essay are to George R. Noyes, *The Poetical Works of Dryden*.

[86]

assesses the "moral"—one might say the social utility—of Homer and Virgil, concluding that "Virgil's [epic] was as useful to the Romans of his age, as Homer's was to the Grecians of his." Virgil's work reflects, Dryden feels, his "having maturely weigh'd the condition of the times in which he liv'd." [22] We have come a long way from Davenant's assumption that all epics attempt the same thing.

We hear regrettably little from Dryden about the evolution of epic form. He does, however, defend Virgil against charges of undue reliance on Homer, arguing first that Homer did not invent the story of the Trojan war, and secondly that the two poets had very different "designs" in mind.[23] We may deduce from this argument that Dryden approved of Virgil's learning "to imitate like" Homer and felt that he had avoided "servile copying" by adapting his design and moral to the needs of his age. Almost explicitly here Dryden is treating change as the modification of literary form by national circumstance.

Dryden is always excellent at giving an account of a single writer, and the "Discourse" demonstrates his ability to compile an annal. Although he plainly wants to account for the growth and change in literary forms, he never really manages to do so. At times he seems to toy with the theory of influence by climate adopted by Temple,[24] but he never works it out explicitly. More often Dryden simply assumes that authors write to the needs of their ages, without making any effort to suggest how or why the ages change.

Persius was grave, and particularly opposed his gravity to lewdness, which was the predominant vice in Nero's Court at the time when he published his satires. . . . Horace was a

22. Noyes, pp. 492, 494.   23. Noyes, pp. 504–506.
24. See Spingarn, III, 45, 103–104.

mild admonisher, a Court satirist, fit for the gentle times of Augustus. . . . Juvenal was as proper for his times as they for theirs. His was an age that deserved a more severe chastisement. Vices were more gross and open, more flagitious, more encouraged by the example of a tyrant, and more protected by his authority [II, 135].

Insofar as Dryden has any systematic idea of change, he relies on his old standby, refinement. As a society matures its language and literature grow more polished, and in each country the process must be repeated, though increasingly with the benefit of prior example. Thus in excusing the remaining "barbarities" of the English language Dryden says, "the Greeks, we know, were labouring many hundred years upon their language, before they brought it to perfection" ("Dedication," II, 246). Tracing the origins of satire Dryden concludes: "When they began to be somewhat better bred, and were entering, as I may say, into the first rudiments of civil conversation, they left these hedge-notes for another sort of poem, somewhat polished, which was also full of pleasant raillery, but without any mixture of obscenity. This sort of poetry appeared under the name of satire" (II, 107).

By the standards we are accustomed to employ, Dryden's attempts at literary history are no better than a promising beginning. Wellek is absolutely right when he says that Dryden does not comprehend the "genius" of an age in the "sense of a pervading temper common to all cultural activities at a given time"; [25] he does no more than assume a simple harmony of writers, country, and age. Dryden's uniformitarian view of human nature makes it impossible

25. Wellek, p. 30.

[88]

for him to conceive radical shifts in *Weltanschauung*.[26]
But we should not be too ready to condemn Dryden by
our own standards, particularly since something of a reaction is now underway against what George Watson aptly
calls the "Tidy School" of literary history.[27] We find it
convenient to assume that writers are the products of the
age in which they live, and that there is an intelligible continuity of development from age to age. Unhappily this
assumption can lead to monstrous distortion and over-
simplification—as in the early twentieth-century notions
of Augustan peace and monolithic neoclassical rigidity,
clichés which still resist extermination.

Probably Dryden underestimates cultural temper no
more than we overestimate it. His uncertainty about the
causes of change is probably not as ridiculous, *sub specie
eternitatis*, as the neat little periods in which many modern
critics have believed. Plainly Dryden is pushing toward a
theory of evolution; he wants to explain the "springs and
motives" of literary change. And though he is not very
successful, we can only grant, after politely deriding him,
that neither are we.

III

Since Dryden's understanding of English literary history
is unsystematic and severely distorted by lack of factual
knowledge, we may learn almost as much from what he
fails to say as from his actual pronouncements. His sense of

26. Wellek's utterly different outlook is made plain in his famous
essay "The Concept of 'Romanticism' in Literary History," *CL*,
1 (1949), 1–23, 147–172, and in his *A History of Modern Criticism*
(New Haven, 1955—).

27. *The Literary Critics* (Baltimore, 1962), pp. 10–11.

his own place is odd; being part of an English tradition is very important to him, and yet his belief in a radical split between Renaissance and Restoration is perhaps the most prominent feature of his discussions of English literature. In this respect Dryden shares the viewpoint of his age: before Cromwell was before the flood. Wellek cites Edward Phillips (Milton's nephew) as a pioneer in the establishment of "a choice of *English* writers" from Chaucer to Settle, and yet as Wellek says, the *Theatrum poetarum* (1675) is "testimony to the break in poetical tradition created by the Civil Wars"—for Phillips knew precious little about even the quantity of Elizabethan and Jacobean writing.[28]

Much the same thing can be said of Dryden. Even in the annals sense his historical knowledge appears sketchy in the extreme. "Queen Gorboduc" aside, earlier drama seems to consist for Dryden of Shakespeare, Jonson, Beaumont, and Fletcher. At least this is the impression given by the critical essays. A glance at *The London Stage*[29] tells us that a theatrical man living in London could easily have been familiar with a considerable variety of Jacobean and Caroline plays. Evidently Dryden was: Arthur Kirsch argues fairly convincingly that his heroic plays draw not only on epic ideas, but "are greatly indebted to Beaumont and Fletcher's tragicomedies and to Jacobean and Caroline court drama."[30] This is puzzling. We would expect, given Dryden's theory of refinement, that he would, like Flecknoe,

28. Wellek, pp. 17–18.
29. Vol. 1 (1660–1700), ed. William Van Lennep, critical introd. by Emmett L. Avery and Arthur H. Scouten (Carbondale, Ill., 1965).
30. Arthur C. Kirsch, *Dryden's Heroic Drama* (Princeton, 1965), p. 12. The sources of heroic drama have long been the subject of heated debate.

seize eagerly on such intermediate figures as Suckling. His failure to do so we might ascribe to a desire to emphasize his own innovations (at least in the 1670s), or to a spottier knowledge of his immediate predecessors than our hindsight would lead us to expect. Dryden did know and work with Davenant, and we cannot tell how much of the Caroline court practice he may have absorbed directly from him.

I have already noted that Dryden is surprisingly incurious about the traditions on which Shakespeare drew; one might expect him, always so conscious of literary models, to wonder where Shakespeare had sought instruction. By 1692 Rymer was aware of this problem: *"Gorboduck* is a fable, doubtless, better turn'd for Tragedy, than any on this side the *Alps* in his [Buckhurst's] time; and might have been a better direction to *Shakespear* and *Ben. Johnson* than any guide they have had the luck to follow." [31] Nor does Dryden ever remark on Shakespeare's adaptation of a Roman source in *The Comedy of Errors,* although he evidently knew the first folio, or one of its descendants, and was anxious to find "regular" plays in Shakespeare's canon— hence his praise of *The Merry Wives of Windsor* (I, 66). Dryden shows almost no awareness of chronology in the earlier period: he dispraises Jonson's "dotages" (I, 69), but never comments on any pattern of development in Shakespeare or Fletcher. He does assume that Jonson and Fletcher learned from that prominent child of nature, William Shakespeare, "who," he says, "(taught by none) did first impart/ To Fletcher wit, to labouring Jonson art" (Prologue to *The Tempest,* I, 136). This takes us little beyond Shakespeare warbling his native woodnotes wild.

Dryden's occasional references to his knowing Milton

31. *A Short View of Tragedy,* in *Critical Works,* p. 130.

give us an agreeable sense of his contemporaneity with a man whom we usually regard as a Renaissance writer. Similarly the relative objectivity with which Dryden appraises Shakespeare, Jonson, and Fletcher helps us feel that he lived close enough to these people to view them without undue awe. Dryden reveres Shakespeare, but bardolotry is not yet in full swing. We must try to realize, though, how little knowledge Dryden actually had of Renaissance practices. For instance, he says of *Troilus and Cressida*, "so lamely is it left to us, that it is not divided into acts; which fault I ascribe to the actors who printed it after Shakespeare's death" ("Preface," I, 240). Plainly he did not realize that many Elizabethan and Jacobean writers did not work in acts and scenes, nor had he any conception of the unlocalized nature of Elizabethan staging, as the Preface to *Troilus and Cressida* makes clear. This ignorance is less surprising, since Dryden inherited the masque and court drama tradition of scenery and specific location, and since nowhere in his criticism does he display any interest in the conventions of theatrical production.

Dryden's understanding of the conventions and conditions of the earlier period does not extend beyond excusing Shakespeare's use of the supernatural because "he writ as people then believed" (Prologue to *The Tempest*, I, 137), or supposing that the realistic comedy of Jonson merely reflects a cruder age. In fairness we should note that after the Dedication of *The Rival Ladies* (1664) Dryden is guilty of relatively few factual howlers—the celebrated case of Chaucer's pronunciation is more his misfortune than his fault. But since Dryden's standards are those of the Restoration, little tempered by historical considerations, his high estimation of earlier English writers is greatly to his credit—and this estimation is far more consistent than has sometimes been supposed.

Except for a passing compliment in the Dedication of *The Rival Ladies,* Dryden's first assessment of the earlier playwrights comes in *Of Dramatic Poesy.* Shakespeare

was the man who of all modern, and perhaps ancient poets, had the largest and most comprehensive soul. All the images of nature were still present to him, and he drew them not laboriously, but luckily; when he describes any thing, you more than see it, you feel it too. . . . He was naturally learned; he needed not the spectacles of books to read nature; he looked inwards, and found her there. . . . He is many times flat, insipid; his comic wit degenerating into clenches, his serious swelling into bombast. But he is always great when some great occasion is presented to him [I, 67].

Dryden goes on to praise the liveliness and courtliness of Beaumont and Fletcher and the judicious regularity of Jonson, whom he takes as a pattern in the examen of *The Silent Woman.* But

if I would compare him with Shakespeare, I must acknowledge him the more correct poet, but Shakespeare the greater wit. Shakespeare was the Homer, or father of our dramatic poets; Jonson was the Virgil, the pattern of elaborate writing; I admire him, but I love Shakespeare [I, 70].

This high praise is echoed near the end of the essay when Dryden insists that Restoration writers must seek new paths. Shakespeare, Fletcher, and Jonson

are honoured, and almost adored by us, as they deserve; neither do I know any so presumptuous of themselves as to contend with them. Yet give me leave to say thus much, without injury to their ashes, that not only we shall never equal them, but they could never equal themselves, were they to rise and write again. We acknowledge them our fathers in wit; but they have ruined their estates themselves before they came to their children's hands. There is scarce an humour, a character, or any kind of plot, which they have not blown upon [I, 85].

Hence Dryden sees good reason "to attempt some other way." We must recollect that in this essay he is speculating on the best method of writing modern drama; his purpose is not analysis or judgment of the earlier writers. They come off remarkably well, considering that Neander (their spokesman here) is supporting the rimed heroic play.

Many critics have supposed that in the period between *Of Dramatic Poesy* and *Aureng-Zebe* (written 1675) Dryden turned against and seriously undervalued the Elizabethans.[32] This view rests on Dryden's criticisms of Renaissance dullness and coarseness in comparison with Restoration polish and refinement in the Epilogue to Part II of *The Conquest of Granada* (1672), and in the ensuing "Defence of the Epilogue." Since Hoyt Trowbridge long ago showed the fallaciousness of this interpretation, no elaborate refutation is needed.[33] Indeed, such a change in Dryden's attitude would have had to be very quick indeed. In the Prologue to the adaptation that he and Davenant made of *The Tempest* (1670) he speaks of "old Shakespeare's honoured dust" and says that his "power is sacred as a King's" (I, 136).[34] In 1671 he comments that "we were excelled by

32. Wm. E. Bohn's classic statement of this interpretation is still referred to with respect. See "The Development of John Dryden's Literary Criticism," *PMLA*, 22 (1907), 56–139, especially 76–100.
33. See "Dryden's 'Essay on the Dramatic Poetry of the Last Age,'" *PQ*, 22 (1943), 240–250.
34. Admittedly Dryden is trying to peddle his product here. But why revive the play if he did not think well of it? In the

[94]

Ben Jonson . . . [in] humour and contrivance of comedy"
(Preface to *An Evening's Love*, I, 144). His assessment
seems utterly fair:

Ben Jonson is to be admired for many excellencies; and can be
taxed with fewer failings than any English poet. I know I have
been accused as an enemy of his writings; but without any
other reason than that I do not admire him blindly, and without looking into his imperfections. For why should he only
be exempted from those frailties from which Homer and Virgil
are not free? [I, 148].[35]

The actual strictures in the "Defence of the Epilogue"
are, as Trowbridge demonstrates, largely concerned with
language, and many of them are clearly foreshadowed in
Of Dramatic Poesy. Dryden is trying to improve the stage,
and he believes that the manners and language of his age
are more refined than those of two generations earlier.[36]

"Preface" he says that the play "was originally Shakespeare's: a
poet for whom he [Davenant] had particularly a high veneration,
and whom he first taught me to admire" (I, 134).

35. For a very high estimation of Jonson (not atypical of the
time) see Shadwell's Prefaces to *The Sullen Lovers* (1668) and
The Humorists (1671); in the latter preface Dryden is attacked
for disrespect to Jonson, and we may suppose that this passage is
a reply.

36. This does represent a change in his views on language. In
Of Dramatic Poesy he places the Jacobeans highest: "I am apt to
believe the English language in them [Beaumont and Fletcher]
arrived to its highest perfection: what words have since been taken
in, are rather superfluous than necessary" (I, 69). The opinions
of the "Defence of the Epilogue" are foreshadowed in the Preface
to *An Evening's Love:* "I have also prepared to treat of the improvement of our language since Fletcher's and Jonson's days, and
consequently of our refining the courtship, raillery, and conversation of our plays" (I, 145).

His criticisms are minute and cranky: Dryden has put himself in the role of a peevish teacher of elementary composition. But his concern about these matters is both genuine and lasting; similar points are belabored much later in a letter to William Walsh (early 1691?). Being much less concerned about refinement, we have little patience with Dryden's carping. We must, however, grant that he mingles much praise with his blame: he "can never enough admire" the "excellencies" of Shakespeare, Jonson, and Fletcher (I, 177); he is ready to "imitate" much in all three; and he concludes: "Let us render to our predecessors what is their due, without confining ourselves to a servile imitation of all they writ . . . " (I, 182–183). This is not the language of contempt and condemnation.[37]

By 1675 the heroic play was in decline, and though Dryden was no more awed by "Shakespeare's sacred name," he was at any rate readier to yield "foremost honours" to "an age less polished, more unskilled" (Prologue to *Aureng-Zebe*, I, 192). The "Heads of an Answer to Rymer" (1677) and "The Grounds of Criticism in Tragedy" (1679) rate Shakespeare and Fletcher very high indeed, even when, in the latter case, they are judged by French neoclassical standards.

Dryden's comments on plays in his later years are rela-

37. Gerard Langbaine, a very hostile critic, seizes (in 1691) on the "Defence" and lambasts Dryden for disrespect to great writers (see Spingarn, III, 113ff.), and his twisted interpretation was long followed by other critics. Dryden dropped the "Defence" from the 1687 edition of *The Conquest of Granada* (and it was not reprinted again in his lifetime); this was probably less because Dryden was ashamed of it than because he realized that it was open to misinterpretation. And its point—that Elizabethan language was obsolete—was no longer disputed.

tively few, but he says enough to make it plain that he considers Elizabethan tragedy the greatest ever written.[38]

I cannot but conclude with Mr Rym[er] that our English comedy is far beyond any thing of the Ancients. And notwithstanding our irregularities, so is our tragedy. Shakespeare had a genius for it; and we know, in spite of Mr R——, that genius alone is a greater virtue (if I may so call it) than all other qualifications put together. You see what success this learned critic has found in the world, after his blaspheming Shakespeare. Almost all the faults which he has discovered are truly there; yet who will read Mr Rym or not read Shakespeare? [Letter to John Dennis, c. March 1694; II, 178].

In other words Dryden admits Shakespeare's faults but finds them outweighed by his virtues.

His estimation of Shakespeare, Jonson, and Fletcher is consistently very high. During his most active period as a playwright he hoped that they could be improved upon, if not surpassed in their own modes. He placed his hopes on refinement, and was disappointed, for as he puts it in "To My Dear Friend Mr Congreve" (1694): "Our age was cultivated thus at length;/ But what we gain'd in skill we lost in strength" (II, 170). By no means has Dryden abandoned hope of further progress—but it will be possible only when refinement is coupled with the "strength" born of "genius." Time has proved the hopes he placed in Congreve illfounded, though the supposition behind them is not unreasonable.

38. See the "Discourse on Satire," II, 81, and the Dedication of the *Examen poeticum* (1693), II, 159–161: "Peace be to the venerable shades of Shakespeare and Ben Jonson! None of the living will presume to have any competition with them: as they were our predecessors, so they were our masters."

Dryden's high opinion of the earlier dramatists is quite typical of his age; his views are unusual only in consistently giving Shakespeare preference over Jonson. This judgment accords well with current (and presumably permanent) estimates of the two, though it is not, I think, solely the result of intrinsic good taste on Dryden's part. He associates Shakespeare with tragedy, Jonson with comedy, and not only did he accept the usual genre-valuation which put tragedy higher, but he had a strong personal preference for it—which accounts, I believe, for one of his most marked divergences from the opinion of his day.[39]

39. There is some dispute about the relative standing of Shakespeare and Jonson in the Restoration. G. E. Bentley, in *Shakespeare and Jonson: Their Reputations in the Seventeenth Century Compared*, 2 vols. (Chicago, 1945), tried to show that right to the end of the century, Jonson's reputation stood higher, though Shakespeare was gaining rapidly after 1680. David L. Frost, in *The School of Shakespeare* (Cambridge, England, 1968), chap. 1, has attacked this conclusion as a "Romantic legend." Frost criticizes both Bentley's methodology and his reasoning, and succeeds, at the very least, in casting serious doubt on his conclusions. Frost does not refer to *The London Stage*, but its listing of known performances (admittedly based on sketchy evidence) tends to bear him out. Shakespeare's plays apparently were performed at least as frequently as Jonson's, and if adaptations are taken into account, vastly more often. Of course such evidence does not begin to settle the matter of "reputation." My reading of Restoration plays suggests to me that Jonson was the more seminal writer, and as Frost insists, frequency of reference proves little by itself anyway. Restoration critics give Shakespeare higher praise than many scholars realize, and his genius is much touted, but Jonson is generally allowed precedence as the more polished craftsman, playing, as Dryden liked to say, Virgil to Shakespeare's Homer. Shakespeare was admired, Jonson more copied. In any case, it is surely to Dryden's credit that from the beginning he rated Shakespeare higher. Shadwell chided him for this (rather gently—see the Pref-

[98]

Dryden's discussions of his English predecessors are largely concerned with their suitability as models. He gives little purely "explanatory" account of them—he is trying to use these writers, and he knows relatively little about them. Their work, in his view, is powerful but crude, and he hopes to refine upon it. But because he regards English literature as part of a larger tradition he must try to ensure that English superstructures will not lack accord with classical foundations. Dryden hopes that, with an eye on both, Restoration writers may correct their predecessors without abandoning the particularities of local tradition. He is in search of a delicate balance.

As we have seen, he generally conceives progress as a refinement in language and manners, as well as a discovery of the potentiality inherent in literary forms. Refinement was a Restoration obsession, and Dryden never abandons the concept. He does, however, come to recognize that "strength" must not give way to mere nicety. Dryden always loves polish, but even late in his career he insists:

A work may be over-wrought as well as under-wrought: too much labour often takes away the spirit by adding to the

---

ace to *The Humorists*, 1671; Spingarn, II, 157–158), and Dryden was obviously stung by other critics: "I know I honour Ben Jonson more than my little critics, because without vanity I may own I understand him better" (Dedication of *The Assignation*, 1673; I, 188). It seems significant that in the early 1670s cracks at the Elizabethans apparently drew responses from defenders of Jonson, not of Shakespeare. (For a generally similar middle-of-the-road conclusion, see Gunnar Sorelius' excellent study, *The Giant Race before the Flood: Pre-Restoration Drama on the Stage and in the Criticism of the Restoration*, Studia Anglistica Upsaliensia, No. 4 [Uppsala, Sweden, 1966].)

polishing, so that there remains nothing but a dull correctness, a piece without any considerable faults, but with few beauties; for when the spirits are drawn off, there is nothing but a *caput mortuum* ["A Parallel of Poetry and Painting," II, 207].

First and last, Dryden's critical standard is *effectiveness*. He asks, does it work? Does it affect the audience? He excuses the faults of the Elizabethans because their works succeeded; he hopes that by avoiding their faults still better results can be achieved.

Because Dryden believes that earlier writers, to the extent that they are good, must be taken as models, he tends to judge them against what he regards as permanent standards of excellence. These are based on effective imitation of nature (largely conceived in terms of classical foundations), and a refined, decorous style. Consequently Dryden is not well equipped to analyze earlier literatures in their own terms, and does little beyond making a minimal allowance for language, religion, and local custom. But his criticism is not procrustean: he manages to use his fixed standards with surprising flexibility to show what is best in a writer, for he always insists that the business of a critic is not merely to find faults [40]—and he lives up to his own prescription.

Inevitably Dryden does treat earlier English writers as part of a fixed development toward a more polished perfection. He does not see, any more than we do, precisely how Chaucer is related to the Elizabethans, but he assumes that

40. For example: "They wholly mistake the nature of criticism who think its business is principally to find fault. Criticism, as it was first instituted by Aristotle, was meant a standard of judging well; the chiefest part of which is to observe those excellencies which should delight a reasonable reader" ("Apology for Heroic Poetry," I, 196–197).

they are all part of a steady growth toward maturity. He supposes that all writers try to do much the same thing: their success varies with natural genius and rhetorical skill, as well as with their particular moral objects. His strictures on his predecessors are almost invariably based on what he sees as their relative crudity of language and construction. Dryden remains convinced that "some great genius may arise to equal any of the Ancients" ("Discourse on Satire," II, 81): he always hopes that with proper attention to both classical foundations and local language, religion, and temper, refinement may yet lead to ever greater perfection— and this peculiar blend of belief in both the classics and progress is central to his view of literature.

CHAPTER 4

Rymer and Others

Where does Dryden stand in relation to other Restoration critics? Some attention has already been paid to such mid-century figures as Davenant and Flecknoe. Here we can turn to the major figures of the last quarter of the seventeenth century. Of these men Rymer is by far the most important: Mulgrave produced only a few pages of criticism; Temple was not primarily a literary man; Dennis had just started to work in Dryden's lifetime.[1] That

1. The inclusion of Rymer, Temple, and Dennis needs no justification. Mulgrave I select as a critic widely read and influential in that time, and one who was highly praised by Dryden, Addison, and Pope, among others. Dryden dedicated both *Aureng-Zebe* (1676) and his translation of the *Aeneid* (1697) to him. (John Sheffield, Earl of Mulgrave, 1648–1721, was created Marquess of Normanby in 1694 and later Duke of Buckingham.) Dryden's compliments to his patron we may take with a grain of salt, but there seems little doubt that Dryden thought highly of Mulgrave. The two of them collaborated on a translation of Ovid's Epistle 13 (1680); Mulgrave and Waller are coupled as "two of the best judges of our age" (Dedication of the *Examen poeticum*, II, 167), and Dryden quotes him as an authority in "A Parallel of Poetry and Painting" (II, 186).

Dryden is the best of the lot is beyond dispute, but one result of this assessment has been a longstanding claim that he was much ahead of his time or even revolutionary in outlook—a very questionable proposition.[2]

I

A key item in the debate is Dryden's "Heads of an Answer to Rymer," a work which has received less critical attention than it deserves.[3] Possibly this neglect is a result of its omission from Ker's long-standard edition of the critical essays or because Dryden disappoints modern critics by failing to cast off what they regard as a yoke of clas-

2. References will be to *The Critical Works of Thomas Rymer*, ed. Curt A. Zimansky (New Haven, 1956); *The Critical Works of John Dennis*, ed. E. N. Hooker, 2 vols. (Baltimore, 1939, 1943); *Five Miscellaneous Essays by Sir William Temple*, ed. Samuel Holt Monk (Ann Arbor, 1963). My quotations from Mulgrave are from *The Works of John Sheffield, Earl of Mulgrave, Marquis of Normanby, and Duke of Buckingham*, 3d. ed., 2 vols. (London, 1740). I have limited my discussion of Dennis almost entirely to works published in Dryden's lifetime.

3. The "Heads" consists of notes made by Dryden in 1677 in his copy (sent to him by the author) of Rymer's *The Tragedies of the Last Age*. The notes were printed by Tonson in 1711 and, in a different order, by Johnson in his *Life of Dryden* (1779). The original text was destroyed in a fire in the 1780s and the resultant textual problems have undoubtedly contributed to the work's neglect. Happily, they have finally been satisfactorily solved by George Watson and need no longer concern us: see "Dryden's First Answer to Rymer," *RES*, n.s. 14 (1963), 17–23, and the text in his edition of the critical essays (I, 210–220). Parenthetical references are to the numbered paragraphs in this edition. Watson's order (basically Tonson's) is internally consistent, and he offers sensible solutions to the problems raised in earlier studies. Cf. James M. Osborn, *John Dryden: Some Biographical Facts and Problems*, (2d. ed., Gainesville, Florida, 1965), pp. 283–285; *The Critical Works of Thomas Rymer*, ed. Zimansky, pp. xxxiv–xxxv.

sical rules. But whatever the cause, the "Heads" has been subjected to little close critical study. Indeed, basic questions of definition remain unsolved. Is the "Heads" merely a series of marginal jottings? The outline of an essay Dryden never dared write? A rough draft for "The Grounds of Criticism in Tragedy"? Not only is the "Heads" largely uninterpreted, but its place in Dryden's thought remains unevaluated.[4]

The importance of these issues is plain, for our assessment of Dryden's relation to other Restoration critics must to a considerable degree rest on our interpretation of the "Heads." It presents the appearance, in part at least, of a revolutionary manifesto; if this is what it is, then Dryden is indeed breaking away—in private at least—from most of his contemporaries. George Watson says flatly:

The cardinal importance of the 'Heads of an Answer to Rymer' can be simply stated: it is the one critical document in English between the Restoration and Johnson's Shakespeare in which the *Poetics* of Aristotle are attacked frontally and without qualification.[5]

Watson would like to see Dryden denounce both Rymer and the Ancients; hence he is pained to find him "oddly respectful" of Rymer and complains that he "never dared to repeat in public this lucid exposure of 'Aristotelianism' " (I, 211; headnote). But in point of fact Dryden seems to

4. The "Heads" has usually been regarded as a collection of preliminary notes for "The Grounds of Criticism in Tragedy" (1679). This relationship was first suggested by Fred G. Walcott, "John Dryden's Answer to Thomas Rymer's *The Tragedies of the Last Age*," *PQ*, 15 (1936), 194–214, and it is accepted, with modifications, by Watson (I, xiv and 238) and, surprisingly, by Zimansky (pp. xxxv–xxxvi).

5. Watson, *RES*, p. 20.

have been much impressed by Rymer's work and to have agreed with much of what he said.[6] I suspect that Dryden was stimulated into examining possible grounds of refutation, and that in doing so he explored lines of argument that he did not wholly accept. As a practicing playwright Dryden was readier than Rymer to allow whatever seemed effective in the theater, but in the 1670s their notions of literary theory were not so different as has been supposed.

Rymer remains a critic more ridiculed than read; the notoriety of his attack on *Othello* in *A Short View of Tragedy* (1692) obscures for us his real virtues and makes incomprehensible the esteem in which Dryden undoubtedly held him. But since Dryden was responding—with respect and interest—to Rymer's work, we can scarcely expect to make sense of his comments if we are uninformed about his subject. Any analysis of the "Heads" must offer at least a brief account of Rymer.

Those who know Rymer only by hearsay do not realize that the acerbic *Short View* is considerably different from his earlier work. *The Tragedies of the Last Age* (1677) is tart and incisive, but basically genial. Rymer's scholarliness in the eyes of his contemporaries can lead us to suppose that his work is crabbed and formal. Actually, his style is vigorous and racy (much more so than Dryden's), and Rymer specifically disclaims any pretense of academic pre-

6. This is certainly what Dryden himself says. About *The Tragedies of the Last Age* he wrote to Dorset: "Mr Rymer sent me his book . . . 'tis certainly very learned, and the best piece of criticism in the English tongue; perhaps in any other of the modern. If I am not altogether of his opinion, I am so in most of what he says" (I, 209). Perhaps Dryden was simply being diplomatic, as Zimansky suggests (p. 194nn.), but the "Heads" too is very complimentary (see pars. 1 and 44).

cision and thoroughness in his statement that he is "not cut out for writing a *Treatise*." His exuberance and informality make the work enjoyable reading. He frequently addresses characters directly with sarcastic questions and comments: "Well *Amintor, de gustibus non est disputandum*."[7]

Some critics have supposed that Rymer was French-oriented, rigidly Aristotelian,[8] of the party of "Ancients," and a nonbeliever in progress. Actually he is consistently patriotic and is interested in the French (of whose writing he entertained a rather low opinion) only because of their classical studies.[9] Speaking of tragedy he concludes the introduction to *The Tragedies of the Last Age:*

But I have elsewhere declar'd my opinion, that the *English* want neither *genius* nor *language* for so great a work. And, certainly, had our Authors began with Tragedy, as *Sophocles* and *Euripides* left it; had they either built on the same foundation, or after their *model;* we might e're this day have seen Poetry in greater perfection, and boasted such *Monuments* of wit as *Greece* or *Rome* never knew in all their *glory*.[10]

Rymer's basic position is that English tragedy has developed improperly and needs correction.[11] His standards are not what might be supposed. His title for his Rapin translation (1674) speaks of Aristotle's necessary, rational, and universal rules for various kinds of poetry, and Aristotle is mentioned with the greatest respect throughout Rymer's

7. *The Tragedies of the Last Age* (hereafter *TLA*), in *Critical Works,* ed. Zimansky, p. 71.

8. The significance of Rymer's "Aristotelianism" has been over-estimated. See, for example, Marvin T. Herrick, *The Poetics of Aristotle in England* (New Haven, 1930), pp. 57–63. Herrick's assessment of Dryden's feelings about "rules" (pp. 60, 64–65) is, however, sound and helpful.

9. Zimansky, p. xxxii.   10. *TLA*, p. 21.   11. *TLA*, p. 18.

work. But the full title to *The Tragedies of the Last Age* is more indicative of his real viewpoint. There he speaks of "the Practice of the Ancients" (not the "rules") and "the Common Sense of all Ages." Rymer's concerns may really be summarized as probability and decorum.[12] He accepts the emotionally and factually commonplace as reasonable; his decorum is basically a demand for ideality in noble characters. Rymer supports the conventions of heroic drama (though like Dryden he later changed his mind): tragedy, in his view, should serve a moral function by presenting life as it ought to be.

Today we find incongruous Rymer's combination of ideal characters and commonsensical standards of probability. Indeed, as a prescriptive critic Rymer is clearly a failure. But he spends little time on rules and makes few absolute demands. He is not, for example, rigid about the "unities." [13] The bulk of *The Tragedies of the Last Age* consists of close analysis of three plays: *Rollo, A King and No King*, and *The Maid's Tragedy*. Rymer was not merely beating a dead horse. Dryden had singled out *Rollo* for praise in *Of Dramatic Poesy* (I, 48), and modern scholarship has substantiated his assertion of Fletcher's popularity; all three plays were frequently performed between 1660 and 1677.[14]

12. For example, he objects with some justice that the repentance of Evadne in *The Maid's Tragedy* is thoroughly unconvincing (*TLA*, p. 66). Similarly, on decorum: "I question whether in Poetry a King can be an accessary to a crime" (*TLA*, p. 65). We may find this silly, but we must remember that Dryden subscribed to much the same code.

13. *TLA*, p. 18.

14. Cf. Watson, I, 69 (*Of Dramatic Poesy*); and *The London Stage 1660–1800*, Part I, ed. William Van Lennep (Carbondale, Ill., 1965). For all that Rymer's intention was to reform the stage, all three plays continued to be popular during the Restoration.

Rymer maintains, and few modern critics would care to disagree, that the three plays suffer from absurdities of plot and monstrosities of characterization. The considerable force of his arguments derives from his effective dismemberment of the plays, not from his rather cursory references to the rules of the Ancients. But Rymer is perfectly correct in claiming that Elizabethan and Greek drama are incommensurable. As Zimansky puts it, "the dramatic practice of the Elizabethans could not be reconciled to the current theory of literature," [15] and Dryden's "rebuttal" ultimately founders on this point.

No matter how the "Heads" is organized, it cannot be construed as an outline for an integrated essay. Dryden makes a number of starts, repeats some arguments, and blunders into contradictory positions. His purpose seems two-fold: to examine the grounds on which Rymer's position might be challenged, and to defend the English dramatic tradition. We must recognize, however, that Dryden was not working from a firmly established position of his own. Though his evaluation of Elizabethan drama was changing somewhat, he did not disagree with Rymer's general claim that the classics should serve as models. None of Rymer's criticisms of Fletcher would sound out of place in Dryden's own "Defence of the Epilogue" to Part II of *The Conquest of Granada* (1672), in which he too censures Fletcher, among others, for indecorum and absurdities of plot (I, 172). But by 1677 Dryden's purposes had shifted, and in the "Heads" he searches for lines of defense or extenuation against Rymer's relentlessly logical condemnations. He is unlucky in having three mediocre examples of Elizabethan tragedy to defend, but the real

15. Zimansky, p. 195nn.

reason for the inconclusiveness of the "Heads" is Dryden's unwillingness to cut loose from Rymer's classically-oriented premises. The result is an inconsistency in Dryden's thought—his respect for the rules clashes with his love of Elizabethan drama. Dryden was not a rigid thinker and could contemplate heresies with interest, but he was satisfied with the notion that a great wit could gloriously offend; he was not prepared to discard the "rules" born of veneration for the classics.

Logically enough, Dryden recognized that "he who undertakes to answer this excellent critique of Mr Rymer, on behalf of our English poets" must either grant his premises and dispute his conclusions, or deny his premises (pars. 1–2). The basic points at issue are whether Greek drama should serve as a model for English, and if so, to what extent this supposition invalidates Elizabethan dramatic practice.[16]

Dryden toys with four major lines of argument against Rymer's position,[17] but he is always in the unhappy position of being unable to deny Rymer's premises and so having to argue ineffectively against conclusions which follow them all too well. Dryden can do no more than claim that Fletcher is better than Rymer admits. Actually none of his arguments is fully developed; he is examining

16. Although both *TLA* and the "Heads" are explicitly concerned with Elizabethan tragedy, both pertain, by implication, to Restoration drama as well. The proper relation between the two becomes Dryden's subject in the "Grounds."

17. These are, loosely, (1) a debate on the standards of judgment in literary theory (pars. 1–14); (2) an appeal to practical reason (pars. 15–28); (3) an analysis of the "parts" of drama (pars. 29–33, 35–37, 51–53); (4) an evaluation of the aim or "ends" of tragedy (pars. 34, 38–44). These distinctions are strictly analytic; that is, they are not related to a planned structure in Dryden's text.

the possibilities, not concentrating his forces for a *coup de grâce*.

The first attempt is the most exciting, though the least conclusive. Dryden challenges Rymer's position by questioning outright the adequacy of his standards of judgment (pars. 7–8). Greek and English tragedy can be compared with reference to Aristotle's definitions of tragedy, its "end," "beauties," and "means," but the applicability of these definitions to English drama can be disputed, since Aristotle drew his standards empirically from Greek drama.[18] In short, has Aristotle really defined what constitutes good tragedy? Dryden does not say no, though he raises the question.

More specifically, he asks what makes a good tragedy. Rymer assumes that it is a fable conducive to pity and terror; Dryden suggests that the Greeks may indeed be superior in this respect without being superior over all (par. 2), since "characters, manners, thoughts, and words" as well as fable all contribute to the effectiveness of tragedy (par. 5).[19] It is this argument against Rymer's conclusions that Dryden pursues furthest in the "Heads."

18. Rymer was perfectly aware of Aristotle's inductive procedure. "The Poets were his Masters, and what was their practice, he reduced to principles. Nor would the *modern Poets* blindly resign to this practice of the *Ancients*, were not the Reasons convincing and clear as any demonstration in *Mathematicks*" (Preface to Rapin, *Critical Works*, p. 3).

19. Hence Dryden could say without contradiction in the Preface to *All for Love* (1678): "I have endeavoured in this play to follow the practice of the Ancients, who, as Mr Rymer has judiciously observed, are and ought to be our masters. . . . Yet, though their models are regular, they are too little for English tragedy, which requires to be built in a larger compass" (I, 230–231). Actually, Rymer too recognized a valid difference between

Two questions are implicit. What is the object of tragedy? and is English tragedy different in kind from Greek? Dryden answers the first question clearly: tragedy should make us love virtue and hate vice "by shewing the rewards of one, and punishments of the other; at least by rendering virtue always amiable, though it be shown unfortunate; and vice detestable, tho' it be shown triumphant" (par. 12). In this moral assessment he is not inconsistent with Rymer. Dryden did see clearly that the English had altered the content of tragedy, but he recognized its greater variety, its broader plot, and its heroic love interest without seeing that such differences made it another sort of drama (pars. 9–11). Dryden was prepared to see improvement, for he always believed that "no art or science is at once begun and perfected, but that it must pass first through many hands, and even through several ages" ("Discourse on Satire," II, 139). But this very tendency to see English writing as part of an unbroken chain of development from the Ancients made it impossible for Dryden to recognize what the perspective of literary history makes plain to us: that the English dramatic tradition was indigenous and unique.

To borrow modern analytic terms, Elizabethan drama aggregates and synthesizes many incidents and processes while Greek drama isolates and analyzes a single situation. The former enriches; the latter refines. Elizabethan drama

---

Greek and English plots: "If the *English Theatre* requires more *intrigue*, an Author may multiply the *Incidents*, may add *Episods*, and *thicken* the *Plot*, as he sees occasion; provided that all the *lines* tend to the same *center*" (*TLA*, p. 26). Dryden does not object to Rymer's demand for unity of plot—indeed, he often praises tragicomedy for managing to retain it.

aims for maximum emotional impact; Greek drama aims at maximum clarity of analysis.[20] To free English drama from Rymer's French-classical strictures Dryden would have had to assert a radical differentiation in kind. But though he recognized that the adequacy of Aristotelian rules could be challenged, he was unwilling or unable to deny their relevance. The result is a peculiar compromise. Dryden is basically content to view literature in an Aristotelian perspective, but he does insist on making allowances for historical development. Consequently he is driven to the conclusion that English drama represents a development of and an advance upon the Greek. Here Dryden's first line of argument has collapsed, and so he abandons theory in favor of practical reason.

Dryden's second method of refutation is an appeal to theatrical experience. Rymer's criticisms must be excessive since these three plays "have moved both those passions [pity and terror] in a high degree upon the stage" (par. 16), and good acting cannot conceal lack of dramatic merit, as Rymer says it can (par. 18).[21] Dryden rests his argument on the opinion of the multitude, something he almost never does, saying that common sense decrees that what pleases many must be good (par. 19), and "the poet's business is certainly to please the audience" (par. 22). This argument might be employed today against any attempt to improve television programs.

20. For these terms and a lucid differentiation of these sorts of drama, see Elder Olson, *Tragedy and the Theory of Drama* (Detroit, 1961), chaps. 7–9. Olson explains in detail why the standards of French theory and drama (Rymer's principal source) are so inapplicable to Elizabethan drama.

21. *TLA*, p. 19. This seems inconsistent with Dryden's usual opinion on the subject. See above, chap. 2, note 21.

In an attempt to escape the logical counterargument that the "general taste" of his time is "depraved," Dryden argues that it is merely different from Greek taste (pars. 20–22).

Shakespeare and Fletcher have written to the genius of the age and nation in which they lived; for tho' nature, as he [Rymer] objects,[22] is the same in all places, and reason too the same, yet the climate, the age, the dispositions of the people to whom a poet writes, may be so different that what pleased the Greeks would not satisfy an English audience.

Again Dryden is on the verge of escaping the jurisdiction of classical dicta, but his belief in the uniformity of human nature restrains him, and so he cannot make his argument conclusive by saying that since Greek and English drama are different in kind their quality cannot be directly compared. Dryden was willing to see the differences only in terms of degree and development. Hence he backtracks to say that even if an author ought to mold the taste of his audience, the English theater does not need "this total reformation," since Rymer has "wittily aggravated" its faults, and these faults only detract from the drama, they do not completely ruin it (pars. 23–25). He concludes:

If the plays of the Ancients are more correctly plotted, ours are more beautifully written; and if we can raise passions as high on worse foundations, it shows our genius in tragedy is greater, for in all other parts of it the English have manifestly excelled them [par. 28].

Dryden's standard here is the response of the audience, which is a feeble prop, since he has not really answered the charge of depraved taste. From this perspective the

22. *TLA*, p. 19.

test of a work is the amount of audience reaction, and the aim of tragedy must be to rouse as much passion in the spectator as possible.[23] Precisely as in his first set of arguments Dryden has jettisoned his claim that English tragedy is different and must be differently judged, and he arrives at the same instinctive assertion: the English have excelled the Greeks at their own game—the rousing of pity and terror.

The third line of argument is based on a comparison of the "parts" of tragedy.[24] Dryden's claim is that the thoughts and words in English drama are "more noble and more poetical" than in the Greek (par. 32). In a rare citation of outside authority he quotes Rapin: " ' 'Tis not the admirable intrigue, the surprising events, the extraordinary incidents that make the beauty of a tragedy; 'tis the discourses when they are natural and passionate' " (par. 52). Here Dryden is seeking the basis of the English superiority he has claimed. His comments are frustrating, not only because they are sketchy, but because he fails to take advantage of his

23. Although he had no way of measuring *Greek* response to Greek drama Dryden was on firm ground in claiming that English plays raise more emotion than Greek. But if Olson is correct (see note 20 above) in saying that this is the primary aim of English drama but not of Greek, then Dryden's claim that the English surpass the Greeks on their own ground collapses. The "Heads" is weakest where it rests on Dryden's assumption that a tragedy must raise as much emotion as possible in the audience. And as Zimansky observes (p. xxxv), Dryden made the unfortunate assumption that the "emotions imitated by the actors" are the same as those "raised in the spectators." In the "Grounds" Dryden extricated himself from this morass by adopting the French-Aristotelian theory of "purgation" (I, 245). In retrospect, this solution undercuts those arguments in the "Heads" which are based on mere *quantity* of emotion.

24. Fable, order, manners, thoughts, words (par. 35).

material. He sees clearly that English plots are composed of many pieces, "like the links of a curious chain" (par. 37); he understands that its turns and complexities make English drama "more diverting" and keep "the audience in expectation of the catastrophe," whereas the simplicity of the Greek drama allows us to "see through the whole design at first" (par. 29); but once again he fails to establish the differences in kind which are implicit in his comments. Without such differentiation his preference for the parts of English tragedy remains merely a matter of taste, and here Dryden is no more impartial than Rymer (see par. 32).

His fourth attempt concerns the aim of tragedy. He defines the end (reformation of manners) and means (arousal of emotions) in order to see who has best fulfilled them (par. 38). Poetic justice is the key concept: "The punishment of vice and reward of virtue are the most adequate ends of tragedy, because most conducing to good example of life" (par. 41). All this is consistent with Rymer; Dryden's question is what emotions are to be aroused. He challenges the supposed centrality of pity and terror by objecting that love is a more profound emotion (pars. 34, 42) and one which touches us more nearly. Therefore it should be allowed a place with pity and terror.

Once more Dryden verges on claiming that English and Greek drama have different functions. He insists that pity and terror are not the only "ends" of tragedy: " 'Tis not enough that Aristotle has said so, for Aristotle drew his models of tragedy from Sophocles and Euripides; and if he had seen ours, might have changed his mind" (par. 40). But all that he can do with this telling point is to claim that permitting the poet to arouse love, joy, and indignation (par. 38) increases the moral utility of tragedy (par. 41). He and Rymer agree that, in Rymer's words, "whoever writes a Tragedy cannot please but must also profit." [25] Dryden simply feels that the addition of love to pity and terror makes English drama more effective than the Greek.

Dryden's assessment of *The Tragedies of the Last Age* reflects his own confusion; he believes that the Ancients should be imitated, but he still admires Shakespeare and Fletcher. We may guess that out of this puzzle came "The Grounds of Criticism in Tragedy."

My judgment on this piece is this, that it is extremely learned; but that the author of it is better read in the Greek than in the English poets; that all writers ought to study this critique as the best account I have ever seen of the Ancients; that the model of tragedy he has here given is excellent and extreme correct; but that it is not the only model of all tragedy, because it is too much circumscribed in plot, characters, etc.; and lastly, that we may be taught here justly to admire and imitate the Ancients, without giving them the preference with this author in prejudice to our own country [par. 44].

Given his beliefs, Dryden had no choice but to maintain that English drama was an extension and development of the Greek. This leads him to the dubious conclusion that Rymer "therefore unjustly blames us for not building on what the Ancients left us, for it seems, upon consideration of the premises, that we have wholly finished what they began" (par. 43).

The "Heads" is known for its boldness, but Dryden's

25. Cf. pars. 46–48 and *TLA*, p. 75. On Dryden's view of tragic effect see Baxter Hathaway, "John Dryden and the Function of Tragedy," *PMLA*, 58 (1943), 665–673. Cf. Edward Niles Hooker's reply in *PQ*, 23 (1944), 162–163.

temerity is confined to hypothesis. Three times he comes to the point of denying the relevance of classical rules (pars. 8, 21, 40) and each time backs off, failing to make a decisive distinction between the two types of tragedy. From this we can conclude that he did not really disagree with Rymer's general critical position. Dryden is prepared to stretch tradition, but not to abandon it. He believes firmly in literary continuity and cannot deny the relevance of the classics, and so falls prey to what we see as a logical contradiction: he upholds both rules and the Elizabethans, struggling manfully to comprehend both within a single system. The classical orientation of contemporary culture was beginning to crumble (and Dryden himself was a "Modern"), but its influence was strong enough to prevent him from assessing English literature wholly in its own terms.

The place of the "Heads" in Dryden's thought is a crucial problem. Those critics who view it as a document of revolutionary conviction have tended to read "The Grounds of Criticism in Tragedy" as a diplomatic dilution of it.[26] That the two works cover some of the same ground is undeniable, but I believe that they are not as closely related as has been supposed.

The "Grounds" is attached to the Preface to *Troilus and Cressida* (1679), Dryden's revision of Shakespeare's play. The subject, of course, is "how far we ought to imitate our own poets, Shakespeare and Fletcher" (I, 243), and as I have indicated, the essay relies heavily on French authority. Dryden quotes extensively from Rapin and Le Bossu and actually takes as a starting point what he regards as Aristotle's definition of tragedy. Dryden agrees outright

26. See note 4 above.

with Rymer's criticisms of Elizabethan plots, insists on decorum of manners, and concludes triumphantly by quoting Rapin's justification of rules as methodized nature (I, 246–247; 251–252; 260–261).

Modern critics have not liked this essay. Walcott's general thesis is that Dryden was noncommittal to avoid offending Rymer, but that his real feelings can be inferred.[27] George Watson goes much further:

The 'Grounds' are infinitely cautious, and only a student practised in reading between Dryden's lines can regard them as a document of much interest. Dryden's craving for Aristotelian respectability now leads him into concession after concession to Aristotle's case in the *Poetics*. . . . Dryden's former advocacy of Shakespeare and 'Fletcher' is now perverted to a boot-licking reverence for authority which does not even have the merit of honesty, in that it pretends a continuity of praise for the Elizabethans which is quite unreal.[28]

And Zimansky correctly observes that "at no point does he [Dryden] quarrel with Rymer's principles. In fact, he shows as much interest in citing rules as Rymer does, and rather more in showing the interconnection of these ideas into a system." [29] Rymer, after all, says of criticism: "Certainly there is not requir'd much Learning, or that a man must be some *Aristotle*, and *Doctor* of *Subtilties*, to form a right judgment . . . common sense suffices." [30] Watson can explain the "Grounds" only as a product of Dryden's timidity and hypocrisy.

He knew the force of neo-classical fashion, and ached to be respectable. The notes he scribbled in his copy of Rymer's

27. Walcott, pp. 206, 208. 28. Watson, *RES*, p. 22.
29. Zimansky, p. xxxvi. 30. *TLA*, p. 18.

[118]

book, which he never dared to publish . . . *contain in outline the full force of his convictions,* and even presume to attack the most sacred of all critical documents in Renaissance Europe, the *Poetics* of Aristotle, raising questions of hair-raising implications. . . . But 'The Grounds of Criticism in Tragedy' (1679), his principal public reply to Rymer, is a weak dilution of his private notes [I, xiii–xiv, Introduction; italics added].

I think it important to reply to three implicit claims: first, that the "Heads" represents the real Dryden; second, that the "Grounds" is a reply to Rymer; third, that the "Grounds" is insincere. To begin with, the subjects of the two works are clearly different. The "Grounds" is an enquiry into how far Shakespeare and Fletcher may properly be imitated, while the "Heads" is a hypothetical refutation of Rymer's proposition that English dramatists should work from Greek principles and foundations. The assumption behind the "Grounds" is Rymer's: that the drama of all ages has similar standards and is conformable to a single set of rules. As I believe I have shown, this assumption is quite consistent with Dryden's beliefs as they are displayed in the "Heads." Even there he does not "attack" the *Poetics;* rather, he considers the possibilities of a denial of their adequacy for English drama. And what Dryden thrice concludes is that change and development must be allowed for, not that classical rules and models should be abandoned. He says much the same thing in the "Grounds": customs change from country to country, but the foundation of tragedy remains the same.

The "Grounds" is indubitably much more formal, prescriptive, and historically oriented than the "Heads." Watson complains that the "Grounds" is "much less radical,

[119]

much less frankly anti-Rymer" (I, 238, headnote)—but
what evidence have we that the "Grounds" was written
in opposition to Rymer at all? Neither in tone nor in content is even the "Heads" "anti-Rymer"; Dryden examines
Rymer's premises critically, but is content finally to accept
them. In both essays he attempts to show that admiration
for the Elizabethans is not inconsistent with respect for
classical models. Watson says that the "Grounds" is "occasionally" "slyly forceful" in its demonstration that
"Greek tragedies were not much more Aristotelian than
the Elizabethan" (I, xiv). This he interprets as a jab at
Rymer. But it can more simply be taken as part of Dryden's proof that the "rules" do not invariably demand
rigid adherence. Both Walcott and Watson base their
analyses on the supposition that the "Heads" is an attack
on Rymer, and so they are disappointed by the noncom-
bativeness of the public essay. But taken by itself, the
"Grounds" cannot be construed as a contradiction of Rymer. Indeed, it starts from Rymer's position and attempts
to reconcile Elizabethan dramatic practice with it as far
as possible.[31]

Dislike of the "Grounds" leads to Watson's claim that
in the "Heads" we have the "real" Dryden, and by implication to its corollary, that the "Grounds" is insincere.
But these conclusions are open to two objections: first, the
"Heads" does *not* actually overthrow Rymer's premises,
and so its assumptions are not inconsistent with those of
the "Grounds"; and second, if they were so, we could only
infer that Dryden was monstrously and consistently hypo-
critical throughout most of his life and work.

If Dryden really believed (contrary to what I find is
the true import of the "Heads") that classical precedent

31. See Zimansky's analysis, pp. xxxv–xxxvi.

had no relevance for the English literary tradition, then he was an astonishingly successful dissembler. His defenses of rules, decorum, and poetic justice are frequent.[32] Are we to suppose that he did not believe what he consistently said? Surely we should rather assume that the "Grounds" better reflects Dryden's considered opinion in the late 1670s. We find his effort to reconcile Greek rules and English practice somewhat ridiculous, but since a close examination reveals the same endeavor in the "Heads," we have no reason to doubt that Dryden believed in what he was doing.

The "Heads" is particularly interesting because it exhibits almost no dependence on authority, though all that this shows us is that left to himself Dryden arrives at much the same conclusions anyway. Undeniably its informality makes the "Heads" more attractive to the modern critic than the formal, authoritative "Grounds." The one is an excited reaction, a speculative response to an impressive essay. The other is a carefully considered attempt to stake out tenable middle ground between strict rules and license. Written less than two years apart and both touching on Elizabethan drama, they naturally have some similarities. But their differences are of aim and orientation, not merely degree. The "Heads" examines—and basically upholds— Rymer's premises; the "Grounds" assumes their validity and tries "to make Rymer's materials workable." [33]

32. For example, on rules: "I have that veneration for Aristotle, Horace, Ben Jonson, and Corneille. . . . [I] fight under their protection. . . . If nature be to be imitated, then there is a rule for imitating nature rightly" ("Defence of *An Essay*" [1668], I, 121–122). Cf. similar references in the "Grounds" and "A Parallel of Poetry and Painting" (1695), as well as innumerable passing comments (e.g., II, 47–48).
33. Zimansky, p. xxxvi.

In neither work was Dryden attacking Rymer, and even in the "Heads" he was not seriously attempting to overturn the premises of *The Tragedies of the Last Age*. T. S. Eliot once noted that he had never seen a "cogent refutation" of Rymer's later objections to *Othello*, extreme as they are.[34] Certainly Dryden could not have produced one, for as examination of the "Heads" makes clear, Rymer's arguments cannot be rebutted, though their extremism can be tempered. His conclusions can be rejected only by denying his premises—which Dryden could not do, since one of his most stable convictions was that modern literature represented a development from the classics.

The "Heads" is then much less radical than has been supposed. Although Dryden does indeed presume to question the assumptions of his age, he does not carry his arguments far enough to threaten his belief in the stability and continuity of tradition. The supposedly revolutionary side of the "Heads" is not a statement of serious conviction but rather an analysis of forensic possibilities. We should not be surprised that Dryden could challenge a position with whose premises he was in substantial agreement. His temper is always sceptically speculative, and he could have no better way of testing and clarifying his convictions than by questioning them. That he did write the "Heads" is perhaps a clue to his undeniable superiority to Rymer as a critic. For though he did not—and could not—refute Rymer's premises, the "Heads" is solid evidence of his reluctance to accept conclusions which contradicted English theatrical experience, and we can honor his good sense without wishing away his principles. Undeniably, his most abiding critical concern, evidenced in both the "Heads"

34. *The Sacred Wood* (New York, 1960), p. 96n.

and the "Grounds," is the reconciliation of the English dramatic tradition with classically derived rules. In this endeavor Dryden reflects the cultural orientation of his time, and no amount of modern critical hindsight can alter the situation.

II

I have analyzed the "Heads of an Answer to Rymer" at such length because the work is our most substantial evidence on Dryden's opinion of contemporary criticism. Unfortunately in this instance it has been necessary to proceed on the *disjecta membra* of earlier critics. The conventional nature of "The Grounds of Criticism in Tragedy" has encouraged the very misleading supposition that the essay represents a compromise between Dryden's allegedly revolutionary convictions and the supposed demands of neoclassical respectability. George Watson in particular (and his is currently the standard interpretation) has glorified the "Heads" as a revolutionary document. His position, like that of some other recent scholars, reflects a desire to see Dryden as a critic ahead of his time, free from the prejudices and limitations of his age.

The first part of this chapter has been directed against such a reading of Dryden. To some extent, I grant, one must sympathize with the desire to give Dryden all possible credit. And to trace (as Aden does) Dryden's anticipation of Coleridge's conceptual and terminological distinctions can be both interesting and illuminating. But to pursue such studies very far—which is to treat Dryden as the beginning of something he was not—must lead to either frustration or fatuity.

If I may be allowed a brief, Drydenesque excursion, I

would like to comment that to find a satisfactory perspective from which to deal with Dryden's criticism is tricky. The critic has a natural tendency to applaud his appreciations and hush up his principles, for most of us find Dryden's pronouncements on moral utility and decorum in literature rather unpalatable. Yet to ignore the principles is to leave us with Saintsbury's belief that Dryden was a great intuitive reader hampered by the conventions of his time—a view to which Dryden himself would have objected strenuously, we may be sure. But how to treat his principles and conventional opinions? We tend to feel deprecating and apologetic about them. Even worse, we may, like Watson, become irritated by Dryden's failure to be what we want to find him—and if we convince ourselves that Dryden "really believed" what we think he should have, we may want to accuse him of timidity or worse. Just as bad as this sort of critical twisting is the pompous assumption that Dryden must, like a sacred cow, be treated strictly "in his own terms." We may say that the critic should explain, not judge, his subject, but this principle becomes an excuse for evading serious questions of worth. If by every sign in the modern critical zodiac Dryden was misguided, why does he deserve our attention? The simplest answer is that studying criticism can help us understand the aesthetics of the literature of a period. My purposes here are less utilitarian than this; I believe that Dryden's criticism is of interest in itself as it reflects and records his responses to contemporary standards and problems. We cannot look to Dryden for solutions to our problems, but we can find in his work the history of a struggle to deal with critical issues which must have appeared no less tangled than ours do now. In dealing with

[124]

such work we must somehow compromise between apology and blindness. With our respect for Dryden and attentiveness to him, we must combine a healthy sense of his shortcomings. It does him a disservice to treat his work in an antiseptic vacuum or to try to ignore the drastic changes in literary theory that differentiate the Restoration period from our own.

A fair view of Dryden places him in his contemporary surroundings, but includes a look at them in the cold light of hindsight. When Dryden solemnly worries about presenting a criminal king, and invokes Rymer's warning on the subject, we tend to respond with either pity or contempt.[35] But we should be able to understand this notion, and to treat it with sympathy and even respect, without having to pretend that we take it seriously—the critic who does so appears a fool to anyone not playing the same game. Standards change—as Dryden's are, ours will be—but we must retain enough of our modern perspective to be able to see that much of Dryden's outlook is the result of particular circumstances at a particular time. And insofar as we unwarrantably differentiate Dryden from his fellows, we do him a grave injustice, for when he is treated by our standards, careful examination of what he says simply makes him look foolish or, as Watson would have it, dishonest.

I am trying then to set Dryden in the context of other

35. See *The Vindication of the Duke of Guise*, in *The Works of John Dryden*, ed. Sir Walter Scott, rev. George Saintsbury, 18 vols. (Edinburgh, 1882–1893), VII, 159; Dryden's reference is to *TLA*, pp. 42, 65. He refers to the same convention with respect seven years later in the Preface to *Don Sebastian* when he says it is "necessary, according to the laws of the drama, that Sebastian should no more be seen upon the throne" (II, 47).

Restoration critics. The "Heads" has been particularly useful because it is the one extended document known to us in which Dryden deals specifically with the views of one of his contemporaries. No such handy source exists to tell us what he thought of Rymer's later work or that of other men; consequently we must proceed by means of more general comparisons, drawing on Dryden's occasional asides when we can.

Dryden's view of Rymer after the 1670s is complicated by the two men's disagreements on nonliterary matters. Rymer supported the revolution of 1688 and, for what reasons we do not know, lampooned Dryden in a verse epistle (c. 1689; "Dryden, thy Wit has catterwauld too long"). On the death of Shadwell in 1692 Rymer was given Dryden's old post of historiographer royal (which, incidentally, he filled with real distinction). Some ill will on Dryden's part is then to be expected. The evidence on specific critical disagreements is sketchy. Rymer pays Dryden an obviously sarcastic compliment at the end of chapter 1 of *A Short View of Tragedy*, coupled with what appears to be a sneer at his conversion to Catholicism.[36] Dryden was evidently irritated,[37] but publicly he replied only indirectly (if angrily) in the Dedication of the *Examen poeticum* (II, 159–160).

A Short View of Tragedy (1692) has been so grossly maligned that we may wonder if it will ever escape its

36. *A Short View of Tragedy* (hereafter *ASV*), in *Critical Works*, pp. 92–93.
37. See *The Letters of John Dryden*, ed. Charles E. Ward (Durham, N.C., 1942), nos. 24, 26. I find no warrant for Ward's statement (p. 164nn.) that Dryden was "reserving for himself an attack on Rymer," other than his suggestion to Walsh in no. 24 that Walsh enter "the lists, though not against Rymer; yet as a champion of our cause, who defy the Chorus of the Ancients."

reputation as a monstrosity.[38] It is, as Zimansky says, one of the earliest attempts to write an English literary history which is more than an annal. The gaps in Rymer's knowledge are enormous, and his lack of formal control over his material can be dizzying, but in concept, at any rate, *A Short View* is an impressive piece of work, and it represents a considerable advance over *The Tragedies of the Last Age*. In both works Rymer's purpose is explicitly to reform the stage; in the earlier one he merely exposes faults, but in the later he does so only to prove his general thesis—that English tragedy needs to be corrected according to lessons drawn from the evolution of earlier national literatures. The faults that Rymer finds in Elizabethan works are the same in both cases, and the models he upholds are also the same: what has been added is the cyclic perspective in which Rymer places English literature.

The deformity of structure caused by Rymer's digressive informality seriously detracts from what Zimansky has shown to be a sensible outline. Evidently Rymer meant to start by indicating the need for reform of the stage; then to show the cycle of rise and fall among the Greeks and Romans; to discuss the opposition of Christianity to the stage as a reason for general decline; and finally to discuss the rise of poetry and drama in England, using *Othello*, *Julius Caesar*, and *Catiline* as illustrations of the need for reform. Rymer's concept here is historically quite—perhaps even spectacularly—sophisticated: he treats national

38. The only good discussion of it (to my knowledge) is in the notes to Zimansky's edition, pp. 227–233. Nigel Alexander, in "Thomas Rymer and *Othello*," *ShS*, 21 (1968), 67–77, has recently attempted to provide the "cogent refutation" of Rymer's arguments on *Othello* demanded by T. S. Eliot. He successfully ridicules Rymer, and exposes his inaccuracies, but does not, I think, shed much light on *A Short View*.

[127]

literatures as independent cyclic entities, all functioning within the pattern of a broader development. This approach makes explicit in a sensible way the place of English evolution in European tradition. Dryden, by contrast, is always very fuzzy on this relationship, and tends to slough off consideration of national declines and the reasons for them.[39]

A Short View suffers not only from disorganization but from a snappishness of tone and manner that makes it less enjoyable than its predecessor, whose boisterous spirits and genial tone soften the harshness of Rymer's criticisms. But perhaps more damaging, from the modern reader's point of view, is the savaging of a play we have all been taught to revere—and in contemporary reactions we can see the beginning of this pious attitude. What we can accept as comment on Rollo becomes inadmissible on Othello. Even in the 1690s some critics objected to Rymer's "blaspheming" Shakespeare, as Dryden put it. But however misguided Rymer undoubtedly was, we cannot in fairness beat him with the club of Shakespeare idolatry.

In discussing Othello Rymer holds up a clear set of standards and finds the play wanting. All that we can say is that he applied the wrong criteria, for his judgment certainly follows from his premises. Rymer demands realistic construction, decorum, and an instructive fable. He does

39. For example, Dryden says in his Dedication to Virgil's *Pastorals:* "I will say nothing of the *Piscatory Eclogues,* because no modern Latin can bear criticism. 'Tis no wonder that rolling down through so many barbarous ages, from the spring of Virgil, it bears along with it the filth and ordures of the Goths and Vandals" (II, 220). Plainly he is aware that Latin literature went to pot, but why "barbarous ages" should have intervened to cause such a decline is a question he never considers.

not find them, and we can scarcely deny that "never was any Play fraught, like this of *Othello*, with improbabilities." [40] Rymer wonders why the Venetian court, sitting at midnight on matters of national security, stops to listen to a personal dispute; asks when Cassio could have seduced Desdemona; and complains at length that the handkerchief device is ridiculous. He seizes on numerous factual contradictions and improbabilities and does manage to show that by Restoration standards Shakespeare was remarkably careless in putting his play together. But what most offends Rymer is the lack of poetic justice: believing that tragedy must instruct, he is led to demand a moral, and finding no real justification for the various characters' agonies and deaths, he concludes that "the tragical part is, plainly none other, than a Bloody Farce, without salt or savour." [41] In Rymer's view Othello is a booby for becoming jealous so easily, but the original fault is Desdemona's, for having been so unnatural as to marry a Moor—hence Rymer's ironic praise of the "Moral" of this "very instructive" fable:

1. First, This may be a caution to all Maidens of Quality how, without their Parents consent, they run away with Blackamoors. . . .

Secondly, This may be a warning to all good Wives, that they look well to their Linnen.

Thirdly, This may be a lesson to Husbands, that before their Jealousie be Tragical, the proofs may be Mathematical.[42]

The violence of this attack on *Othello* has almost completely obscured Rymer's purposes in making it. He wanted

40. *ASV*, p. 134.   41. *ASV*, p. 164.
42. *ASV*, p. 132.

to show that English tragedy fell sadly short of the high standard of probability, decorum, and moral utility that Restoration writers were agreed in demanding. The extent to which *A Short View* reflects Restoration thinking must be assessed in three questions: were Rymer's criticisms accurate? were they well balanced? were his solutions sensible? Contemporary opinion is well summed up by Dryden:

After I have confessed thus much of our modern heroic poetry, I cannot but conclude with Mr Rym[er] that our English comedy is far beyond any thing of the Ancients. And notwithstanding our irregularities, so is our tragedy. Shakespeare had a genius for it; and we know, in spite of Mr R——, that genius alone is a greater virtue (if I may so call it) than all other qualifications put together. You see what success this learned critic has found in the world, after his blaspheming Shakespeare. Almost all the faults which he has discovered are truly there; yet who will read Mr Rym or not read Shakespeare? For my own part, I reverence Mr Rym's learning, but I detest his ill nature and his arrogance. I indeed, and such as I, have reason to be afraid of him, but Shakespeare has not [Letter to John Dennis, *c.* March 1694; II, 178].

"Almost all the faults which he has discovered are truly there"—this flat admission, unpalatable though we find it (and modern critics tend to gloss over its implications), is the key to Dryden's thought on the subject. As we shall see, he disagrees with both Rymer's prescriptions and his evaluation of Shakespeare, but what Rymer saw as faults Dryden did too. We may be prepared to dismiss Rymer's objections as ridiculous, but Dryden was not. This position is quite consistent with his lifelong convictions. His revision of *Troilus and Cressida* and his imitation of *Antony and Cleopatra* betray much of Rymer's concern for realistic construction. The same sense of decorum leads Dryden to say in *The Vindication of the Duke of Guise* (1683) that the "laws of poetry" had compelled him to minimize the vices of a prince, and he had received Rymer's dictates on poetic justice with enthusiasm ("The Grounds of Criticism in Tragedy," I, 245–246). Even in the Preface to *Don Sebastian* (1690), after his personal relations with Rymer had deteriorated, Dryden still invokes "the learned Mr Rymer" and upholds "poetical justice" and decorum, "according to the laws of the drama" (II, 47–48). Did Dryden think *Othello* well constructed, decorous, and properly instructive? He does not say so, and we cannot suppose it.[43]

As in the "Heads," Dryden does not really disagree with Rymer's specific criticisms; he differs about the weight which they should be given. Dryden always admires the imaginative power of genius, particularly as it appears in fine rhetoric: hence his love of the "excellent thoughts" buried in the piles of Shakespeare's "rubbish" (I, 240). His lesser interest in fable leaves him less bothered by Shakespeare's considerable irregularities.

By the 1690s both critics had become more concerned about factual and emotional probability than they had been earlier. Rymer had grown openly contemptuous of the conventions he associated with heroic drama: "We want

43. Rowe comments in the Introduction to his 1709 edition of Shakespeare (I, xvff.) that Rymer's model for a tragedy (*ASV*, pp. 89–93) is no improvement on Shakespeare, and indeed we would find it easy to ridicule Rymer's proposal. But before doing so we should recollect that Dryden's suggested plot for a Christian epic (which most critics prefer to pass over in silence) is just as open to criticism, if not more so (see the "Discourse on Satire," II, 88–90).

a law for Acting the *Rehearsal* once a week, to keep us in our senses, and secure us against the Noise and Nonsence, the Farce and Fustian which, in the name of Tragedy, have so long invaded, and usurp our Theater."[44] Doubtless Dryden would have preferred to dispense with *The Rehearsal*, but by 1681 he had come to similar conclusions.[45]

The point on which he takes complete, even violent, exception to Rymer is over the latter's corrective prescriptions. Casting about for a device to help maintain unity of time and place and to hold the writer to a more straightforward structure, Rymer hit on one recently revived from classical drama by Racine—"*The* Chorus *keeps the Poet to Rules.*"

The *Chorus* was the root and original, and is certainly always the most necessary part of Tragedy.

The *Spectators* thereby are secured, that their Poet shall not juggle, or put upon them in the matter of *Place*, and *Time*, other than is just and reasonable for the representation.

And the *Poet* has this benefit; the *Chorus* is a goodly *Show*, so that he need not ramble from his Subject out of his Wits for some foreign Toy or Hobby-horse, to humor the Multitude.[46]

Rymer looked to this device for the "Reformation" he sought. Dryden, more conscious of the conventions of English drama, flatly rejects the chorus as "an unprofit-

44. *ASV*, p. 170.
45. See the Dedication of *The Spanish Friar*, I, 276. Perhaps even more striking than this confession of personal "extravagance" is his later admission that "love and honour" were "the mistaken topics of tragedy" (Preface to *Don Sebastian*, II, 45)—a reversal of longstanding theory and practice.
46. *ASV*, p. 84.

able encumbrance" (Dedication of the *Examen poeticum*, II, 161).⁴⁷ His objection to Rymer's procedure here is heated. In an attack on false critics he speaks first of those who commend the Elizabethans not to "commend their writings, but to throw dirt on the writers of this age," and he continues:

But there is another sort of insects, more venomous than the former; those who manifestly aim at the destruction of our poetical church and state; who allow nothing to their country-men, either of this or of the former age. These attack the living by raking up the ashes of the dead; well knowing that if they can subvert their original title to the stage, we who claim under them must fall of course. Peace be to the venerable shades of Shakespeare and Ben Jonson!" [II, 159–160].⁴⁸

This is in part patriotic bluster; Dryden is always ready to evade French and classical-based criticism by demanding

47. Three years later Dryden notes that tragedy had developed from a chorus, grants that like a "group" in a picture it can have a place, but insists that "a good tragedy may subsist without a chorus: notwithstanding any reasons which have been given by Dacier to the contrary" ("A Parallel of Poetry and Painting," II, 199–200).

48. The heat of this passage we may attribute at least in part to extrinsic circumstances. Rymer had just "spoken slightly of me in his last Critique," as Dryden put it, and he had been told that Mary II "had commanded her Historiographer Rymer to fall upon my Playes. . . . I doubt not his malice" (Letter to Tonson, 30 August 1693; Ward no. 26). Watson suggests that the "explosion" against Rymer "was based on personal pique rather than critical principle" (II, 159n). But whether the verse lampoon attributed to Rymer was involved (as Watson speculates) seems questionable: in January 1690 Dryden was quoting "the learned Mr Rymer" with approval (II, 48). Without more facts, further speculation is idle, but in any case it seems unlikely that so old a wound would have provoked Dryden so thoroughly.

to "be tried by the laws of my own country" (Preface to *All for Love*, I, 225). But beneath this evasiveness there remains a solid substratum of conviction that there is real worth in and point to English tradition. That Dryden was correct in rejecting the chorus we have no doubt (though we should recollect that T. S. Eliot hoped it might be useful); to what extent Dryden's rejection of Rymer's procedure—looking abroad—is based on intellectual conviction we cannot say, since he provides no real justification for it. At no point does Dryden deny that the Ancients "are and ought to be our masters" (I, 230), but he consistently makes more allowance than Rymer for local tradition.

Dryden and Rymer have often been regarded as the opposite poles of Restoration criticism—the one supposedly rule-bound, the other intuitively free. Clearly enough their purposes and perspectives are quite different, as are their valuations of the "parts" of drama. But about the use and conventions of tragedy they are substantially in accord, both believing in regular construction, decorum, and moral utility. Dryden's saving grace, from our point of view, is his relative flexibility in being able to admire beauties in spite of what he regarded as faults; Rymer's concentration on the faults makes him a far less agreeable critic. Like his contemporaries, Dryden seems to have admired Rymer's brilliance and learning while finding him too severe. His final reference to Rymer is in the Preface to *Fables* (1700), and it is wholly laudatory, though Dryden no longer had anything to fear from the "learned Mr Rymer." Mentioning Chaucer's language, Dryden says: "But this subject has been copiously treated by that great critic, who deserves no little commendation from us his countrymen"

(II, 272). Since the reference is to *A Short View*, we may infer that neither disagreements nor personal animus kept Dryden from admiring Rymer's most extreme and controversial work.

III

To compare the various Restoration critics is tricky because their work differs in a variety of ways. I need to start therefore by indicating the diversity of their perspectives, purposes, and methods. Dryden and Dennis may be called "explanatory" critics (though "controversial" or "polemical" might describe the latter more precisely). Rymer is composition-oriented, and his practice consists largely of specific, corrective criticisms. Mulgrave too addresses himself to writers, though what he has to say amounts to a collection of commonplace observations on the nature and utility of satire, poetry-in-general, and criticism. Temple's discussions of literature are a part of his considerations of the use and history of culture, and so they cannot be considered criticism in the usual sense at all.

The forms in which these men cast their productions are equally diverse. Dryden and Rymer write informal, often epistolary, discourses. Mulgrave's little essays, whether in verse ("Essay on Satire" and "Essay on Poetry") or prose ("On Criticism"), consist of the sort of general observations and prescriptions which were codified, and vastly better expressed, in Pope's *Essay on Criticism* (1711). Temple's much longer essays are well organized and focused, though quite broad in their subjects, but one would have to look to Bentley in this period for specific and scholarly study. Dennis, a younger man, adopts a very different form. His work is immensely organized—he is a "Treatise" writer with a vengeance.

We may say generally that as the century draws to an end a change is apparent in the dominant critical mode. The informal discursiveness of Dryden and Rymer and the platitudinous prescriptions epitomized by Mulgrave's writings are giving way to more systematic considerations of specific works and problems. Consider, for example, Dennis' *Remarks on a Book Entituled, Prince Arthur* (1696) and *The Usefulness of the Stage* (1698). We see in both Dennis' aggressiveness: the one is an attack on Blackmore, the other on Collier. Both pieces, characteristically for Dennis, are as long as any of Dryden's efforts. Dennis prefaces the *Remarks* with an explanation of his aims and procedures:

I think my self obliged to give the Reader an account of the Method which I propounded to use in the following Remarks. In the first Part I intended to shew that Mr. *Blackmore*'s Action has neither unity, nor integrity, nor morality, nor universality, and consequently that he can have no *Fable* and no *Heroick Poem*. In the second Part I design'd to come to the Narration; and to shew that it is neither probable, delightful, nor wonderful. I propounded to show that there are three things that make a Narration delightful; The Persons introduc'd, the Things related, and the Manner of relating them. I resolv'd to consider the first of these, and to prove that the Poetical Persons ought to have manners, and that those manners ought to have the following qualifications: That they ought to be good, convenient, resembling, and equal, and that besides there ought to be an unity of Character in the principal person; and that that unity of Character like an universal Soul was to run thro' the whole Poem. Next, I determin'd to make it appear that Mr. *Blackmore*'s Characters have none of the foremention'd qualifications. Then, I pretended to convince the Reader that the things contain'd in Mr. *Black-more*'s Narration are neither in their own natures delightful, nor numerous enough, nor various enough, nor rightly disposed, nor surprizing, nor pathetick.[49]

Nothing in Dryden's criticism can be adduced as a parallel. Dennis produces his critique in two "Parts" of eight chapters each. Every chapter has a clear focus (for instance, "That the Incidents in *Prince Arthur* are not surprizing") and forms a step in a logical progression from general theory to specific proof.

The Usefulness of the Stage is designed and announced as a formal proof of its proposition in three parts. In part I Dennis undertakes to show

First, That the Stage is instrumental to the Happiness of Mankind in general.

Secondly, That it is more particularly instrumental to the Happiness of *Englishmen*.[50]

In the second part he tries to demonstrate "That the Stage is useful to *Government*," especially to the English government, and in the third "That the Stage is useful to the Advancement of Religion." Each one starts with Dennis' claim and concludes with chapters answering anticipated arguments from "Reason" and "Authority." Dennis plainly tries to make his proofs as "Mathematical" as ever Rymer demanded of jealous husbands. A greater contrast to Dryden in this respect would be hard to find.

In studying this collection of critics we can usefully survey contemporary reactions to Rymer's *A Short View*, which has represented for many modern critics—quite unjustly—the nadir of Restoration criticism. Dryden's com-

49. Dennis, I, 46.   50. Dennis, I, 148.

bination of respect for Rymer with objections to his severity is quite typical.[51] As Motteux puts it: "Mr. *Rymer* has a little too violently inforc'd the Errors" in Shakespeare. Dennis' reaction, set forth in the five dialogues of *The Impartial Critick* (1693), is similar to Dryden's—he accepts the specific criticisms but denounces the application of Greek devices to English drama.[52] The conclusion gives Rymer as much approval as censure:

> *Beaum.* I find then, that you do not dissent from Mr. *R*—— in every thing.
> *Freem.* No, I should be very sorry if I should do that; for his Censures of *Shakespear* in most of the particulars, are very sensible and very just. But it does not follow, because *Shakespear* has Faults, that therefore he has no Beauties.[53]

Dennis objects to Rymer's faultfinding, particularly when Shakespeare is the subject, but takes real exception to the chorus. His preface begins:

51. Zimansky includes a useful discussion of contemporary comment in his notes (pp. 227–231), to which I am indebted.
52. Zimansky (p. 229), in noting this parallel, says that "it has been suggested that he [Dennis] used material given him by Dryden (Hooker's note in Dennis, *Works*, I, 434)." What Hooker actually suggests is that Dennis used the "Heads of an Answer to Rymer" (Dennis, I, 434–435, 438, 445). This conjecture seems dubious to me. We have no evidence that Dryden recollected or passed the "Heads" about. More important, the apparent similarities of argument are on matters so general that no specific source need be suspected—that Greek plots were more regular was not disputed, and to defend love in tragedy was by 1693 a commonplace, even though Dryden himself had apparently suffered second thoughts. The theory of the influence of climate on national taste more probably came, I should think, from Temple's recent essays than from the "Heads."
53. Dennis, I, 41.

Upon reading Mr. *Rymer's* late Book, I soon found that its Design was to make several Alterations in the Art of the Stage, which instead of reforming, would ruine the *English Drama*. For to set up the *Grecian* Method amongst us with success, it is absolutely necessary to restore not only their Religion and their Polity, but to transport us to the same Climate in which *Sophocles* and *Euripides* writ.[54]

We have here, explicitly bolstered with the theory of climatic influence, Dryden's objection to "the destruction of our poetical church and state."

Gildon's replies, in his *Miscellaneous Letters and Essays* (1694), are far more bluntly anti-Rymer. Gildon does what Dryden had failed to do in the "Heads": he flatly rejects the authority of Aristotle for English drama. But though Gildon does reject rules, his position is not wholly outside the norms of his day, for he defends Shakespeare by arguing that he does profit and delight, and, interestingly, Gildon makes the historical argument that Shakespeare's faults must be excused as those of his age.

We should note that not one of these critics, nor any to come, makes a systematic attempt to show that Rymer's criticisms of *Othello* are unfounded. The attack which makes *A Short View* notorious to us was accepted with little dissent by Rymer's contemporaries. They do criticize him, as Zimansky notes, for failing to balance Shakespeare's beauties against his admitted faults. The more rancorous objections do not concern *Othello* at all, but Rymer's application of Greek methods to the English stage. Indeed Gildon, who had attempted "a Vindication of Shakespear" in 1694, had by 1710 backed off: "I have drawn the Fable with as much favour to the Author, as I possibly cou'd,

54. Dennis, I, 11.

[139]

yet I must own that the Faults found in it by Mr *Rymer* are but too visible for the most Part." [55]

The factor which most differentiates Rymer from his fellows is not principles or specific judgments but his concept of criticism. For Rymer it is correction by negative example; scarcely ever, after the "Preface to Rapin" (1674), does he pause to note "beauties." Dryden, Mulgrave, and Dennis make a major point of saying that the critic's main business is to explain what is right and to note the beauties—evidently they felt it necessary to disclaim faultfinding "hypercritics," as Dryden terms them (I, 198; II, 158). Thus Mulgrave says:

The business of a Critick is mightily mistaken among us; for our Town-sparks think it consists in nothing but finding fault, which is but the least half of their work. Every man who drinks his pot, can judge a paultry picture in an alehouse to be worth nothing; but how few can discern the best touches, and judge of a good collection![56]

Dryden's condemnations of faultfinders are frequent, especially in his prologues, when his plays are likely to be their target; that he had a positive sense of "criticism" is made clear both in his brief definition ("Apology for Heroic Poetry," I, 196–197), and in such statements as his complaint in "The Life of Lucian" that "criticism is now become mere hangman's work, and meddles only with the faults of authors" (II, 213). Dennis, the most contumacious of these critics, argues at great length that criticism serves a constructive function, and not merely by negative ex-

55. Charles Gildon, in Nicholas Rowe's *The Works of Mr. William Shakespear* (1710), VII, 410, cited by Zimansky, p. 230.
56. Mulgrave, *Works*, II, 284.

ample. In the Preface to his *Remarks* on *Prince Arthur* he says to the reader:

But that he may come with the less prejudice to the Reading the following Criticism, I desire to prepare him, by Answering some Objections which have been made against Criticism.

Three Objections have been made against Criticism in General: The First, That it is an invidious ill-natur'd thing. The Second, That it is a vain and successless Attempt. And the Third, That it tends to the certain diminution of the happiness of the reader.[57]

Dennis goes on to refute these objections at great length, and we may guess that he thought it necessary, for this justification of adverse criticism precedes a long and savage attack on Blackmore's epic. In Dennis' defense we should note that he does explain and explore the positive standards by which he feels Blackmore falls short.

We may deduce simply that many of the contemporary objections to Rymer were based on his failure to follow the usual procedures of balancing beauties against faults. Of these other critics Dennis comes closest to him in this respect, and he was to become notorious for his ill-temper and critical quarrels.

Within their diversity of purposes and methods, these critics have much in common; on matters of the construction, proprieties, and function of literature they display an essential unanimity. A few examples of Dryden's general opinions will indicate the extent to which he is at one with his fellows. "A Parallel of Poetry and Painting" can serve as a convenient source.

Dryden tells us that "the moral (as Bossu observes) is

57. Dennis, I, 48.

the first business of the poet, as being the groundwork of his instruction. This being formed, he contrives such a design, or fable, as may be most suitable to the moral" (II, 186). This is the principle on which Rymer starts all his analyses: he begins by outlining the fable and enquiring what moral it is meant to convey. Similarly Dennis commences his discussion of epic with an explanation of its purpose: "The Design of every Man who Writes an Epick Poem, is to give Moral Instructions to Mankind, and particularly to his own Country-men": therefore "An Epick Poem is a Discourse invented with Art to form the Manners by Instructions disguis'd under the Allegory of an Action." [58] The doctrine of pleasure and profit, however arid it appears to us, was a central article of faith for all these men. A poem that does not please will not instruct —and hence the poet's immediate object must be to please —but "the chief design of poetry is to instruct" (II, 186).

Pleasure, Dryden says, is the result of successful imitation.

The imitation of nature is therefore justly constituted as the general, and indeed the only, rule of pleasing. . . . Both these arts [poetry and painting], as I said before, are not only true imitations of nature, but of the best nature, of that which is wrought up to a nobler pitch [II, 193–194].

Much of Rymer's objection to *Othello* follows from just such a sense of decorum: he cannot accept the lack of class distinctions or grant that a general and a hero could treat a lady as Othello treats Desdemona.[59] This same acute sense

58. Dennis, I, 56, 55.
59. These critics do allow for a difference between drama and epic in ideality of character. Dryden notes that "as this idea of perfection is of little use in portraits . . . so neither is it in the char-

[142]

of propriety appears in Mulgrave's objection to satirists attacking "the grossest Follies," which he calls "ignoble Game" and considers an indecorous subject: he asks the satirist "with sharp Eyes those nicer Faults to find,/ Which lie obscurely in the wisest Mind." [60] Mulgrave was not thinking of our meaning of "nicer," but in a sense that was what he meant. Restoration critics have a horror of what would in the first part of this century have been called the "common." Subjects are to be noble, preferably exalted, and the style must be suitable: where realism is desired, the familiar (in Pope's term) is permissible, but never the low. Dryden's preference for "high" to "low" burlesque is but one outcropping of a pervasive attitude in this age. Another is Rymer's constant demand that the manners of the nobility be shown as suitably refined. This concern is entirely shared by Dennis, who says in lambasting Blackmore:

So that we may observe, that these two Princes having longed to see one another: *Hoel* to express his share of the Joy, greets *Arthur* with a Speech of about forty Lines, which he begins with a couple of Similies; because you know Similies are proper for Passion, and a Man that is transported always makes a long Speech.

I have indeed heard of a King, that has been entertain'd at this rate, in an University Quadrangle: But can any one be-

---

acters of comedy and tragedy, which are never to be made perfect, but always to be drawn with some specks of frailty and deficience" ("A Parallel of Poetry and Painting," II, 184). This is of course part of his reason for preferring epic, which does admit of ideal characters.

60. "An Essay on Satire," *Works*, I, 113. It is worth noting that when it appeared (anonymously), this essay was thought to be by Dryden. See Charles E. Ward, *The Life of John Dryden* (Chapel Hill, 1961), pp. 143-144.

lieve, that ever any one King greeted another so? Is there any thing like this in Nature, and in the world? If not, I think I may venture to affirm, that there ought to be no such thing in an Epick Poem. For tho' true Sublimity, like Grace, may exalt Nature, it can never invert it.[61]

In more formal fashion, this is the manner and method of Rymer, who, we may observe, is at least no sillier than his fellows.

Classical models are a subject on which each of these critics expresses himself warmly; their differences lie entirely in the weight that they allow local tradition. Dryden and Rymer have already been quoted on the utility of the classics. Mulgrave's comment is, as usual, utterly typical of the age: "I confess I am still very difficult in matters of writing, and seldom find any thing worth commending, because of those great Ideas I have of the Antients." [62] Temple echoes the usual estimate of Homer and Virgil:

I think no Man has been so bold among those that remain [i.e., whose works are preserved] to question the Title of *Homer* and *Virgil*, not only to the first Rank, but to the supream Dominion in this State, and from whom, as the great Law-givers as well as Princes, all the Laws and Orders of it are or may be derived. *Homer* was without Dispute the most Universal *Genius* that has been known in the World, and *Virgil* the most accomplish't.[63]

Dennis exceeds the other critics in his knowledge of the classics, and his respect for them is immense, but he shares the dilemma in which Restoration critics were caught.

Beaum. Now then, let me hear your Objections to Mr. *Rymer*'s Design; for nothing can seem more commendable to

61. Dennis, I, 91.   62. "On Criticism," *Works*, II, 285.
63. "Of Poetry," Spingarn, III, 82.

me, than his intention, which is to restore Tragedy to its primitive purity, by re-establishing the Ancient Method, and reviving the Rules of *Aristotle*.

Freem. I am for observing the Rules of *Aristotle*, as much as any Man living, as far as it can be done without re-establishing the Ancient Method. But because the Ancients Tragedies had little Love in them, that therefore ours must have little too; because the Ancient Tragedies had a Chorus, that therefore we must ridiculously ape them; this is what I cannot endure to hear of.[64]

The issue of classical jurisdiction is not really a matter of Ancients versus Moderns, though that was the over-simplification toward which the controversy tended to move. Rymer and Temple are among the critics commonly associated with the "Ancients" position. But we have already noted that Rymer's object was to help English writers surpass the classics, and though Temple rejected the possibility of lasting progress, he refused to believe that the relative perfections of the past were unapproachable.

Among these many Decays, there is yet one sort of Poetry that seems to have succeeded much better with our Moderns than any of the rest, which is *Dramatick*, or that of the Stage. In this the *Italian*, the *Spanish*, and the *French* have all had their different Merit, and received their just Applauses. Yet I am deceived if our *English* has not in some kind excelled both the Modern and the Antient, which has been by Force of a Vein Natural perhaps to our Country.[65]

Dryden and Rymer were alike in touting the possibility (and in some fields the actuality) of progress, without

64. *The Impartial Critick*, Dennis, I, 30.
65. "Of Poetry," Spingarn, III, 103. This opinion is, of course, echoed by the other critics, including even Rymer, for comedy at least.

facing the probability of an eventual decline in England. Temple's uniqueness in this little group lies in his pessimistically cyclic view of culture; he assumes that English literature will follow the pattern of others both in its rise and also in a future decline. He makes two other assumptions of import: if the Moderns excel the Ancients in any way, they do so only because they had the Ancients to build on; and cultural diversity is the product of physical environment. He objects to exalting the Moderns, because "let it come about how it will, if we are Dwarfs, we are still so, though we stand upon a Gyant's shoulders." [66] Temple accounts for the excellence of the English stage by saying:

But as of most general Customs in a Country there is usually some Ground from the Nature of the People or the Clymat, so there may be amongst us for this Vein of our Stage, and a greater variety of Humor in the Picture, because there is a greater variety in the Life. This may proceed from the Native Plenty of our Soyl, the unequalness of our Clymat, as well as the Ease of our Government, and the Liberty of Professing Opinions and Factions, which perhaps our Neighbours may have about them, but are forced to disguise, and thereby they may come in time to be extinguish't.[67]

These two ideas can be variously developed. These Restoration critics all believe that Moderns should build on ancient foundations, trying to improve upon them. How much allowance should be made for national differences seemed problematical. Dryden and Dennis were convinced that Rymer granted too little leeway, but Dryden, at least, seems prepared to admit that English drama might be made

66. "On Ancient and Modern Learning," Spingarn, III, 48–49.
67. "Of Poetry," Spingarn, III, 104.

to evolve toward Greek methods. In rejecting the use of a chorus he says:

I will give no other reason than that it is impracticable on our stage. A new theatre, much more ample and much deeper, must be made for that purpose, besides the cost of sometimes forty or fifty habits, which is an expense too large to be supplied by a company of actors. [Oddly niggling objections, these.] 'Tis true, I should not be sorry to see a chorus on a theatre more than as large and as deep again as ours, built and adorned at a king's charges; and on that condition, and another, which is that my hands were not bound behind me, as now they are, I should not despair of making such a tragedy as might be both instructive and delightful, according to the manner of the Grecians ["A Parallel of Poetry and Painting," II, 200].

The differences, Dryden seems to be saying, are those of a local tradition which is not absolute.

Christianity was regarded by all of these men as demanding some alteration of classical practice by modern poets. Dennis goes so far as to make religion a basic point of differentiation. In his long treatise, *The Advancement and Reformation of Modern Poetry* (1701), he concludes that the excellence of the Ancients lay in their combination of regularity and religion,[68] but that the Moderns may

68. Enquiring into his preference for *Oedipus* over *Julius Caesar* Dennis says: "I find then, my Lord, That there are Two very signal Differences between the *Oedipus*, and the *Julius Caesar*. First, The *Oedipus* is Just and Regular, and the *Julius Caesar* is very Extravagant and Irregular. Secondly, The *Oedipus* is very Religious, and the *Julius Caesar* is Irreligious. For, with Submission to your Lordship's Judgment, I conceive, that every Tragedy, ought to be a very Solemn Lecture, inculcating a particular Providence, and shewing it plainly protecting the Good, and chastizing the Bad. . . . Thus, my Lord, I have a great deal of Reason to suspect, that

[147]

surpass them by combining Christianity, a greater religion, with rules. We may be reminded of Dryden's similar claim that the use of Christianity is both proper and necessary for the production of a great modern epic ("Discourse on Satire," II, 85–91).

To gloss over the very real differences among these critics would be wrong, but the extent of their agreement and common ground must be acknowledged. Dryden's principles are by no means revolutionary, or even unusual; they consist, as he believed proper, largely of commonplaces. Few scholars have cared to see much common ground between Dryden and Rymer, but if we read the "Heads" and scattered later comments as they appear to have been meant, we can see that, far from attacking Rymer or rebelling against his "neoclassical" restrictions, Dryden actually shared much of his outlook. The two men differ in the rigor with which they apply principles rather than in the principles themselves. And in fairness we should remember in Rymer's favor that his textual critical methods are far more modern than the procedures of Dryden or Dennis.

That Dryden is the best critic of his age is no more in need of demonstration than that Shakespeare is the best playwright of his. But each deserves to be studied in his proper context. We will understand Shakespeare poorly if we fail to recognize his use of the conventions of his age, and the same must be said for Dryden. Shakespeare's lesser

---

the *Oedipus* derives its Advantage, from its Regularity, and its Religion; and the Presumption grows still more strong, when, upon Enquiry, I find, that the fore-mention'd Regularity, is nothing but the bringing some Rules into Practice" (*The Advancement and Reformation of Poetry*, Dennis, I, 200).

[148]

efforts are surpassed by the best plays of Marlowe, Jonson, Fletcher, and Webster. Similarly Dryden's criticism exists in the same world as that of Rymer, Temple, Dennis, and even Mulgrave. Deification is a poor compliment. To say why Dryden is the best of these critics, without taking refuge in the fact that his opinions are closest to ours, is difficult. My answer, really only a guess, is that Dryden's status as a practicing writer helped him shift the focus of his critical concern away from his general principles toward more specific problems of construction and effectiveness, to which he could respond with greater flexibility.[69]

69. For a mechanistic but useful account of Dryden's notion of critical "latitude," see Thomas A. Hanzo, *Latitude and Restoration Criticism*, Anglistica XII (Copenhagen, 1961).

CHAPTER 5

Neoclassicism

Dryden's intellectual context is most commonly described as "neoclassical"—a term to which a bewildering variety of meanings has been attached. Thus Dryden has been called both one of the great exemplars of "neoclassicism" and the leading rebel against its restrictions: the disagreement is as much terminological as substantive. Though the neoclassical designation for the 1660–1800 period has been sharply challenged in recent years, it has also been powerfully reaffirmed. How well does such a general characterization, carefully defined, seem to fit Dryden's critical opinions? The subject is complex, but after some necessary groundwork and a consideration of the traits neoclassicism has been said to comprise, I will attempt at least a brief sketch of Dryden's place in the intellectual currents of his time.

I

A survey of the uses to which the term "neoclassicism" has been put demonstrates strikingly how ill defined it is.

[150]

Most broadly it is used in contradistinction to "romanticism"—a pairing which, when used to describe "essences"
of periods, is so vague as to be almost meaningless.¹ When
"neoclassicism" is used more specifically to describe or define Restoration and eighteenth-century literature its usages
seem to me to fall into a few fairly distinct types.

"Neoclassical" is occasionally used simply as a descriptive term to designate works falling within the 1660–1800
period. In a similar way, "Victorian" can be taken to mean
a work produced between the death of Scott and the end
of the nineteenth century. No value judgment need be implied; nor must any particular quality or origin be assumed.
Thus R. S. Crane's "English Neoclassical Criticism: An
Outline Sketch"² includes a great deal that other critics
might call "preromantic." In his essay "On Writing the
History of Criticism in England, 1650–1800," Crane remarks that it is to literary theory associated with the
" 'mechanical rules' " that "the name of 'neoclassicism' in
its stricter meaning has been most commonly applied," but
that there are other (and radically different) "modes of
critical discussion" which can "also claim the prestige of

1. Such a distinction is most helpful when it is based on a contrast of specific characteristics rather than supposedly pervasive
"essences." Thus M. H. Abrams says that neoclassical writing is
tradition and craft oriented, often about man, aimed at "what
men possess in common," and postulated on the limitation of man;
romantic writing emphasizes innovation, spontaneity, nature, and
the individual, and assumes that man is "a being of immense potentialities." See *A Glossary of Literary Terms* (New York, 1957),
pp. 55–58. All sorts of exceptions and qualifications can be made,
but some of the differences between the two periods can be usefully be put in these terms.

2. *Critics and Criticism*, ed. R. S. Crane (Chicago, 1952), pp.
372–388.

antiquity and hence of being 'neoclassical' in any but the narrowest sense of that word."[3] Crane is suggesting here that a respectable pedigree may be found for a variety of critical theories, which is true. But when we recollect that the theory of rules and genres contains as much modern accretion as classical prescription, we may wonder whether the term is simply misleading unless little beyond period is implied by it.

In its most restricted sense "neoclassicism" can be used to mean French literary theory of the later seventeenth century—basically the ideas of Boileau, Le Bossu, and Rapin—a usage that has two real advantages. First the term is explicitly associated with the rigidly codified and considerably elaborated theory of the modern (particularly seventeenth century) period. Second, the French critics did make a deliberate effort to return to classical practices, and if relative fidelity is any criterion, they are more genuinely "classic" than their English contemporaries—as Rymer noted with regret. One advantage of defining "neoclassicism" as French orthodoxy is evident in Atkins' otherwise unimpressive book: the impact of consciously "classical" ideals on English literature can be put in terms of the influence of a clearly defined set of theories largely originating in and filtering through France.[4] Such a view is an oversimplification, but particularly for the Restoration period it is substantially accurate.

"Neoclassicism" is often used to mean the orthodox literary doctrine of a period which is assumed to run from Dryden to Johnson. Thus Book V of Saintsbury's *History*

3. *The Idea of the Humanities*, 2 vols. (Chicago, 1967), II, 169–171.
4. See J. W. H. Atkins, *English Literary Criticism: Seventeenth and Eighteenth Centuries* (London, 1951), pp. 3–18.

of Criticism and Literary Taste in Europe is entitled "The Crystallising of the Neo-Classic Creed" and Book VI "Eighteenth-Century Orthodoxy"; similarly Sherburn's history of the period is divided into parts: "The Rise of Classicism" is said to take place in the Restoration, its "Disintegration" in the later eighteenth century. But this use of the term is more than a characterization—it is a condemnation, for it rests on the assumption that writers were under pressure to conform to standards with which the best of them were presumably not in sympathy. J. H. Smith believes that Dryden gave in to current literary fashions; Wm. Bohn says unhappily that "he seemed predestined by nature to become a supreme conformist." [5] This outlook is not simply old-fashioned: George Watson, one of the most acute and stimulating of recent critics, postulates his whole view of Dryden on this sort of assumption: "On the one hand, he was held fast by deeply instinctive affection for his Elizabethan masters; on the other, *he knew the force of neo-classical fashion*, and ached to be respectable" (I, xiii; italics added). Quite literally, Watson believes that Dryden's fear of nonconformity made him unwilling to show his real convictions. I will not reargue this point. Undeniably Dryden publicly professed much of the literary theory held by Rymer. And unless we determine what this "orthodoxy" was, when it flourished, and how dominant it appeared, we may suspect that the orthodox bogey consists of everything in the period disliked by more recent critics.

Perhaps most commonly "neoclassicism" is used to desig-

5. John Harrington Smith, "Dryden's Critical Temper," *Washington University Studies*, Humanistic Series xii, no. 2 (1925), 214; Wm. E. Bohn, "The Development of John Dryden's Literary Criticism," *PMLA*, 22 (1907), 63.

nate the general literary outlook of writers between 1660 and 1800. The assumption which underlies this usage is that a "characteristic idea-complex," as Lovejoy calls it,[6] somehow defines any era in literary history. Such an "idea-complex" can be conceived not merely as an orthodox creed, or as an arbitrarily cohesive "system," but as an organically evolving spirit-of-the-age which comprises all of the vital elements in the period. Thus in *Literary Criticism: A Short History*, W. K. Wimsatt entitles chapter 10 "English Neo-Classicism: Jonson and Dryden." He says outright that "Dryden's views are hardly the ideal ground from which to launch a discussion of English neo-classic theory"—but he chooses to use them anyway.[7] In these terms "neoclassicism" is not a creed to which Dryden was forced to subscribe, but a general *Weltanschauung* which he largely shared. This usage has the very great advantage of not being arbitrarily exclusive; the only difficulty lies in defining the "idea-complex" in a way specific enough to be meaningful without starting to become exclusive.

The variety of meanings given "neoclassicism" can be exceedingly confusing. Thus the "Tendency Toward Platonism" and the "Psychology of Imagination" which Bredvold and Donald Bond find in English "Neoclassicism" are for Paul Spencer Wood part of the "Opposition to Neoclassicism 1660–1700."[8] I want simply to point out

6. A. O. Lovejoy, "The Parallel of Deism and Classicism," *MP*, 29 (1932), 281–299; reprinted in *Essays in the History of Ideas* (Baltimore, 1948), p. 78.
7. William K. Wimsatt, Jr., and Cleanth Brooks, *Literary Criticism: A Short History* (London, 1957), p. 208.
8. See Donald F. Bond, "The Neo-Classical Psychology of the Imagination," *ELH*, 4 (1937), 245–264; Louis I. Bredvold, "The Tendency Toward Platonism in Neo-Classical Esthetics," *ELH*, 1

some of the obvious objections to the various usages, trying to see how we can best understand Dryden's intellectual context.

First, we may say that to try to use "neoclassical" as a neutral period designation is rather silly, since the term carries the clear implication of a revival of or a returning to an earlier culture. If this is what we mean, then we are getting into an "idea-complex" definition and the term is no longer neutral—we are characterizing the period. As a period description "Augustan" is probably a less misleading term (despite Jonathan Swift's opinion of it), if only because its connotation is fuzzier.[9]

Second, we may say that to try to limit the application of "neoclassicism" to French literary theory is unrealistic both because French doctrine is as much neo as classic, and because as the period went on an increasing amount of genuine classicism appeared which was not imported by way of France.

Third, I think that to call "neoclassicism" a restrictive orthodox creed is both inaccurate and misleading. Certainly Restoration and eighteenth-century critics hold much in common—as I have just spent a chapter trying to demonstrate. But the concept of a powerful orthodoxy is postulated on the old notion that "neoclassicism" was a frigid monolith which gradually cracked as the eighteenth

---

(1934), 91–119; Paul Spencer Wood, "The Opposition to Neo-Classicism in England Between 1660 and 1700," *PMLA*, 43 (1928), 182–197.
    9. For an unsettlingly lucid demonstration of the shortcomings of "Augustan," see James William Johnson, *The Formation of English Neo-Classical Thought* (Princeton, 1967), chap. 1. But his preference for "Neo-Classical" is based on assumptions about the character of the age which are not indisputable.

century wore on and was finally destroyed by a romantic revolution. Critics like Paul Spencer Wood have long supposed that after a struggle in the Restoration neoclassicism of an essentially French variety triumphed in England and that the early eighteenth century is consequently a period of rigid literary conformity. George Watson says that Dryden is incipiently revolutionary, since the "Heads of an Answer to Rymer" "even presume to attack the most sacred of all critical documents in Renaissance Europe, the *Poetics* of Aristotle, raising questions of hair-raising implications" (I, xiv). The "Heads," Watson says, is "the one critical document in English between the Restoration and Johnson's Shakespeare in which the *Poetics* of Aristotle are attacked frontally and without qualification." [10] However we may choose to interpret the "Heads," this is simply untrue. We might dismiss something like Sir Robert Howard's objection to rules in the Preface to *The Duke of Lerma* (1668) as too early to be important, but in 1694 Charles Gildon's *Miscellaneous Letters and Essays* explicitly rejects rules, the French, and the authority of Aristotle with a vehemence far surpassing Dryden's private questionings of seventeen years earlier. Gildon was writing when the triumph of neoclassicism was supposedly nearly complete, but he was not torn limb from limb by hordes of ravening Aristotelians; we may deduce that denying Aristotle was at least no more blasphemous than demolishing Shakespeare, and probably much less so. But by 1718 Gildon himself had become severely Aristotelian. Have we merely set too early a date for the triumph of neoclassical orthodoxy? I think not, for if Addison's papers on the

10. George Watson, "Dryden's First Answer to Rymer," *RES*, n.s. 14 (1963), 20.

Imagination (1712) are the jumping-off point for the aesthetics of romanticism,[11] we can only conclude that the neoclassical monolith had fractured before it congealed. Undoubtedly French classicism was fashionable in Restoration England, but it was never crushingly dominant.

Finally, we must admit that the use of "neoclassical" to suggest the character of the age cannot be lightly dismissed, and that its convenience is undeniable. The supposition that writers in any period hold a great deal in common is not unreasonable, and apparent anomalies (Blake for instance) are more rooted in their times than was once thought. So, this argument runs, to define the characteristic literary theory of any period can help us understand the common factors in the work of many writers—all of which is very true. The danger lies in defining the spirit of an age and then blindly reading every work in accordance with the definition, a procedure that can lead the critic into merciless twisting.[12] The issues here take us beyond simple criticisms of the use of a term and demand some detailed consideration.

That Dryden largely shared the *Weltanschauung* of his

11. See Ernest L. Tuveson, *Imagination as a Means of Grace: Locke and the Aesthetics of Romanticism* (Berkeley, 1960). Tuveson's argument is stimulating but highly debatable; I am inclined to go along with most of what he says about the incipience of the romantic concept of imagination in the empirical tradition of Hobbes and Locke (see section III of this chapter).

12. As an example unlikely to offend any of my readers, I offer the theories of D. W. Robertson, Jr., which seem revealing in much medieval literature but wide of the mark when applied to something like *The Miller's Tale*. R. S. Crane has argued the case against Robertson in his essay "On Hypotheses in 'Historical Criticism': Apropos of Certain Contemporary Medievalists," in *The Idea of the Humanities*, II, 236–260.

age I absolutely agree: the question is what this "characteristic idea-complex" consists of and whether it is properly described as neoclassical. In defining a spirit-of-the-age, the critic may deal in specific attributes, or in the generalities of intellectual disposition. Critics who attempt to follow the first course are often confounded by myriads of niggling contradictions; those who follow the latter tend to blur real distinctions by subordinating every writer to principles drawn from excessively general common denominators. Here I will try to assess attempts of both kinds.

Back in 1932 A. O. Lovejoy made a brief outline of the characteristic beliefs which constituted "classicism" (or "rationalism of the Enlightenment") in a period he did not trouble to define.[13] From his examples we can deduce that the phenomenon he was discussing flourished somewhere between Hooker (1594 is the date quoted) and the end of the eighteenth century, and that its zenith came early in that century. Lovejoy expresses the hope that all of his observations will be "generally familiar": he assumes that the characteristics he is ascribing to men in the period are beyond dispute. The relationship of these beliefs to literature is said to be straightforward: "The neoclassical theory of poetry, and of the other arts, was in great part the application of the same set of preconceptions to aesthetics." [14] Very well—Lovejoy suggests that neoclassicism consists of certain general intellectual preconceptions carried into practice.[15] Let us see whether Dryden possesses these preconceptions. Not all of them are relevant

13. Lovejoy (see note 6 above).   14. Lovejoy, p. 79.
15. Both his procedure and his conclusions have been challenged recently. See Roland N. Stromberg, "Lovejoy's 'Parallel' Reconsidered," *ECS*, 1 (1968), 381–395.

to his critical opinions, but we can at least get some idea of how well he fits the pattern conceived by Lovejoy. The elements of this complex are nine in number.

(1) *Uniformitarianism.* The mind of man is assumed to be the same in all places and ages. Certainly this is one of Dryden's basic principles. We must note though that Dryden makes significant allowance for the change in national character and taste which may result from difference in climate. He does not go as far as Lovejoy in saying that "differences in opinion or in taste are evidences of error." [16]

(2) *Rationalistic individualism.* "Because all individuals, *qua* rational, are fundamentally alike . . . truth is to be attained by every individual for himself, by the exercise of his private judgment uninfluenced by tradition or external authority." [17] To some degree Dryden would go along with this—but as a Catholic, obviously, not all the way. And how, we may wonder, is a description of "deism" suppose to characterize a practicing Catholic, or even Anglicans like Swift and Johnson?

(3) Belief in the *consensus gentium.* Unlike Johnson, Dryden makes little use of this appeal; although he believes that it is a writer's duty to please his audience, he holds a low opinion of all but a few readers and suggests, for example, that the popularity of Statius is maintained by consistent ill-taste (I, 276–277; cf. II, 243).

(4) *Cosmopolitanism.* This fits only to the extent that Dryden could and did read French. He was consistently (and to some critics obnoxiously) patriotic and is always concerned about coming out ahead of the French, even though he drew freely on them.

(5) *Antipathy to "enthusiasm" and originality.* Cer-

16. Lovejoy, pp. 79–80.   17. Lovejoy, p. 82.

tainly Dryden is no friend of the Dissenters, and he has little concept of "originality" as we think of it. But his admiration of Shakespeare and Homer, men whose "genius" was said to give their work a grace beyond the reach of art, should make us qualify any blanket statement about a rejection of "special insights attained by individuals of exceptional endowment." [18]

(6) *Intellectual equalitarianism*. Belief in uniformity of reason produces "a democratic temper in matters of religion and morals and taste, even in persons not democratic in their political views." [19] Again Dryden does not fit: in matters of taste he is an arrogant elitist (see the Dedication of the *Aeneis*, II, 242–245), despite his injunctions that the writer must please his audience.

(7) *Rationalistic anti-intellectualism*. This distrust of subtle, intricate reasonings on abstruse subjects Dryden possesses (though to a lesser degree than Bredvold supposed), and certainly in his criticism he avoids elaborate reasonings. Rymer gives colorful expression to this attitude when he says that in criticism "there is not requir'd much Learning, or that a man must be some *Aristotle*, and *Doctor* of *Subtilties*, to form a right judgment." [20]

(8) *"Rationalistic primitivism."* A belief that the truths of "nature" were at least as accessible to the uncivilized man as to the civilized runs directly counter to Dryden's trust in refinement and his biological metaphor for the evolution of literature. For him the "rudeness" of poetry in its "infancy" is deplorable, not admirable.

(9) "From all this followed *a negative philosophy of*

18. Lovejoy, p. 84.   19. *Ibid*.
20. *TLA*, in *Critical Works*, ed. Curt A. Zimansky (New Haven, 1956), p. 18.

history." Change is probably for the worse and certainly no lasting improvement is possible. Dryden is in flat disagreement with this supposedly central article of neoclassical faith, for he is a firm believer in progress.[21]

Quite plainly Dryden does not possess the intellectual preconceptions which, according to Lovejoy, constitute the foundation of neoclassicism. Is he then part of an opposition? I think not, for I can find no major Restoration figure who *could* represent the supposed orthodoxy. Rymer ought to be the logical candidate (Wimsatt describes him as a critic of "fanatically classic temper"),[22] but he fits Lovejoy's scheme little better than Dryden does. Rymer is rather more of a uniformitarian, but he is even harder on the *consensus gentium*, is anything but a cosmopolite, and is a firm believer in the existence and further possibility of progress. Among later so-called neoclassicists it is easy to find some major figures who subscribe to the theory of a negative philosophy of history—Pope, Swift, and Gibbon, for example. But none of these men fits Lovejoy's earlier "elements" at all well. Are Pope and Swift "intellectual equalitarians"? Singly, the various elements may be found in almost any writer between 1660 and 1800, but gathered together as an idea-complex they do not describe writers satisfactorily either individually or in the aggregate. We should see on reflection that they could not be expected to do so. No amount of mental gymnastics will produce a useful definition which can apply to both Swift and Defoe. At best then an idea-complex can be developed to describe a limited group of essentially similar

21. See Earl Miner, "Dryden and the Issue of Human Progress," *PQ*, 40 (1961), 120–129; and see chap. 3, section I.
22. Wimsatt, p. 205.

writers. Lovejoy's suggestions cannot usefully be applied to Dryden, and since he failed to indicate the limits of their applicability, they are not really useful at all.[23]

Perhaps we can find a better way of defining neoclassicism. Is it best viewed as a general outlook rather than as a specific system of ideas? To reconcile the diverse beliefs of a multitude of authors is impossible, but conceivably they may share what Paul Fussell calls "a quality of mind." [24] Fussell restricts himself to a group of six writers whom he calls "Augustan Humanists," but James William Johnson has recently made a powerful defense of the term "neoclassicism" as the proper description of what he calls the "intellectual disposition" characteristic of writers in the 1660–1800 period, and we need to give his arguments serious consideration.

Between 1660 and 1800, a "classicist" was the man who saw within preserved Greco-Roman literature a total and applicable world. . . . The term which has come to vie with "Augustanism" as the inclusive critical epithet, "Neo-Classicism," is a latter-day coinage, but it may well prove the more useful, once it loses its ersatz connotations. Nowadays, "classicism" can be conveniently defined as the intellectual disposition to find in ancient culture, particularly Greek and Roman, the values which recurrently appear in human experience. "Neo-Classicism" may be concomitantly designated that variation of classicism characteristic of English thought and literature between 1660 and 1800. It is temporally and ideologically differentiated from the earlier "Humanism" and the later

23. For an example of a properly limited description of an "idea-complex" see Paul Fussell, *The Rhetorical World of Augustan Humanism* (Oxford, 1965), chap. 1 (discussed below).
24. Fussell, p. viii.

"Romantic classicism" (often identified with Romantic Hellenism).[25]

This discussion helpfully gives us a suitably limited referent for "classics," and it suggests that the dominant—not necessarily the only—literary characteristic in the period was an *attitude* toward these classics, not a collection of specific beliefs. And the principal assumption on which this attitude must rest—uniformitarianism—was indeed very widely held. Public dissent is obvious by the time of Sterne, and some nonsubscribers to this "intellectual disposition" are easy to find, but objections do not rise thick and fast, as they do to Lovejoy's scheme.

How viable is James W. Johnson's definition? The application of Greek and Roman literature to contemporary life and problems was widespread in the Restoration and eighteenth century and its importance is undeniable. But whether this habit should be regarded as the central, the *defining* characteristic of the period is less clear. After all, a great deal in literature throughout the age is distinctly nonclassical. The novel and heroic drama are modern developments, only occasionally (as in *Tom Jones* and *Amelia*) influenced directly by the classics. *Cato* is classical to be sure, but *The Fair Penitent* and *The Conscious Lovers* are not. Pope's Horatian imitations and Johnson's Juvenalian ones are satires of the classic sort, but the burlesque satires that we find most typical of the age (*Mac Flecknoe*, the *Dunciad*) have little classical precedent.[26] Can we ignore all this in defining the literary temper of the time?

25. James William Johnson, p. 29.
26. *Absalom and Achitophel, Gulliver's Travels,* "sentimental" comedy, "bourgeois" (or "domestic") tragedy, Restoration "wit" comedy, *Hudibras, The Lives of the Poets,* and Thomson's *Sea-*

James Johnson's concern is principally to explore "the intellectual geography of the Neo-Classical *polis*," a task he carries out with some distinction. As he says, the source of a great many ideas current in the period is the classics. But in the matter of the intellectual disposition of the age I am inclined to turn Johnson's own words against him. "Augustanism," he says, "was but one aspect of Restoration and eighteenth century classicism,"[27] and the classicism of the time is, I would continue, but one aspect of the temper of the age. Specifically, we may enquire how well the quality of mind Johnson describes can define Dryden's outlook and endeavors.

II

What is Dryden's attitude toward the classics? As the translator of the whole of Virgil and parts of many other classical poets he certainly directed much of his attention to them, and his critical essays abound with Greek and Roman examples intermixed with English. His sense of the primacy of the classics is frequently expressed:

I have endeavoured in this play to follow the practice of the Ancients, who, as Mr Rymer has judiciously observed, are and ought to be our masters [Preface to *All for Love*, I, 230].

. . . all who, having rejected the ancient rules, and taken the opposite ways, yet boast themselves to be masters of this art, do but deceive others, and are themselves deceived; for that is absolutely impossible ["A Parallel of Poetry and Painting," II, 191].

---

sons are a few random examples of the literature of this period which lacks solid classical precedent. In fact, precious few works of the Restoration and eighteenth century *can* claim it.

27. James Johnson, p. 29.

Dryden's respect for the classics does not need to be demonstrated again. He feels the weight of tradition and looks constantly to the past for precedent and justification, especially for modest departures from regularity. In an excellent essay Mary Thale has shown how consistently he tries to reinterpret and use classical dicta in the criticism of contemporary literature[28]—and in this respect his procedure differs little from that of men today who reinterpret the scriptures or Marx for modern use.

But how, more precisely, does Dryden treat the classics? What constitutes their authority, and to what degree of detail does it descend? In a famous passage he rejects unquestioned submission to the past:

We live in an age so sceptical, that as it determines little, so it takes nothing from antiquity on trust. And I profess to have no other ambition in this essay than that poetry may not go backward, when all other arts and sciences are advancing ["Defence of the Epilogue," I, 169].

This disclaimer must be qualified: Dryden was excusing in advance what were to be rather severe strictures on his Elizabethan predecessors, and doubtless he hoped that this swipe at ancestor worship might help undercut incipient opposition. But though he venerates the greatest classical writers, he does not accept their every practice, any more than he does all the practices of Shakespeare, whom he venerates equally. Homer and Virgil are accepted because they mirror nature well, not for any magical virtue of their own. In the last chapter I noted Rymer's comment on this point: "Nor would the *modern Poets* blindly re-

28. Mary Thale, "Dryden's Dramatic Criticism: Polestar of the Ancients," *CL*, 18 (1966), 36–54.

sign to this practice of the *Ancients,* were not the Reasons convincing and clear as any demonstration in *Mathematicks"* [29]—a claim later echoed by Pope. Dryden does believe in the applicability of ancient practice, but he never uses it blindly; as Thale shows, he selects and reinterprets what he chooses to apply. To return to my analogy, we may say that there is a difference between blind importation of scriptural dicta into the contemporary world and the attempt to reinterpret some of them to make them applicable. Similarly we must make an important distinction—to which I will return—between returning to classical practice and working in a tradition which stems from it.

Dryden's most extended commentary on this difference is the first debate in *Of Dramatic Poesy,* and his opinion of 1668 was modified only in details during the remainder of his life. Crites argues in behalf of the Ancients that any excellence in the Moderns is the result of being able to imitate their predecessors, but that on the whole they do so rather badly (I, 25–27). He makes an extended survey of the "Three Unities," concluding that by failing to observe them the Moderns have imitated nature inexactly. Finally he turns to the most potent of English writers, at least in the estimation of the 1660s.

I must desire you to take notice that the greatest man of the last age (Ben Jonson) was willing to give place to them [the Ancients] in all things: he was not only a professed imitator of Horace, but a learned plagiary of all the others; you track him every where in their snow: if Horace, Lucan, Petronius Arbiter, Seneca, and Juvenal had their own from him, there are few serious thoughts which are new in him: you will pardon

29. "Preface to Rapin," in *Critical Works,* p. 3. Pope makes the same point in his *Essay on Criticism* (1711).

[166]

me, therefore, if I presume he loved their fashion, when he wore their clothes. But since I have otherwise a great veneration for him, and you, Eugenius, prefer him above all other poets, I will use no farther argument to you than his example: I will produce Father Ben to you, dressed in all the ornaments and colours of the Ancients; you will need no other guide to our party, if you follow him; and whether you consider the bad plays of our age, or regard the good ones of the last, both the best and the worst of the modern poets will equally instruct you to esteem the Ancients [I, 31].

Eugenius replies that the Moderns have used the rules of the Ancients to excel them (I, 32). Most of his argument consists of a demonstration that Greek and Roman plays can be quite irregular; his claim for modern superiority rests on the assertion that though classical plays are more regular, they are too narrow in compass and have too few characters to engage us fully (I, 37), and that their expression lacks the tenderness and passion of the English (I, 42)—in a word, their plays are less effective.

Dryden resolves the debate by saying that Eugenius "seemed to have the better of the argument," but he commends the "moderation of Crites" in granting that a writer "might accommodate himself to the age he lived in." Crites follows this admission with an interesting conclusion: "Yet in the mean time, we are not to conclude any thing rashly against those great men, but preserve to them the dignity of masters, and give that honour to their memories (*quos Libitina sacravit*) part of which we expect may be paid to us in future times" (I, 43). This implies that Restoration writers may in time attain the status of "classics" (in a general sense of the word); even the champion of the Ancients does not hold that contemporary literature is utterly debased. The key to the debate is neatly summed up by Crites: "Eugenius and I are never like to have this question decided betwixt us; for he maintains the Moderns have acquired a new perfection in writing, *I can only grant they have altered the mode of it*" (I, 42; italics added). Crites wants to return to something more like classical practice; Eugenius insists that the alterations are improvements, not blemishes—and Dryden agrees with him.

How then would Dryden have assessed his own status? James Johnson says that Dryden, Swift, and Samuel Johnson should not be called "pseudo-classical" since "these men after all believed they *were* classical; they were not pretending at being classical, in their own minds." [30] I simply do not believe that this is true, particularly for Dryden. He knew very well that his plays and poems were of their age and country. In the third chapter I tried at some length to show that though Dryden's roots in the classics run very deep, he defends the accretions of English tradition with consistent tenacity. He refuses to countenance departure from what he regards as immutable foundations, but in the superstructures he is quite ready to applaud change.

James Johnson correctly observes that Dryden, among others, saw an analogy between the England of this period and the Rome of Augustus Caesar; [31] the parallel seems to have been compounded from equal parts of admiration of Virgil's style and a desire for patronage on a lavish scale. But the imagery of "Astræa Redux" has little to do with the literary theory of the time.

30. James Johnson, p. 14.
31. James Johnson, pp. 17–27. Johnson notes that the "Augustan" analogy was applied to Cromwell and William III as well as to Charles II.

Obviously Dryden works in what he regards as a classical tradition: the Ancients are his "masters" and he hopes to build on their beginnings. But he is not really *returning* to classical practice in the way that Rymer, for instance, recommends at the outset of *A Short View of Tragedy*. This distinction is important. When Rymer insists upon the use of a chorus, he is cutting across a deeply ingrained local tradition, something that Dryden flatly refuses to do. Rymer is ready to import classical practice into the contemporary theater, assuming that it will be right in any case. The drama he wishes to produce would be far more genuinely classic than that championed by Dryden, who was able to convince himself that "we have wholly finished what they began" (I, 218), and so could approve the changes. Here Rymer returns to the classics while Dryden builds from them, and though both procedures are in a sense neoclassical, some differentiation between them seems necessary.

A still more genuinely classic procedure is described in Milton's "Of That Sort of Dramatic Poem which is Call'd Tragedy," prefaced to *Samson Agonistes* (pub. 1671). We seldom think of Milton as a neoclassical writer, and yet on this evidence he has a better claim to the title than Dryden.

Tragedy, as it was anciently compos'd, hath been ever held the gravest, moralest, and most profitable of all other Poems: therefore said by *Aristotle* to be of power by raising pity and fear, or terror, to purge the mind of those and such like passions, that is to temper and reduce them to just measure with a kind of delight, stirr'd up by reading or seeing those passions well imitated. . . . *Gregory Nazianzen* a Father of the Church, thought it not unbeseeming the sanctity of his person to write a Tragedy, which he entitl'd *Christ Suffering*. This is mention'd to vindicate Tragedy from the small esteem, or rather infamy, which in the account of many it undergoes at this day with other common Interludes; happ'ning through the Poet's error of intermixing Comic stuff with Tragic sadness and gravity; or introducing trivial and vulgar persons, which by all judicious hath been counted absurd; and brought in without discretion, corruptly to gratify the people. . . . In behalf of this Tragedy coming forth after the ancient manner, much different from what among us passes for best, thus much beforehand may be Epistl'd; that *Chorus* is here introduc'd after the Greek manner, not ancient only but modern, and still in use among the *Italians*. . . . The measure of Verse us'd in the Chorus is of all sorts, call'd by the Greeks *Monostrophic*, or rather *Apolelymenon*, without regard had to *Strophe, Antistrophe* or *Epode*, which were a kind of Stanzas fram'd only for the Music, then us'd with the Chorus that sung; not essential to the Poem, and therefore not material. . . . Division into Act and Scene referring chiefly to the Stage (to which this work never was intended) is here omitted; it suffices if the whole Drama be found not produc't beyond the fifth Act.

Of the style and uniformity, and that commonly call'd the Plot, whether intricate or explicit, which is nothing indeed but such economy, or disposition of the fable as may stand best with verisimilitude and decorum; they only will best judge who are not unacquainted with *Aeschylus, Sophocles,* and *Euripides*, the three Tragic Poets unequall'd yet by any, and the best rule to all who endeavor to write Tragedy. The circumscription of time wherein the whole Drama begins and ends, is according to ancient rule, and best example, within the space of 24 hours.[32]

Milton goes straight back to classical procedures, chorus and all, abandoning English dramatic tradition as debased. His knowledge of the classics, and in particular of Aris-

32. *John Milton: Complete Poems and Major Prose,* ed. Merritt Y. Hughes (New York, 1957), pp. 549–550.

totle's theory of purgation, is a good deal more accurate than Dryden's. He condemns tragicomedy, utilizes a Greek verse form suitably adapted to nonmusical presentation, adopts a fable of classical simplicity and clarity, and holds with utter regularity to all three unities.[33] The story is not English, but it is Biblical, and so suitable for a Christian age. The praise of "verisimilitude and decorum" even *sounds* neoclassical.

Here, I believe, is a more genuine *return* to classical procedures and standards than Dryden ever gives us. Elizabethan and Jacobean tragedy—the high point of English literary development—might never have been. Rymer wants to use classical dicta to reform the existing English stage; Milton is content to ignore it. Dryden is vastly more concerned with the classics than we are in the mid-twentieth century, and so, comparatively speaking, he seems quite classical. But although by James Johnson's lights neoclassicism implies the full applicability of Greek and Roman literary theory to modern work, Dryden imposes some significant modifications on it. His uniformitarianism is only slightly qualified, but his reservations are firm and they assume considerable importance. He refuses to countenance the abrogation of tradition, even when its conflict with classical standards is radical. Despite Dryden's immense respect for the classics and his constant use of them he never goes back to them in the way that Milton does and he vehemently rejects Rymer's demand that such a return be attempted. The attitude of these three men toward the classics is much the same, but we would make a serious error in supposing that they could agree in practice on what use should be made of them.

Distinctions of degree enter here. Is "neoclassicism" to

33. On this last point Milton is more neoclassical than classical.

mean just the tendency to look to the past for guidance—specifically the Greco-Roman past? Or should it be taken to mean an actual *return* to the classics, a resurrection of earlier practices and principles? And when there is an attempt at such a return, how literal or accurate must it be to count as genuinely classical? In a brilliant debunking of the whole concept of neoclassicism (one which goes too far, in my estimation), Donald Greene comments that "Pope's and Johnson's 'imitations' of Horace and Juvenal could no more be mistaken for Horace and Juvenal than Brahms's *Variations on a Theme by Handel* could be mistaken for Handel," [34] which is true enough, even discounting the differences imposed by language and musical evolution respectively. But is it the author's intention or the accuracy of his copy which should weigh more heavily? After all, however unlike the originals these eighteenth-century imitations may be, they *are* imitations. As poets and critics, Dryden, Pope, and Johnson look more to the classics than Coleridge does, and so in some sense of the term they are more classical. But whether their literary endeavors are best characterized as neoclassical is another question.

To work under the uniformitarian assumption that certain principles are always valid is not, to my way of thinking, neo anything. I must insist, once again, that there is a fundamental difference between looking to earlier experience for guidance and correction, and trying to jettison established tradition in order to return to earlier ways. *A Short View* recommends the latter, and *Samson Agonistes* exhibits the principle in practice, even though no one

34. "Augustinianism and Empiricism: A Note on Eighteenth-Century English Intellectual History," *ECS*, 1 (1967), 36.

would mistake it for the work of Sophocles. Sidney's attempt to write quantitative verse is literally a revival of classical practice, and in this sense he is more neoclassical than Dryden, who is quite ready to adapt his poetry to the particular character of the English language. A conclusion is obvious: given his acceptance of English tradition, Dryden's neoclassicism is an "intellectual disposition" rather than a basic principle of artistic practice. But might not much the same thing be said of a very different critic—Matthew Arnold, for instance? Arnold certainly looks to the Greeks for guidance (and, like Dryden, to his French contemporaries); the Preface to *Poems* (1853) relies quite as heavily on Greek examples as Dryden's essays tend to rely on Roman ones. We could carry this parallel further by noting that Arnold makes similar allowance for cultural change,[35] and in "The Function of Criticism at the Present Time" he even makes similar modifications in literary theory to suit contemporary needs, which in his case were being influenced by the rise of science and the decline of religion. Arnold is every bit as ready as his eighteenth-century predecessors to find preserved in "Greco-Roman literature a total and applicable world," as James Johnson puts it. But few critics have supposed from Arnold's comments on Pope and Dryden that he was a neoclassical writer *manqué*. Unless we are prepared to compartmentalize in a radical way, so general a use of "neoclassical" becomes exceedingly misleading.

"Neoclassical," when used to characterize a man or a

35. For example, he notes that Antigone's dilemma in Sophocles' play of that name "is no longer one in which it is possible that we should feel a deep interest." *Poetry and Criticism of Matthew Arnold*, ed. A. Dwight Culler (Boston, 1961), p. 212.

work, is a meaningful term only when it is describing an actual revival of classical principles or practice. Again, we may ask how accurate such a revival must be in order to "count." In a recent essay, "When was Neoclassicism?" [36] Bertrand Bronson has suggested that only toward the *end* of the eighteenth century does neoclassicism (or plain classicism) attain its fullest development, and classicism in painting and architecture becomes a major style early in the nineteenth century. Genuine—meaning accurate— classicism is, Bronson points out, a late-century phenomenon. Donald Greene adds the wry comment that perhaps "it would make more sense to call the 'Romantic period' the 'Classical period'." [37] Are Shelley and Tennyson less under the spell of the classics than Dryden, Swift, and Pope? asks Greene. Probably not. Should "Romantic Hellenism" receive the title neoclassical? In Bronson's terms, why not? But Dryden is not much like Shelley: is he not neoclassical at all?

This sort of terminological game leads quickly into nonsense. Obviously the bulk of the literature of the early nineteenth century is not much like the classics and is written without much reference to them. At the same time, clearly *some* of the late-eighteenth and early-nineteenth century literature is more accurately classical than most of the work done in the preceding century. Nonetheless, probably *more* was written with one eye on the classics in the early eighteenth century than a hundred years later. These contradictions make nonsense out of any attempt to char-

36. *Studies in Criticism and Aesthetics 1660–1800* [Essays in Honor of Samuel Holt Monk], ed. Howard Anderson and John S. Shea (Minneapolis, 1967), pp. 13–35.
37. Greene, p. 34n.

acterize an age as neoclassical. Two major points need to be made.

First, no period is monolithic. Contradictory practices and tendencies appear in every age: any attempt to characterize them in the aggregate must either do violence to some part of the subject or fade into meaningless generality. If we are studying a deliberate return to classical practice in England, we find it in varying degrees in Spenser, Jonson, Milton, Rymer, Pope, Johnson, Arnold, and T. S. Eliot. As a movement it probably reaches its peak of influence and exactness around the beginning of the nineteenth century—a time in which it was far from being the only, much less the dominant, style.

Second we must make a basic differentiation between *the nature of a work of art* and the *cultural orientation* of the artist. In general, Restoration and early eighteenth-century writers thought more about the classics and looked to them oftener than did their counterparts in the romantic age. The wealth of classical exempla and allusions in Restoration poetry and criticism tells us that these writers lived far more intimately with the classics than the romantics did. A writer may revive an earlier style whatever his beliefs or the nature of his age. The Romantic Hellenists go back to the past in much the way that Ruskin does. But such writers as Dryden, Pope, and Swift seem to feel no need to *go back:* they believe that they are carrying on a live tradition. All writers of the Restoration and early eighteenth century look to the classics as a matter of course; intellectually their age has a classical orientation. By the time of the "Classical Revival"—the very name betrays it—this was not really true. Some writers and artists return to the classics, and with far more scholarly accuracy, but by and large the

[175]

cultural concerns of the period have far less to do with
them.

III

A general concept of neoclassicism as an idea-complex is of no use in discussing Dryden, and the suggestion
that it is "a quality of mind" is of little more help. I have
made this lengthy excursion into the terminology of intellectual history in order to clarify a widely-used term,
hoping to give a broader perspective on Dryden in the
process of the exploration. At this point I have done little
more than raise objections to some common assumptions
about the nature of Dryden's cultural milieu. To conclude
this survey of Dryden's context I want to offer a brief
account of his intellectual milieu as I understand it.

In order to avoid the distortions of gross oversimplification, any attempt at a capsule characterization must be
eschewed: the currents of intellectual history are singularly
resistant to codification in tidy idea-complexes. To start
with, the Restoration is not an intellectually homogeneous
period. Its temper—if it is possible to speak of such—must
be seen as an inharmonious blend of incongruous elements.
I find three major constituents in the literary outlook of the
time: a classical orientation, French classicism, and empiricism. In practice they are far from discrete and they
become complicated by such extrinsic factors as religion.
Obviously any analytic separation of them is artificial. I
undertake merely to provide a trial interpretation after the
fashion of Spingarn, whose categorizations I find stimulating even though I do not wholly agree with them.

The primary element in Restoration culture was a longstanding classical heritage. From the beginning of the

sixteenth century all educated Englishmen had been taught to look at Greek and Roman literature as a paradigm. Recent scholars have emphasized that there remained a strong medieval and native English current which was more important in determining the course of literary development than was once supposed,[38] but the influence of what we now call a classical education remained enormous throughout the sixteenth and seventeenth centuries. This classicism is English-humanist in origin, but in full force it carried right through the seventeenth century; Spenser, Jonson, Milton, and Dryden all bear its mark.[39] The practice of looking to the classics for guidance is anything but a Restoration innovation, despite what handbooks say about the "rise of classicism" in this period. Without becoming enmeshed in debate about "classical disposition" we may say that in the Restoration there remained a basic conviction that English literature had its roots in the classics, ought to follow them, and was in some sense an outgrowth from them. This belief is reflected in the plethora of classical examples cited by critics in this period and in their assumption that English literary development would necessarily follow the pattern of Rome and France.[40]

38. See, for example, David M. Bevington, *From 'Mankind' to Marlowe: Growth of Structure in the Popular Drama of Tudor England* (Cambridge, Mass., 1962).

39. The influence of a classics- and rhetoric-oriented education is evident in Milton of course; for a demonstration of similar influence on Dryden see Lillian Feder, "John Dryden's Use of Classical Rhetoric," *PMLA*, 69 (1954), 1258–1278.

40. As I understand the situation, all Restoration writers had a "classical orientation." In this respect the difference between Dryden and Rymer is merely one of the degree to which they supported actual return to classical practices. In an important article, Louis I. Bredvold has argued that English classicism is essentially

To this classical orientation were added in mid-century two conflicting elements, French classicism and empiricism. French classicism consists of the codifications and rules which handbooks usually call "neoclassical" (in the narrowest sense of the term). Boileau and company demanded "ideal" imitation, a rigid sense of decorum, and an actual return to what they defined as classical practice—such as the use of the chorus, a device which never took in England. This French literary theory was avowedly classical, though it actually included many accretions. It was modish for a time in Restoration court circles, and we may guess that it bolstered the classical orientation indigenous to seventeenth-century England, although much of the doctrine (filtered through Castelvetro and other Italians) had already been bruited about in England for fully a century. This more deliberate classicism must have been in the air by the time of *An Essay of Dramatic Poesy* (written 1665–6?); it appears in such places as Rymer's translation of Rapin (1674), and in the relatively classical construction of such plays as *All for Love* (1677) and Dryden's adaptation of *Troilus and Cressida* (1679). The importance of French classicism lies at least as much in the procedure it preached—return to the classics—as in its actual system of doctrines, which were never fully carried into practice in England.

The third element, empiricism, had its immediate origin in Hobbes' mechanistic and materialistic "philosophy of

a native culture, not an importation from France. Obviously I agree with this, but would add that the influence of French classicism did tend to bolster English at a time when the latter was already declining. See "The Rise of English Classicism: Study in Methodology," *CL*, 2 (1950), 253–268.

sense." Science and psychology, not the classics, are the natural province of the empiricist. Thus in sharp contra-distinction to French classicism, empiricism is concerned with the present, and far from supporting ideal imitation it demands *vraisemblance*. The fanciful flights of heroic drama reflect in part the French-classical passion for the ideal; the later Restoration demand for accuracy of presentation (by what Spingarn calls the "School of Sense") is an out-growth of Hobbes' views. From ridicule of the super-natural to Rymer's denunciation of improbabilities is an easy jump.

These three elements seem to be the crucial components of Dryden's intellectual milieu. Naturally they did not rest in a static balance. Without tracing their combinations and permutations in detail, I will try to indicate some general trends.

Most broadly, we may say that by the end of Dryden's life the classical orientation of the period was breaking down. In science and philosophy, Newton, Hobbes, and Locke were supplanting the Ancients. And although Aris-totle's *Poetics* retained its authority a little longer than did the *Physics*, by the last decade of the century the growth of an English literary tradition greatly reduces the attention paid by critics to the classics. Dryden wrote rather little on other English poets; Rymer was a pioneer in such work; but by 1730 such essays were very com-mon indeed. Renaissance writers look almost wholly to Rome and the continent for literary sustenance and guid-ance; by the mid-eighteenth century this is no longer true. The sense of continuity with the classics which Dryden feels so strongly was vanishing—even Samuel Johnson does not, I think, possess it to anything like the same degree; vastly more of his attention is devoted to *English* writing.

This collapse of the classical orientation has been somewhat obscured because many literary scholars have assumed that certain major figures characterize the eighteenth century. "The age of Pope and Swift" and "the age of Johnson" are still phrases in common use. But Dryden's mental cast is far more typical of the age he lived in than are those of his Augustan successors. Paul Fussell, in a book devoted to explaining the "Augustan Humanist" tradition of Pope, Swift, Johnson, Burke, Reynolds, and Gibbon, says:

The dependence of the Augustan humanists on Shakespearian and Miltonic figures and motifs bespeaks their close alliance with a conservative literary past, a literary past which is perhaps as justly termed "Renaissance" as "classical." Their cause was beginning to look thoroughly old-fashioned even by the early years of the eighteenth century, and by Johnson's time the English humanist found it quite natural to conceive of himself as a small fortified city besieged by Goths.

Modern scholars and critics are perceiving increasingly that the Augustan humanists, far from being "representative" of the general tendencies of their time, constitute actually an intensely anachronistic and reactionary response to the eighteenth century. . . .

Once we perceive the fundamental unity of the ethical tradition articulated by Swift and Pope and transmitted to Johnson and Reynolds, to Gibbon, and finally to Burke, we are in a position to measure its "great rejection" of what is sometimes thought of as "the eighteenth century." Against the humanist tradition running from Swift to Burke we must place the optimistic tradition bounded on one end by Defoe and on the

[180]

other by Burns and Blake, and including writers like Addison and Steele, James Thomson, Samuel Richardson, Edward Young, Robert Blair, Mark Akenside, William Shenstone, Oliver Goldsmith, Thomas Chatterton, and William Cowper. This other tradition, although it may draw some strength from classical literature, tends to operate as if the classics are largely irrelevant to the modern experience; regardless of its occasional quarrels with industrialism, it tends to draw its real strength from the new industrial and commercial evidence of the validity of the idea of progress.[41]

If the classical orientation of English culture was falling apart by the time of Dryden's death, then such writers as Pope, Swift, and Johnson, so often called neoclassical, may be seen as fighting a vain rearguard action against the encroachments of new scientific (or empirical) and evangelical traditions. Of course neither Fussell nor I would claim for a moment that these writers do not to a considerable degree reflect their times. But insofar as they are "neoclassical" ("Augustan-humanist" is a more precise description) they are, by the more common spirit of the time, anachronistic.

What was happening in the Restoration? Very generally, empirical rationalism was driving out classical humanism. More specifically, a peculiar interaction between French classicism and rationalism is apparent. To describe the resultant changes in the neat terms of a Hegelian synthesis (as it is always tempting to do) would be misleading; we can only describe some of the forces operating in what is best regarded as a muddle.

In what remains one of the sanest treatments of Restoration criticism J. E. Spingarn says that "the seventeenth

41. Fussell, pp. 20, 22.

century was the great battle-ground" for a "conflict between classicism and rationalism." [42] Looking to the more limited context of Restoration crosscurrents we can see a confused struggle between what is essentially French classicism supported by tradition-minded churchmen, and Hobbesian empiricism. Spingarn is right in feeling that rationalism undermined classicism, but the conflict was masked by the early empiricists' respect for the classics. In retrospect it seems surprising that the two were so successfully synthesized. Some pitched battles were fought (for example, the Cambridge Platonists versus Hobbes), but to a considerable degree classicism and rationalism were combined in a single system. Spingarn describes it with the comment:

In the theory of Boileau and Pope the two conflicting forces were speciously reconciled by the assumption that, since nature and reason were best exemplified in the ancients, classical practice rather than reason or nature itself should be the guide of the poet and critic.[43]

This seems a little harsh. Peculiar as we find the combination—and it did prove tenuous—there is no doubt that the compromise seemed valid to many Restoration writers. Rymer, for example, succeeds in being both very Hobbesian and quite classically minded. He succeeds in believing that Homer, nature, reason, and rules all add up to the same thing, and so he can demand absolute fidelity to factual probability while suggesting (quite erroneously) that it is to be found in the classics.

In the first section of this chapter I described and attacked the cliché about the triumph of French-style clas-

42. Spingarn, I, lxxxi.   43. *Ibid.*

sicism during the Restoration. Actually the influx of French classicism bolstered the waning classical orientation briefly but was quickly absorbed into a combination with rationalism. The basic oppositions and inconsistencies of the two led to a quick disintegration of the synthesis. The Augustan-humanists of the eighteenth century have a foot in the empirical tradition, while those literary theorists who are concerned with affective psychology generally retain a considerable knowledge of the classics (which were, after all, still the principal subject in schools), but as Fussell says, a divergence of the empirical from the humanist tradition is evident. Addison is a convenient example of a pivotal figure: he was capable of writing in a deliberately classical way, as in *Cato*, but the affective aesthetics implicit in many of his *Spectator* essays are part of the empiricist tradition and belong to the early stages of what we loosely call romanticism.

A romantic-intuitive revolt against the restrictions of rationalism is another misleading cliché. "Rationalism" is a term which, like "neoclassicism," is open to misconstruction. The late seventeenth and early eighteenth centuries are not well described as an "age of reason," particularly if the definition is stretched to include the humanists.[44] The basis of the shift into romanticism (whatever it may be) is less an opposition of imagination to reason than a shift from uniformitarian to *tabula rasa* assumptions about the mind. The stress on environment started by Hobbes makes his empirical tradition receptive to such ideas as the influence of climate on national temper. Hobbes does em-

44. See George Boas, "In Search of the Age of Reason," in *Aspects of the Eighteenth Century*, ed. Earl Wasserman (Baltimore, 1965), pp. 1-19.

phasize sense and *vraisemblance*, but he is interested in psychology as well. He postulates an essentially uncontrolled imaging faculty, and since in his view the content of the mind is not predetermined but gained through experience, he is paving the way for affective aesthetics. And from subjective response to subjective creation is but a step. The empirical tradition's stress on "sense" is perfectly compatible with French classicism, but the subjective psychological bias inherent in empiricism tended to undermine such a combination. Spingarn feels that at the end of the seventeenth century a "School of Taste" was developing which respected the classics but emphasized diversity of tastes, and beauties rather than faults, and which led into the affective theories of the eighteenth century. Perhaps this trend is too diffuse to be called a "School," but certainly it does exist, and I would add that it is an outgrowth of the psychological side of empiricism.

The Restoration is then a period of transition, and to a remarkable degree Dryden mirrors his intellectual milieu. The two poles of his literary outlook are his classical orientation and his respect for the English literary tradition. His strong sense of literary continuity with the classics is evident in the "Heads of an Answer to Rymer," where it greatly weakens his defense of English practices—and yet he did defend them, stubbornly and consistently, throughout his life. To his respect for both ends of what he regarded as an unbroken tradition Dryden added an interest in both French classicism and Hobbesian empiricism. The former appears in his many borrowings from Boileau, Bossu, and Rapin, and in the increasingly classical bent of his plays in the 1670s; the latter is the source for Dryden's psychological speculations about literary creation. In the next chapter I will be illustrating some of the resultant conflicts.

To the present-day critic, Dryden's combination of classical and English traditions seems radically inconsistent, but I can detect no signs, even amid all his wobblings, that he felt particularly insecure about it. Although the synthesis was doomed to fairly quick extinction, Dryden seems to have used it comfortably and to good effect—nowhere better than in the Preface to *Fables* of 1700.[45] From our point of view, Dryden ought to have been horribly torn between the traditions he straddled; thus Saintsbury supposes that he struggled to assert an instinctive love of Shakespeare against his respect for the rules. Dryden avoids such a conflict by denying the total applicability of classical practice in order to allow for English tradition and by assuming that a continuing process of refinement will in due course eliminate whatever flaws remain in English writing.

By later "Augustan humanist" standards Dryden's position is an odd one, compounded as it is of a classical orientation and a belief in progress that cuts neatly across the negative philosophy of history that a neoclassicist should supposedly possess. Historically this position is a transitional one: the eighteenth-century possessors of a classical orientation become pessimistic defenders of a crumbling order, while "progress" becomes a rallying cry for Whig mercantilists. Despite his respect for the classics, Dryden has no desire to return to them; he wants to forge ahead toward greater perfections. His easy optimism of the 1660s

45. See John C. Sherwood's demonstration of this point, "Dryden and the Rules: The Preface to the *Fables*," *JEGP*, 52 (1953), 13–26.

and early 1670s gives way by the 1690s to the realization that surpassing the Elizabethans is not as simple as he had supposed, but he remains hopeful. All in all Dryden's outlook is quite representative of the jumble of conflicting elements in Restoration culture. Others balance the elements in different proportions—Rymer has distinctly more French classicism—but the mingle itself is typical of the dominant spirit of the time.

In this chapter and the preceding one I have tried to set Dryden in his intellectual context as clearly as possible. My description of the intellectual milieu is very brief and in no way definitive; doubtless another critic would have come up with different formulations, as others have in the past. But one thing should be clear: neither the 1660–1800 period nor even just the Restoration can be tidily characterized in a phrase or defined in terms of a single, static idea-complex. Sixty years ago Spingarn concluded that "seventeenth-century criticism is really a very troubled stream; winds from every quarter blow across its surface; currents from many springs and tributaries struggle for mastery within it." [46] Despite the many attempts to explain the situation in simpler terms, this description still holds true.

46. Spingarn, I, cvi.

CHAPTER 6

The Stability of
Dryden's Critical Premises

Some major questions remain unanswered at this point. Here I want to leave the specific details of Dryden's critical practice in order to explore some of his general principles and assumptions. Dryden's standing as a critic has long suffered from his reputation for cavalier inconsistency, and I wish to challenge this view of him.[1]

1. For example, George Watson speaks in his Introduction of "infinite excuses for changing his mind" (I, xiii), and in *The Literary Critics* (Baltimore, 1962) he comments that "Dryden is remarkable as a critic . . . for the casual ease with which he contradicts himself" (p. 41). I do not mean to keep picking on Watson; I have drawn on him so often because he is one of the most intelligent, useful, and stimulating of recent Dryden critics—as well as being quite an influential one. On the problem of consistency he is merely the latest of a long line of critics. See, for example, Percy Houston, "The Inconsistency of John Dryden," *SR*, 22 (1914), 469–482; George Williamson, "Dryden as Critic," *University of California Chronicle*, 32 (1930), 71–76. Williamson starts out: "A reading of Dryden's chief critical essays leaves one with at least three conclusions: Dryden had no fixed critical principles of his own, with the exception of a belief in the criticism of

Some scholars have assumed that a man so inconsistent probably had no principles, and since many influential critics have taken the line that Dryden worked intuitively, they have tended to suppose that neoclassical rules (which they held in contempt) merely hampered him. Consequently, rather little attention has been paid to Dryden's literary principles. Some superficial inconsistencies among his various pronouncements are easy to find, but I emphatically deny that he was without stable and meaningful theoretical foundations. I propose, therefore, both to enquire what Dryden's basic premises are, and to follow his "changes" with some care, trying to show that they are far from haphazard. Dryden's concept of the nature and function of poetry is really my subject here: what does he think literature is? How does he think it works? By going back to investigate these basic issues I hope both to pull together some of the specific points discussed piecemeal earlier and to help explain some of Dryden's opinions, attitudes, and apparent vacillations.

I

"I never heard," Dryden tells us, "of any other foundation of dramatic poesy than the imitation of nature" ("Defence of *An Essay*," I, 122). And since, to his way of thinking, all art must be representational, imitation of na-

---

poets by poets; his literary taste, especially outside his own literature, tended to be coarse; he was a writer of admirable prose and critical prefaces. In spite of his inconsistencies, there was a fundamental and arresting honesty in Dryden, and yet an honesty of character rather than of intellect." Dryden, Williamson goes on to say, "does not dissemble," but suffers from "inability consistently to hold a point of view."

ture must be the foundation not only of drama but of all art. This deceptively simple formula is the basis of Dryden's understanding of literature. Unfortunately, the cliché itself tells us little, for two concepts vaguer than "imitation" and "nature" would be hard to find. No seventeenth-century writer believed that a literal representation of observed reality constituted art: though the current French ideal was a play whose action encompassed only the time necessary to put it on, even in France the "representation" was invariably selective. Similarly Rymer's demands for fidelity to life do not take imitation to the point of the camera and the tape recorder. And if, on the one hand, the imitation was to be selective, so, on the other, was the choice of nature to be represented. Dryden was certainly not the man to approve poetry or painting that included dead cats and battered garbage cans.

Critics have tended to acknowledge the nonliteral nature of "neoclassical imitation" by pointing out the demand for decorum and letting it go at that. But to treat "imitation of nature" as a meaningless cliché is a serious mistake, for it leads the critic to ignore and obscure the complexities of a major problem in Restoration literary theory—one on which Dryden and his contemporaries were far from sure of their ground.

In a brief but useful survey Mary Thale has demonstrated the astonishing range of meanings with which Dryden used such terms as "imitation" and "nature" at various times.[2] According to her analyses, "nature" can mean observed, or "particular," reality; *"la belle nature,"* or human life as it *should* be; what is consistently pleas-

2. Mary Thale, "Dryden's Critical Vocabulary: The Imitation of Nature," *PLL*, 2 (1966), 315–326.

ing; and "heightened" reality.[3] "Imitation," she says, "sometimes means the closest possible replica," but in other cases "allows for conscious contrivance."

What can we make of this? There is no neat chronological explanation. Short of hypothesizing that Dryden had taken to heart an early-day form of Emerson's comment on consistency, we are left with one of two possibilities: either he was consciously varying his meanings or he was seriously muddled. Thale herself takes the former view. She suggests that Dryden used "imitation of nature" as "an inclusive phrase *intended* to synthesize apparently opposite features of ancient and modern drama" (italics added)—"justness" and "liveliness" were to be reconciled by a broadly flexible principle. Mary Thale makes a persuasive case, for certainly Dryden always tries to minimize the differences between ancient and modern drama, and in critical practice the wide range of his usages of "imitation" contributes to this goal.

Such a reading, however, seems to contain the implicit assumption that Dryden was a slippery fish who consciously attempted to put something over on his audience by means of specious verbal resolutions of irreconcilable differences. I think it likely enough that Dryden befuddled himself in his attempts to reconcile Greek and Elizabethan drama, but what object could he have in deliberately trying to fool others? Dean T. Mace has suggested in an important and unfairly neglected essay that Dryden's criticism contains a basic conflict between representational and imaginative

3. Of course, as A. O. Lovejoy has shown, this diversity was commonplace. See his " 'Nature' as Aesthetic Norm," *MLN*, 42 (1927), 444–450; reprinted in *Essays in the History of Ideas* (Baltimore, 1948), pp. 69–77.

concepts of art and hence that he was not in full control of his meanings.[4] I agree. Mace works almost entirely with *Of Dramatic Poesy* and devotes much of his attention to possible French sources; what he has done is to establish clearly the existence (and perhaps origin) of a major conflict in literary theory as it appears in Dryden. What Mace has not done is to integrate these findings into a broad survey of Dryden's concept of literature or to explore chronologically the changes in his outlook; with due acknowledgment, I propose to do so here, starting with a detailed examination of the concept of imitation as it appears in *Of Dramatic Poesy*.[5]

When, in defending his *Essay*, Dryden says that the foundation of a play must be its "imitation of nature," he adds: "This I have plainly said in *my* definition of a play: that it is a just and lively *image* of *human nature*, etc." (I, 122; italics added). Three points are noteworthy here: Dryden lays personal claim to Lisideius' definition of a play; this definition, as we will see, is quite distinctly "French"; and he insists that what is imitated is "human nature," not an "action." Lisideius' definition, to which Dryden holds in his "Defence," suggests a startlingly static conception of drama: "*A just and lively image of human*

4. See Dean T. Mace, "Dryden's Dialogue on Drama," *JWCI*, 25 (1962), 87–112. I suspect that the combination of an unrevealing title and a slightly out of the way journal are responsible for the lack of attention given this essay. (Thale's article would be much the better for her having consulted it.) Despite some carelessness and poor structuring, it is clearly one of the most important contributions to Dryden studies in recent years.

5. My disagreement with Mace's reading is sufficiently extensive and my perspective and purposes are sufficiently different to make me risk repeating a few of his points in surveying afresh even *Of Dramatic Poesy*.

nature, representing its passions and humours, and the changes of fortune to which it is subject, for the delight and instruction of mankind" (I, 25). This definition has a distinctly pictorial connotation which is not inappropriate to drama; the subject, however, is not to be a unified series of actions, but rather "human nature" in a general sense. That a play is not conceived as utterly static is indicated by "changes of fortune," but apparently a series of tableaux would more or less meet the case.

It is feelings which are the object of attention here, not the events which occasion them. This outlook is so far removed from our normal assumptions about drama that the implications of what Dryden says are seldom remarked upon. In essence, he is making character rather than action the prime constituent of a play. Mace comments that the omission of "action" from the definition "is somewhat startling in an age whose dramatic critics generally sought out Aristotle, directly or indirectly, as their model and guide." [6] Quite so, but the change, though it betrays a feeble sense of effective drama, is no mere aberration, even within a quasi-Aristotelian framework. To take an analogous case, consider the novel. R. S. Crane, in a deliberately Aristotelian treatment of plot (which, he believes, constitutes "the matter" of the writer's "invention"), suggests that there are "plots of action, plots of character, and plots of thought." The examples he gives are *Oedipus* and *The Brothers Karamazov* for the first; *The Portrait of a Lady* for the second; *Marius the Epicurean* for the third.[7]

6. Mace, p. 89.
7. R. S. Crane, "The Concept of Plot and the Plot of *Tom Jones*," in *Critics and Criticism*, ed. Crane (Chicago, 1952), pp. 620–621.

Presumably in a play an author can similarly make action, character, or thought the primary basis of his "matter." In a rough way we might say that (most commonly) Shakespeare does the first, Dryden the second, and Shaw the third.

Is this reading of Lisideius' definition borne out in the rest of the *Essay* and its "Defence"? I think so. Howard challenges Dryden's defense of rime, and by implication his concept of a play:

Now, after all the endeavours of that ingenious Person, a Play will still be supposed to be a Composition of several Persons speaking *ex tempore*, and 'tis as certain that good Verses are the hardest things that can be imagin'd to be so spoken; so that if any will be pleas'd to impose the rule of measuring things to be the best by being neerest Nature, it is granted, by consequence, that which is most remote from the thing supposed must needs be most improper.[8]

Dryden replies: "I must crave leave to dissent from his opinion. . . . For, if I am not deceived, a play is supposed to be the work of the poet, imitating or representing the conversation of several persons" ("Defence of *An Essay*," I, 114). Howard does not demand actual belief in the representation offered, but for him, the audience (suspending disbelief) is to "suppose" that it is seeing what is acted out. Dryden here dispenses with the illusion of actuality; for him, the audience is to suppose only that it is seeing the conscious contrivance of the playwright. Howard's view demands some fidelity to factual probability; Dryden's does not, provided that there is psychological fidelity to "human nature." The difference is not merely

8. Preface to *The Duke of Lerma* (1668), Spingarn, II, 107.

a matter of semantics—it provides the *raison d'être* for Dryden's heroic drama.

Why is action downgraded in favor of "human nature"? Mace suggests that the change reflects the old Greek problem of trying to justify the products of imagination against the charge of falsehood. Dryden's immediate source on this point, he observes, may be Davenant's Preface to *Gondibert*.

Lucan, who chose to write the greatest actions that ever were allowed to be true, which for fear of contemporary witnesses oblig'd him to a very close attendance upon Fame, did not observe that such an enterprize rather beseem'd an Historian then a Poet: For wise Poets think it more worthy to seek out truth in the Passions then to record the truth of Actions, and practise to describe Mankinde just as we are perswaded or guided by instinct, not particular persons as they are lifted or levell'd by the force of Fate, it being nobler to contemplate the general History of Nature then a selected Diary of Fortune: And Painters are no more then Historians, when they draw eminent persons, though they terme that drawing to the life; but when, by assembling divers figures in a larger volumn, they draw Passions, though they terme it but Story, then they increase in dignity and become Poets.[9]

That Dryden followed this line of thought (or even drew on this passage) seems the more likely since, after his objection to Howard's *ex tempore* theory of drama, he goes on to say that

prose is not to be used in serious plays . . . because it is too near the nature of converse: there may be too great a likeness; as the most skilful painters affirm that there may be too near a resemblance in a picture: to take every lineament and feature

9. Spingarn, II, 3–4.

is not to make an excellent piece, but to take so much only as will make a beautiful resemblance of the whole: and, with an ingenious flattery of nature, to heighten the beauties of some parts, and hide the deformities of the rest. For so says Horace, *ut pictura poesis erit,* etc. ["as with a picture, so with a poem"] ["Defence of *An Essay,*" I, 114].

Quite aside from matters of decorum then, art (whether poetry or painting) is to aim for a truth which is above the merely historical.[10]

We are accustomed to reading *Of Dramatic Poesy* as a debate, a battleground of English versus French and Ancient versus Modern. If, however, the essay is considered as the ground for a struggle between literal and ideal representation, the lines can be drawn in quite a different way. Let us examine the work in this light. Eugenius and Neander accept Lisideius' definition, but Crites raises the "logical objection" that it fails to differentiate drama from other literary forms (I, 25). Immediately a basic line of dispute is clear: Crites upholds and the others tend to belittle generic distinctions. In an earlier chapter I noted that in the definition Dryden was preparing for an explicit denial of them. Near the end of the last speech Neander says in comparing tragedy with epic:

For though tragedy be justly preferred above the other, yet there is a great affinity between them, as may easily be discovered in that definition of a play which Lisideius gave us. The genus of them is the same, a just and lively image of human nature, in its actions, passions, and traverses of fortune:

10. On the subject of "fidelity" versus "Platonism" (as these issues can be called), cf. the very different reading of David Daiches, *Critical Approaches to Literature* (London, 1956), chap. 4.

so is the end, namely for the delight and benefit of mankind. The characters and persons are still the same, viz. the greatest of both sorts; only the manner of acquainting us with those actions, passions, and fortunes, is different. Tragedy performs it *viva voce*, or by action, in dialogue; wherein it excels the epic poem, which does it chiefly by narration, and therefore is not so lively an image of human nature [I, 87–88].

Dryden was to change his mind about the relative merits of the two forms, and during the 1670s he was forced to pay more attention to the generic demands of drama, but nonetheless his tendency to conflate the two forms is apparent even in the 1690s. We might guess then that in *Of Dramatic Poesy* there will be a conflict between a point of view which emphasizes *representation* as the essence of drama and one which regards it as no more than a lively way of conveying the author's imitation to his audience. Crites takes the former view, Lisideius and Neander the latter, and Eugenius tends to agree with them.

The issue is simple: what constitutes the imitation of nature? Crites' two speeches (the first and fifth of the six) contain demands for observance of the three unities and the avoidance of rime; he is for the "nearest" imitation. His arguments are straightforward. First, the illusion of watching an action will be more difficult to maintain if great amounts of time are supposed to elapse. Second, the scene must stay close to the same place,

for the stage on which it is represented being but one and the same place, it is unnatural to conceive it many, and those far distant from one another. I will not deny but, by the variation of painted scenes, the fancy (which in these cases will contribute to its own deceit) may sometimes imagine it several places, with some appearance of probability; yet it still carries the greater likelihood of truth if those places be supposed so near each other, as in the same town or city; which may all be comprehended under the larger denomination of one place [I, 29].

Third, one main action is all that can reasonably be followed at once. Lastly, the condemnation of rime is based on explicitly naturalistic premises.

I am of opinion that rhyme is unnatural in a play, because dialogue there is presented as the effect of sudden thought. For a play is the imitation of nature; and since no man without premeditation speaks in rhyme, neither ought he to do it on the stage. . . . Nor will it serve you to object that . . . 'tis still known to be a play; and, consequently, the dialogue of two persons understood to be the labour of one poet. For a play is still an imitation of nature; we know we are to be deceived, and we desire to be so; but no man ever was deceived but with a probability of truth, for who will suffer a gross lie to be fastened on him? Thus we sufficiently understand that the scenes which represent cities and countries to us are not really such, but only painted on boards and canvas: but shall that excuse the ill painture or designment of them? Nay, rather ought they not to be laboured with so much the more diligence and exactness, to help the imagination? since the mind of man does naturally tend to, and seek after truth; and therefore the nearer any thing comes to the imitation of it, the more it pleases [I, 78–80].

This position is essentially that stated by Howard in the Preface to *The Duke of Lerma;* here, as in Dryden's reply to that work in his "Defence of *An Essay*," the conflict is between literal and nonliteral theories of imitation. The identification of Crites with Howard's position is made essentially explicit when Dryden rather unfairly brings

Crites to an early conclusion with the statement that his arguments against rime "are for the most part already public" (I, 81).[11] It is sometimes objected against the identification of Crites with Howard that Dryden could not properly have made him the champion of the Ancients, since Howard had publicly written that he could "presume to say somthing in the justification of our Nations Plays," which, he claimed, "justly challenge the Preheminence." [12] In this respect, violence is done to Howard's position, but the bulk of what Crites is made to say has less to do with the relative merits of Ancients and Moderns than with the problems of how representation can be made effective.

If we try for the moment to forget the official lines of debate in *Of Dramatic Poesy*, we can see more clearly the basic conflict in the work. The first and third debates, generally regarded as Ancients versus Moderns and blank verse against rime, are actually about different parts of the same subject—whether Crites' demands for near-literal representation are justified. The middle debate, ostensibly French versus English, is postulated on Lisideius' assumption that imitation should *not* be literal; the actual disagreement there is largely on the question of how much literal restriction need remain. The essential denial of Crites' claims is made by Neander near the end of the essay:

It has been formerly urged by you, and confessed by me, that since no man spoke any kind of verse *ex tempore*, that which was nearest nature was to be preferred. I answer you, there-

11. The reference is evidently to Howard's Preface to *Four New Plays* (1665), on which Dryden plainly drew in outlining Crites' position (see Spingarn, II, 97–104).

12. Preface to *Four New Plays*, Spingarn, II, 98, 100.

fore, by distinguishing betwixt what is nearest to the nature of comedy, which is the imitation of common persons and ordinary speaking, and *what is nearest the nature of a serious play:* this last is indeed the representation of nature, but 'tis *nature wrought up to an higher pitch.* The plot, the characters, the wit, the passions, the descriptions, are all *exalted above the level of common converse,* as high as the imagination of the poet can carry them with proportion to verisimility. Tragedy, we know, is wont to image to us the minds and fortunes of noble persons, and to portray these exactly; heroic rhyme is nearest nature, as being the noblest kind of modern verse [I, 86–87; italics added].

If we study the structure of the essay in light of this dispute, it looks something like this.

(1) Crites demands literal representation on the ground that it is most pleasing. Eugenius speaks against the unity of place as an excessive modern restriction (I, 36), but his basic counterclaim is that a serious writer should "stir up a pleasing admiration and concernment, which are the objects of a tragedy" (I, 41). Crites' concern is for the representation, Eugenius' for the effect. In place of an imitation whose exactness is to be admired, Eugenius praises art which affects the spectator, often through display of love and tenderness (I, 41–42). These affective assumptions underlie the second exchange, whose subject (from this perspective) is how the effect is best obtained.

(2) Lisideius praises the unities (of which the French had made a great deal), but, significantly, he devotes most of his attention to unity of action—which Crites had mentioned only briefly and indifferently (cf. I, 29–30). Lisideius follows "Aristotle" in saying that the "end of tragedies *or serious plays . . .* is to beget *admiration,* compassion,

or concernment" (I, 46; italics added).[13] The emphasis on unity of action may seem momentarily surprising. After all, Lisideius' definition omits all mention of action. But his point is that in order to get maximum effect, the dramatist must concentrate on a single, unified incident, refining away all extraneous events and characters in the process.[14] Lisideius does say flatly that "the spirit of man cannot be satisfied but with truth, or at least verisimility" (I, 47)— hence his suggestion that a play be "grounded upon some known history" (I, 46). The object, however, is to *suggest* verisimilitude, not to dramatize history, for the author's job is to interweave truth with "probable fiction" in order to mend the "intrigues of fate" and dispense a pleasing poetic justice (I, 47). Like Eugenius and Neander, Lisideius feels that a story whose end is known to the audience will rouse less concern than one which keeps it in suspense. But the key to Lisideius' whole view of drama lies in his reservations about the effectiveness of representation.

I have observed that, in all our tragedies, the audience cannot forbear laughing when the actors are to die; 'tis the most comic part of the whole play. All *passions* may be lively represented on the stage . . . but there are many *actions* which can never be imitated to a just height: dying especially is a thing which none but a Roman gladiator could naturally perform on the stage, when he did not imitate or represent, but naturally do it; and therefore it is better to omit the representation of it.

The words of a good writer, which describe it lively, will make a deeper impression of belief in us than all the actor can

13. "Admiration" was a sixteenth-century addition. But in it and in the mention of the "serious play" we can see in capsule the theory of the Restoration heroic play.

14. For a helpful discussion of the nature of the French drama which serves Lisideius as a model, see Elder Olson, *Tragedy and the Theory of Drama* (Detroit, 1961), chap. 9.

persuade us to when he seems to fall dead before us; as a poet in the description of a beautiful garden, or a meadow, will please our imagination more than the place itself can please our sight. When we see death represented, we are convinced it is but fiction; but when we hear it related, our eyes (the strongest witnesses) are wanting, which might have undeceived us, and we are all willing to favour the sleight when the poet does not too grossly impose on us. . . . But it is objected that if one part of the play may be related, then why not all? I answer, some parts of the action are more fit to be represented, some to be related [I, 51–52].

Thus he places the verbal and poetic part of drama far above the visual. Representation, the prime differential between drama and other literary forms, becomes here merely a minor adjunct.

Neander starts his reply by saying that he will "grant Lisideius, without much dispute, a great part of what he has urged against us" (referring to his strictures on the Elizabethans). Many of his objections are against Lisideius' concessions to representational verisimilitude. Thus Neander quotes Corneille on the excessive restrictions on invention (and even probability) imposed by the unities, and he is readier to accept dramatic illusion:

The indecency of tumults is all which can be objected against fighting: for why may not our imagination as well suffer itself to be deluded with the probability of it, as with any other thing in the play? For my part, I can with as great ease persuade myself that the blows which are struck are given in good earnest, as I can that they who strike them are Kings or princes, or those persons which they represent [I, 62].[15]

15. Neander seems to be stretching a point here. In a real debate a believer in literal representation would undoubtedly have objected. After all, the spectator is not asked to *believe* any of these pretenses, but merely to suffer the illusion. All men look alike,

Neander's principal claim for the English, however, is that their imitation of nature is *lively* and therefore better fitted to "beget concernment in us" (I, 60) than the relatively "cold" French manner. But Neander agrees with Lisideius on the object of serious drama (to rouse admiration, compassion, and concernment in the audience) and in the proper subject for imitation: "The soul of poesy . . . is imitation of humour and passions" (I, 56).

(3) In the final debate Crites challenges Lisideius and Neander on the use of rime, holding that it renders the author's imitation of nature unnatural. This discussion is often skimmed over, for in and of itself rime is not an issue which enthralls us. Actually, half hidden in this wrangle over the suitability and utility of rime in plays is the more basic issue of literal versus heightened representation. I have already quoted Crites' objections and Neander's reply that rime helps "exalt" a serious play "above the level of common converse." The details are not important. What matters is Neander's conclusion: "A play, as I have said, to be like nature, is to be set above it" (I, 88).[16]

---

whether prince or actor, but very seldom does a feigned blow *appear* real. Neander's point on fighting seems to be a pragmatic allowance on Dryden's part, for as Neander is made to say just before this, "custom has so insinuated itself into our countrymen . . . [that] they will scarcely suffer combats and other objects of horror to be taken from them" (I, 62).

16. Although I owe Dean T. Mace an obvious debt for suggesting this general line of approach to *Of Dramatic Poesy*, I am not altogether in agreement with many of his specific interpretations. Basically, I feel that he overemphasizes the connection of Neander's principle of "variety" to literal representation (p. 107); that in general he does not realize how much of Lisideius' position is actually absorbed into Neander's; and that he exaggerates in saying that Lisideius "offers a dramatic structure unlimited by the

We have all become accustomed to the idea that one of the main objects in *Of Dramatic Poesy* was to put down the French, but whatever Dryden's opinion of the relative merits of contemporary French and English drama, French ideas are both stronger and more pervasive in the essay than has generally been supposed. In both the definition and in Neander's speeches Dryden follows the French stress on passions at the expense of action. In the "Defence of *An Essay*" Dryden is pushed into admitting more explicitly the antinaturalistic nature of his views; grudgingly he admits that he calls rime "natural" not because it is "nearest the nature of that it represents" (which it obviously is not), but because he considers it most fitted to the nature of "a serious subject" (I, 113). And on the issue of dramatic illusion he is driven to grant that he is relying on "the imagination of the audience, aided by the words of the poet, and painted scenes" to compensate for infractions against the unities (I, 125).

The true import of the *Essay* and its "Defence," if I understand them rightly, is essentially that Dryden was pulling away from a literal concept of the representation of nature in drama and moving toward a more imaginative and antirealistic one. Not only was a selection to be made to increase the impact of what was "imitated," but the elements selected were to be worked up, "wrought up to an higher pitch" in order to affect the audience more strongly. And since, obviously, this could not be done visually, the visual aspect of drama is downgraded in favor of the verbal.

----

necessity of conforming to anything but an inward and hidden psychological truth" (p. 110)—this ignores the import of Lisideius' genuine concern for the unities.

By no means was imitation a cut-and-dried matter in the Restoration, and early in Dryden's career we can see a strong inclination toward nonliteral representation which was to be considerably modified by a decade's practical experience in the theater. According to the theory largely shared by Neander and Lisideius, literature consists of heightened imitation, not so much of actions (which are hard to inflate) as of the passions and humours which constitute human nature. The dramatic practice implicitly recommended in *Of Dramatic Poesy* is that which Dryden was to explore during the next few years in his rimed "heroic" plays. These are probably best epitomized by the two parts of *The Conquest of Granada* (1670–1671), in which there is no pretense of factual realism. Fantastic exploits, exalted sentiment, and grandiosely ideal characters are the order of the day, and the action is so preposterous that no question of literal dramatic illusion really arises.

In his essay "Of Heroic Plays" (1672), prefixed to *The Conquest of Granada*, Dryden permits himself to express bluntly the antinaturalistic assumptions which governed his work.

And if any man object the improbabilities of a spirit appearing or of a palace raised by magic, I boldly answer him that an heroic poet is not tied to a bare representation of what is true, or exceeding probable: but that he may let himself loose to visionary objects, and to the representation of such things as depending not on sense, and therefore not to be comprehended by knowledge, may give him a freer scope for imagination. 'Tis enough that in all ages and religions the greatest part of mankind have believed the power of magic, and that there are spirits or spectres which have appeared. This, I say, is foundation enough for poetry [I, 161].

Dryden's purpose is to present "the highest pattern of human life"; he believes, evidently, that the audience will be both pleased and instructed if allowed to identify with a "perfect pattern of heroic virtue" (I, 162–163). Dryden defends his hero Almanzor by saying that though some of the actions he performs are improbable, none is impossible; more important, the imitation of his *nature* is psychologically accurate, for he is not divested of "human passions and frailties" (I, 163–166). This is the sort of accuracy in imitation which concerns Dryden.

The essential weakness of these plays as drama, though, is undeniable. The difficulty seems to lie in what can only be called Dryden's failure to reconcile his aims with the nature of dramatic illusion. As in *Of Dramatic Poesy*, he says that one advantage of the drama over the epic (his stated model) is that "it represents to view what the poem only does relate" (I, 162).[17] But the nature of what he is trying to imitate makes it hard to represent visually at all. The problem is compounded by Dryden's stated desire

to raise the imagination of the audience, and to persuade them, for the time, that what they behold on the theatre is really performed. The poet is, then, to endeavour an absolute dominion over the minds of the spectators; for, though our fancy will contribute to its own deceit, yet a writer ought to help its operation [I, 162].

17. Dryden quotes Horace on this point: *segnius irritant animum demissa per aures, quam quae sunt oculis subjecta fidelibus* ("what enters through the ears stirs the soul less than what is submitted to the trusty eyes") (I, 162). This opinion is common in the period—Addison propounds it in his *Spectator* papers on Imagination, for example.

He seems to aim at the impossible: no audience believes that what it sees is actually happening, or tries to think so, and certainly the emphasis Dryden places on passions at the expense of realistic action undermines any illusion of actuality. The truth is that he was seriously confused on this point. Despite his determination to rise above literal imitation, he was worried enough about the representation carrying conviction to hope (rather improbably) that it could be accepted as real.

For all his debate about *what* should be represented, Dryden had devoted little thought to the actual process by which the imitation was to affect the audience. In *Of Dramatic Poesy* the issue is skirted; the speakers argue mostly about what can be represented successfully, Crites demanding *vraisemblance* for actions, Lisideius and Neander opting for passions. In "Of Heroic Plays" Dryden seems to assume that some kind of imaginative empathy will make the audience respond to the ideal "patterns" he presents. As becomes clear in the "Heads of an Answer to Rymer," he really has little idea of how audience response works, and simply assumes that the writer should "raise passions as high" as possible in the spectators (I, 215). And as far as one can judge, he supposes that the audience would share whatever passions were imitated by the actor. Of course the most cursory reflection reveals the naïveté of Dryden's view of audience response—a view which he modified only at the very end of the 1670s when the bulk of his playwriting was behind him. What is surprising is not that he gradually modified his position but that it took him so long to do so.

The principal products that follow from the theory of heightened imitation expressed in *Of Dramatic Poesy* are the heroic plays—*The Indian Queen* (1664),[18] *The Indian Emperor* (1665), *Tyrannic Love* (1669), and *The Conquest of Granada* (1670–1671). But despite Neander's willingness to differentiate between the demands of serious and comic plays (I, 86–87), the theory has a strong effect on Dryden's comedies in this period as well.[19] This influence appears clearly in the Preface to *An Evening's Love* (1671), where Dryden speaks of his "disgust of low comedy" (I, 145). He grudgingly approves Jonson's "natural imitation of folly" (I, 148), but cannot really like a representation of such a subject. Dryden does grant that comedy is to imitate "the frailties of human nature" in order to make the audience laugh and reject them (I, 152), but we may suspect that he would have been in sympathy with the exemplary "sentimental" comedy of the eighteenth century. What Dryden really does like in comedies is the wit and courtliness of well-born characters (he is vehement about his detestation of farce), and he mentions with approval Restoration writers "refining the courtship, raillery, and conversation of plays" (I, 145).

The influence of heightened imitation was pervasive in these years, and Dryden's outlook changed only gradually. *Aureng-Zebe* (1675) clearly marks a point of transition.[20]

18. *The Indian Queen* is actually a collaboration with Howard—an amusing point in light of their later quarrel about the use of rime in drama.

19. For a sensible and useful account of Dyden's comedy and comic theory in this period see Frank Harper Moore, *The Nobler Pleasure: Dryden's Comedy in Theory and Practice* (Chapel Hill, 1963), chaps. 1–5. Moore's book is vastly better than Margaret Sherwood's monograph, *Dryden's Dramatic Theory and Practice* (Boston, 1898).

20. See Arthur C. Kirsch, "The Significance of Dryden's *Aureng-Zebe*," *ELH*, 29 (1962), 160–174.

Of his rimed heroic dramas it is the least extravagant; rant and superhuman exploits are greatly diminished, and human relations are put on a more ordinary plane. But Dryden grumbles in his dedication that he feels "condemned to rhyme," and he states outright in the Prologue that the author "grows weary of his long-loved mistress, Rhyme" (I, 190, 192). We see here concomitant disgust with the extravagances of heightened imitation and the rime which Dryden had considered proper to it.

Not for a moment do I suggest that Dryden was in the process of flitting from the principles of Neander to those of Crites. Rather, he is embracing more of a mingle than he had done heretofore. Half a dozen years later, having abandoned heroic plays altogether, he was to say "I remember some verses of my own Maximin and Almanzor which cry vengeance upon me for their extravagance, and which I wish heartily in the same fire with Statius and Chapman" (Dedication of *The Spanish Friar*, I, 276). But Dryden did qualify this condemnation: "Neither do I discommend the lofty style in tragedy, which is naturally pompous and magnificent; but nothing is truly sublime that is not *just* and *proper*" (I, 277; italics added). By 1681 he had learned to avoid "abominable fustian" in seeking grand effects.

By concentrating on Dryden's concept of what constituted effective imitation, I am trying to get at a major problem: Dryden's views on literature were shifting in the later 1670s; the cause and nature of the change, however, have never been entirely clear. Some critics have assumed that Dryden was greatly affected by Rymer's *The Tragedies of the Last Age*.[21] That he was impressed and in-

21. For example, George Watson says in his headnote to the "Apology for Heroic Poetry" (written 1674–1677) that the in-

fluenced I have no doubt, but already by the time of *Aureng-Zebe* Dryden was moving in the direction of a more literal representation of nature, a development which undoubtedly made him more receptive to Rymer's literalistic position. To suppose that Dryden abandoned heroic plays because they were theatrically unsuccessful would be a serious mistake. On the contrary, reference to *The London Stage* shows that they were well liked, received critical acclaim, and continued to be staged long after the success of *The Rehearsal* (1671). Nor is such unnaturalistic drama necessarily a contradiction in terms. Racine's plays were flourishing around this time, despite their adherence to neoclassical restrictions, and an "artificial" tradition had long flourished in England. Shakespeare is most emphatically not a naturalistic dramatist. Dryden's dissatisfaction with the heroic play, as far as I can judge, was largely the result of his realization that spectacle tended more to inhibit the "heroic" than to add to it. At a certain point, the sight of a man waving a sword seriously interferes with our believing in the greatness of the character he represents. Further, two practical considerations weighed on Dryden: the increasing emphasis on staging and scenery— a major factor in the success of these dramas—introduced a distracting naturalism; the exaggeration of the heroic mode by other writers (particularly Settle) was making it ridiculous—"a Rapsody of non-sence," as Dryden wrote disgustedly in the Preface to *Notes and Observations on The Empress of Morocco* (1674).

Comparison of the essay on "Heroic Plays" (1672) with

---

fluence of Longinus "might have led Dryden into a freer and more adventurous poetic . . . had not Rymer's *Tragedies of the Last Age* (1678) [*sic*] recalled him to defend neo-classical positions" (I, 195).

the "Apology for Heroic Poetry" prefaced to *The State of Innocence* is instructive.[22] By the time he wrote the latter, Dryden is exhibiting concern about some of the issues on which earlier he had pronounced confidently. Rant has been challenged: Dryden replies "Are *all* the flights of heroic poetry to be concluded bombast, unnatural, and mere madness . . . ?" (I, 199; italics added). He adopts Longinus as a respectable classic authority for what he has learned to call sublimity in heightened imitation. Dryden retains his basic view of the function of imitation.

Imaging is, in itself, the very height and life of poetry. It is, as Longinus describes it, a discourse which, by a kind of enthusiasm, or extraordinary emotion of the soul, makes it seem to us that we behold those things which the poet paints, so as to be pleased with them, and to admire them [I, 203].

Nonetheless, his once confident assertion of the propriety of the supernatural (cf. I, 161) is by now considerably qualified:

If poetry be imitation, that part of it must needs be best which describes most lively our actions and passions, our virtues and our vices, our follies and humours: for neither is comedy without its part of imaging; and they who do it best are certainly the most excellent in their kind. This is too plainly proved to be denied. But how are poetical fictions, how are hippocentaurs and chimeras, or how are angels and immaterial sub-

22. Unluckily we cannot be sure just when this essay was written. It was published at the beginning of 1677 (before Rymer's book had appeared) and must have been written after publication of Boileau's translation of Longinus (1674). The actual adaptation from *Paradise Lost* was evidently done in late 1673. See Charles E. Ward, *The Life of John Dryden* (Chapel Hill, 1961), pp. 104–105.

stances to be imaged; which, some of them, are things quite out of nature; others, such whereof we can have no notion? . . . The answer is easy to the first part of it. The fiction of some beings which are not in nature . . . has been founded on the conjunction of two natures which have a real separate being. So hippocentaurs were imagined by joining the natures of a man and horse together. . . . And poets may be allowed the like liberty for describing things which really exist not, if they are founded on popular belief. Of this nature are fairies, pigmies, and the extraordinary effects of magic; for 'tis still an imitation, though of other men's fancies [I, 203–204].

Dryden was never altogether to abandon this position—angels were to play a part in the Christian machinery of the hypothetical epic he outlined in the "Discourse on Satire" of 1693. But his confidence in heightened representation is plainly shaken. One evidence of this is the attention paid to style in the "Apology for Heroic Poetry"; Dryden is finally turning to specifically verbal means of rousing his audience instead of relying on representation. Though the "Apology" is prefixed to a play, it was an unperformed play, perhaps not altogether a coincidence. Dryden's objectives remain much the same, but in emphasizing language he tends to move out of drama altogether—hence his discussion here of heroic *poetry*.

Much of the essay is devoted to a defense of "hard" metaphor and hyperbole as effective agents in arousing imaginative response. Yet Dryden is by no means returning to the metaphysical extravagance of his youth. More than ever before, he is concerned with the suitability of description to subject.

From that which has been said, it may be collected that the definition of wit (which has been so often attempted, and ever unsuccessfully by many poets) is only this: that it is a propriety of thoughts and words; or, in other terms, thoughts and words elegantly adapted to the subject [I, 207].

Dryden concludes his "Apology for Heroic Poetry" with a final protest against the strictures of "those who pretend [i.e., claim or undertake] to reform our poetry" by denouncing "figurative expressions." Indeed, the whole essay is really a defense of raised or sublime *language*, and in this respect the work shows a marked change from the confident claims for imaginative *representation* made in "Of Heroic Plays" some two to four years earlier.

The "Heads of an Answer to Rymer" (1677) is interesting in this context because it touches on some of the issues in *Of Dramatic Poesy*. Rymer's demands for realistic representation are in the same tradition as Crites', but Dryden's responses, though not greatly dissimilar from those of Lisideius and Neander, have changed somewhat. Much of his reply is still based on a de-emphasis of plot and action in favor of the passions, particularly love—a pattern with which we are thoroughly familiar by now. The relative caution of the "Apology for Heroic Poetry" appears clearly, however, in the seriousness with which Dryden takes Rymer's charges and in his final emphasis on the affective power of *dictio* (I, 219–220). Nowhere in the "Heads" does he make claims for "nature wrought up to an higher pitch"—the power is now explicitly supposed to reside in the imitation, not in the raised nature of what is represented.

The extent of the change in Dryden's outlook is apparent when *All for Love* (first performed in December 1677) is compared with the heroic tragedies which preceded it. It is unrimed, for a start ("I have disencumbered myself from rhyme"). For another thing, it is genuinely a tragedy, and Antony is not allowed to be "a character of perfect virtue." No longer is Dryden holding up a pattern of perfection for emulation. His increased concern for literal representation is reflected not only in the abandonment of rime but in his holding to all three unities, "more exactly . . . than, perhaps, the English theatre requires" he hastens to add. This trend toward regularity is apparent also in Dryden's adaptations: compare the imaginative romancing of the Dryden-Davenant *Tempest* (1668) with the Dryden-Lee *Oedipus* (1678) or Dryden's radically regularized *Troilus and Cressida* of the following year. In the Preface to the latter he appears as obsessed with unity of place ("a due proportion of time allowed for every motion") as ever Crites was (I, 240–241).

"The Grounds of Criticism in Tragedy" (1679), a short treatise attached to the Preface to *Troilus and Cressida*, is a critical expression of the changes we have just observed. The definition of tragedy with which Dryden starts, explicitly adapted from Aristotle, is radically different from Lisideius' definition of a play. " 'Tis an imitation of one entire, great, and probable *action;* not told, but represented; which, by moving in us fear and pity, is conducive to the purging of those two passions in our minds. More largely thus, tragedy describes or paints an action" (I, 243; italics added). Note the emphasis on action and representation. Just as important, Dryden has adopted purgation as the object of tragedy, a notable advance over his assumption only two years earlier that it should simply stir the audience as much as possible. Similarly his views on the probability of the action have changed.

The last quality of the action is that it ought to be probable, as well as admirable and great. 'Tis not necessary that there should be historical truth in it; but always necessary that there should be a likeness of truth, something that is more than barely possible, *probable* being that which succeeds or happens oftener than it misses. To invent therefore a probability, and to make it wonderful, is the most difficult undertaking in the art of poetry; for that which is not wonderful is not great; and *that which is not probable will not delight a reasonable audience* [italics added]. This action, thus described, must be represented and not told, to distinguish dramatic poetry from epic [I, 245].

No longer is Dryden quite so bent on conflating tragedy and epic (cf. I, 87–88), and he no longer approves the improbable-possibles that he had once defended in Almanzor (cf. I, 165–166). Another change is a clear distinction between the emotions acted out and those which are to be raised in the audience.

Under this general head of manners, the passions are naturally included as belonging to the characters. I speak not of pity and of terror, which are to be moved in the audience by the plot; but of anger, hatred, love, ambition, jealousy, revenge, etc., as they are shown in this or that person of the play [I, 253].

Dryden's new concern for *appropriate* language and passion is spelled out at great length.

To describe these [the passions] naturally, and to move them [Watson's text reads "then": I have followed Ker] artfully, is one of the greatest commendations which can be given to a poet. . . . A poet must be born with this quality; yet, unless he help himself by an acquired knowledge of the passions, what they are in their own nature, and by what springs they are to be moved, he will be subject either to raise them where they ought not to be raised, or not to raise them by the just degrees of nature, or to amplify them beyond the natural bounds, or not to observe the crisis and turns of them, in their cooling and decay: all which errors proceed from want of judgment in the poet, and from being unskilled in the principles of moral philosophy. Nothing is more frequent in a fanciful writer than to foil himself by not managing his strength, therefore, as in a wrestler, there is first required some measure of force, a well-knit body, and active limbs, without which all instruction would be vain; yet, these being granted, if he want the skill which is necessary to a wrestler, he shall make but small advantage of his natural robustuousness: so, in a poet, his inborn vehemence and force of spirit will only run him out of breath the sooner, if it be not supported by the help of art. The roar of passion, indeed, may please an audience, three parts of which are ignorant enough to think all is moving which is noise, and it may stretch the lungs of an ambitious actor, who will die upon the spot for a thundering clap; but it will move no other passion than indignation and contempt from judicious men. Longinus, whom I have hitherto followed, continues thus: *If the passions be artfully employed, the discourse becomes vehement and lofty: if otherwise, there is nothing more ridiculous than a great passion out of season* [I, 253–254].

If we consider Dryden's position in "The Grounds of Criticism in Tragedy" in light of the various claims in *Of Dramatic Poesy*, we find that while he has not altogether abandoned Neander's "variety," and imitation of passions retains great importance, a much larger part of his attention is now devoted to producing "a *reasonable* and *judicious* poem" (I, 261; italics added). This concern reappears the next year in the Preface to *Ovid's Epistles:*

If the imitation of nature be the business of a poet, I know no author who can justly be compared with ours, especially in the description of the passions. . . . Yet, not to speak too

[215]

partially in his behalf, I will confess that the copiousness of his wit was such that he often writ too pointedly for his subject, and made his persons speak more eloquently than the violence of their passion would admit: so that he is frequently witty out of season; leaving the imitation of nature, and the cooler dictates of his judgment, for the false applause of fancy [I, 265].

And in 1681, in the Dedication to *The Spanish Friar,* after commenting that "nothing is truly sublime that is not just and proper," Dryden concludes that "in the heightenings of poetry, the strength and vehemence of figures should be suited to the occasion, the subject, and the persons. All beyond this is monstrous: 'tis out of nature, 'tis an excrescence, and not a living part of poetry" (I, 278). We are by now a long way from the transports of heroic drama.

This section has been devoted to tracing briefly the changes in Dryden's literary theory from the principles set forth in *Of Dramatic Poesy* to the drastically modified position sketched out in "The Grounds of Criticism in Tragedy" about a dozen years later. I have gone into so much detail to make clear beyond question that Dryden's literary principles are more than a collection of unvarying clichés, and to emphasize both that Dryden's particular judgments do change, and that they evolve in a logical way. Many critics have thrown up their hands over his opinions on rime, concluding only that his arguments are too inconsistent to be worth serious attention. What they have failed to see is that Dryden's shift on this issue makes perfect sense if it is regarded as a function of the change in his views on imitation in drama. Similarly, I have tried to exonerate him from the charge that he was excessively influenced by Rymer by demonstrating that Rymer's example merely reinforced a trend already well developed in Dryden.

III

Imitation, let me say once again, is Dryden's critical keystone, and in considering his supposed inconsistency I have been at pains to explore the changes in his views on imitation in drama, in order to show that these changes reflect concessions to the exigencies of dramatic form, not a complete reversal of his literary theory. This seems obvious only in retrospect: since practically all of his early criticism is on drama, major alterations seem more fundamental than they really are. We can get a better sense of perspective by examining Dryden's transfer to epic of the essentials of the theory which he had foisted on drama.[23]

The changes in Dryden's outlook, as I understand them,

23. Dryden did write several more plays (the last was *Love Triumphant*, 1694), but he broke no new ground in them, and for the most part his indifference is plain. The few plays of the early 1690s were evidently written purely out of financial need, and their dispirited air lends credence to Dryden's claim that he returned to the drama "against his will" (Preface to *Don Sebastian*, II, 44). This preface displays a theory very little changed—concern for poetic justice, uniformity of design, decorum of parts, and the unities. It is true that the play is not utterly regular, but Dryden is careful to justify his few "broken" scenes and the use of two days instead of one. Basically though, he has lost interest in the drama. During the 1680s there are obvious political reasons for his preoccupation, but the essential cause of change is apparently just his indifference to more literal representation. Dryden had come to realize that it was necessary, and even to accept purgation as the object of tragedy, but by the late 1670s he no longer has the kind of enthusiasm which he had once displayed for heroic drama.

make the explanation of this transfer quite simple. His theory of dramatic representation had grown vastly more realistic (and concomitantly he had become more careful about the propriety of imitation in general), but nonetheless, his desire to imitate the "idea of perfect nature" (II, 183) remained unchanged, and he saw the possibility of doing this in epic form, where the effect would not be undercut by the realities of staging. When we examine the essays of the 1690s, we find that Dryden is still advocating heightened imitation of nature in order to present the reader with an ideal with which he may identify.

The idea of epic starts to assume importance for Dryden during the 1670s when tragedy was proving an unsatisfactory vehicle for ideal imitation. By the time of the Dedication of *Aureng-Zebe* (1676) we find Dryden hoping that he "may make the world some part of amends for many ill plays by an heroic poem" (I, 191). That he continued to see a close connection between tragedy and epic is made plain in his comparative discussions of them in the 1690s. But by that time he had changed his mind about the utility of visual representation.

Many things which not only please, but are real beauties in the reading, would appear absurd upon the stage; and those not only the *speciosa miracula,* as Horace calls them, of transformations, of Scylla, Antiphates, and the Laestrygons, which cannot be represented even in operas; but the prowess of Achilles or Aeneas would appear ridiculous in our dwarf heroes of the theatre. We can believe they routed armies in Homer or in Virgil; but *ne Hercules contra duos* in the drama. I forbear to instance in many things which the stage cannot, or ought not to represent [Dedication of the *Aeneis,* II, 230].

Dryden now sets this advantage of freedom above the extra impact which, he admits, tragedy undeniably gains from actual representation (II, 229)—and certainly he is happy to see the author freed from the restrictions of dramatic representation, as he says at length.

The essential appeal of the epic form for Dryden, though, lies in the opportunity it affords for ideal imitation.

A heroic poem, truly such, is undoubtedly the greatest work which the soul of man is capable to perform. *The design of it is to form the mind to heroic virtue by example;* 'tis conveyed in verse, that it may delight while it instructs. . . . Even the least portions . . . must be of the epic kind: all things must be grave, majestical, and sublime [II, 223–224; italics added].

Here we have once again Dryden's theory of empathetic response to an ideal which is presented in rime for extra effect. To dismiss his demands that literature provide instruction because we find them platitudinous is a serious mistake, for he really believed in them. In the Dedication of the *Aeneis* he discusses at length the religious and social utility of the epics of Homer and Virgil. Unfortunately Watson omits almost all of this material: the casual reader may not realize that for Dryden the great virtue of these works is that they display ideal patterns for emulation. He had claimed this moral purpose as an aim of his own as far back as the Preface to *Tyrannic Love* (1670).

I considered that pleasure was not the only end of poesy; and that even the instructions of morality were not so wholly the business of the poet as that the precepts and examples of piety were to be omitted. . . . Yet far be it from me to compare the use of dramatic poesy with that of divinity: I only maintain, against the enemies of the stage, that patterns of piety, decently represented and equally removed from the extremes of superstition and profaneness, may be of excellent use to second the precepts of our religion. By the harmony of words we elevate the mind to a sense of devotion, as our solemn music, which is inarticulate poesy, does in churches; and by the lively images of piety, adorned by action, through the senses allure the soul; which while it is charmed in a silent joy of what it sees and hears, is struck at the same time with a secret veneration of things celestial, and is wound up insensibly into the practice of that which it admires [I, 138–139].

Allowing for the change in form, this view is very much Dryden's theory in the 1690s.

The most explicit expression of his later preference for epic appears in "A Parallel of Poetry and Painting" (1695), where he discusses the imperfect nature which must be imitated in drama. Introducing his translation of du Fresnoy's *De arte graphica*, Dryden says:

The business of his preface is to prove that a learned painter should form to himself an idea of perfect nature. This image he is to set before his mind in all his undertakings, and to draw from thence, as from a storehouse, the beauties which are to enter into his work; thereby correcting nature from what actually she is in individuals, to what she ought to be, and what she was created. Now as this idea of perfection is of little use in portraits (or the resemblances of particular persons), so neither is it in the characters of comedy and tragedy, which are never to be made perfect. . . . The perfection of such stage-characters consists chiefly in their likeness to the deficient faulty nature, which is their original. . . . That I may return to the beginning of this remark concerning perfect ideas, I have only this to say that the parallel is often true in epic poetry. The heroes of the poets are to be drawn according to this rule. There is scarce a frailty to be left in the best of them; any more than is to be found in a divine nature [II, 183–185].

We may guess that when Dryden came to realize that the characters in drama must be flawed, the form lost much of its appeal for him, since from very early he believed that the best way of affecting an audience is to present an ideal with which it may identify. He can praise *The Plain Dealer* as "one of the most bold, most general, and most useful satires which has ever been presented on the English theatre," but his preference for edification by positive example is made plain ("Apology for Heroic Poetry," I, 199).

Dryden's clearest explanation of the process by which he thinks imitation affects the audience is to be found in "A Parallel of Poetry and Painting." He grants that whatever "comes nearest to the resemblance of nature is the best," but insists that since "truth is the object of our understanding," only that imitation will please which accurately reflects a worthy object—and hence no matter how skillfully represented, dead cats and garbage cans are not allowed.

As truth is the end of all our speculations, so the discovery of it is the pleasure . . . lively imitation of it, either in poetry or painting, must of necessity produce a much greater. For both these arts, as I said before, are not only true imitations of nature, but of the best nature, of that which is wrought up to a nobler pitch. They present us with images more perfect than the life in any individual; and we have the pleasure to see all the scattered beauties of nature united by a happy chemistry, without its deformities or faults. They are imitations of the passions which always move, and therefore consequently please; for without motion there can be no delight [a Hobbesian notion], which cannot be considered but as an active passion. When we view these elevated ideas of nature, the result of that view is admiration, which is always the cause of pleasure [II, 194].

Knowing his tendency to avoid abstractions we should not feel surprised that Dryden promptly adds: "This foregoing remark, which gives the reason why imitation pleases, was sent me by Mr Walter Moyle, a most ingenious young gentleman." Nonetheless, he has adopted the point and made it his own. Certainly Moyle's explanation is consistent with Dryden's belief that if the poet presents "what 'is most beautiful in nature'" (II, 193) the desired effect will be achieved.

When we survey the development of Dryden's views on imitation (the foundation of his critical theory and practice), we find that they are far more stable than they appear at first glance. The inconsistencies in his use of terms found by Mary Thale appear less the product of Machiavellian critical deceit than the result of conflict and confusion in his own mind about the nature of imitation in effective drama. But even the changes of the 1670s do not alter Dryden's basic convictions about the nature and function of literature, as his views on epic show.

In light of this stability of premise, we may well enquire which of Dryden's critical principles actually do change. On a number of basic points he is quite consistent —chief among them uniformitarianism, belief in refinement and progress, and a combination of a general classical orientation with a stubborn respect for English tradition. Most prominent of all, of course, is his love of ideal nature and the sublime, which tie into his empathetic theory of literary response. The one major point on which Dryden does change his mind we have already investigated—imitation *in drama*. During the 1670s he was gradually forced to the realization that ideal imitation is incompatible with stage performance, and consequently he moves toward a more Aristotelian, less antinaturalistic theory. When ideal imitation reappears in his theory of epic it has suffered little change, though he had learned to restrain the imaginative extravagance which characterizes the heroic plays.

And whereas poems which are produced by the vigour of imagination only have a gloss upon them at the first which time wears off, the works of judgment are like the diamond; the more they are polished, the more lustre they receive. Such is the difference betwixt Virgil's *Aeneis* and Marini's *Adone* [Dedication of the *Aeneis*, II, 244].

As early as the Dedication of *The Rival Ladies* (1664) Dryden does speak of imagination submitting images for the approval of judgment (I, 2), but in the later 1660s he adopts a much freer concept of imaginative creation (e.g., I, 98), and only in the mid-1670s does he begin to worry about the extravagance of his creations. Perhaps unbounded faith in imagination is a young man's position, while later on judgment and reason are balanced against it—certainly this pattern of development is shared by Dryden and Blake. The overall result is that even when Dryden is freed of the restrictions of the stage, he is a little more cautious; his obsession with the heroic remains, but it appears as much in style as in imaginative antinaturalism.[24]

24. Dryden's preoccupation with heroic style is apparent by the time of the "Apology for Heroic Poetry," where it has already become the mainstay of the presentation of the ideal. Indeed, Dryden likes to use the elevated style even when he is not working in the heroic mode: his preference for "high burlesque" satire

One of the few marked changes that appears in Dryden's criticism is the increase in his concern with morality. A belief in the moral and educational function of literature goes back to the beginning of his career (it is certainly prominent in the Preface to *Tyrannic Love*, quoted above), but early in his career he did write some rather smutty comedies. By the end of his life he had decided not to make this sort of concession to popular taste. In the Preface to *Fables* he announces his refusal to include any of Chaucer's *fabliaux* and adds, rather primly, "I have written nothing which savours of immortality or profaneness. . . . I wish I could affirm, with a safe conscience, that I had taken the same care in all my former writings" (II, 273–274). At the end of the essay he does object to Jeremy Collier's distortions,[25] but he admits that "in many things he has taxed me justly," and rather like Chaucer, frankly repents and retracts them (II, 293–294). This reversal is the culmination of a long process. Actually, by the end of the 1670s Dryden had become much more concerned with propriety than he had been at the beginning of the decade.[26] In the troubled period of the 1680s, however, his

------

(in which the style elevates the subject) is very marked. For his dislike of "low" satire, see the "Discourse on Satire," II, 147. For a brief analysis of his use of heroic style in satire see H. T. Swedenberg, Jr., "Dryden's Obsessive Concern with the Heroic," in *Essays in English Literature of the Classical Period Presented to Dougald MacMillan*, ed. Daniel W. Patterson and Albrecht B. Strauss, Studies in Philology, extra series, 4 (Chapel Hill, 1967), pp. 12–26.

25. In *A Short View of the Immorality and Profaneness of the English Stage* (1698).

26. For example, he says in the Preface to *All for Love* (1678): "Some actions, though natural, are not fit to be represented; and broad obscenities in words ought in good manners to be avoided:

interest in social and moral matters really deepens. This deepening is not apparent in the few critical essays of the period, but is implicit in the satires and political writings on which he was engaged; during a time when the establishment of which he was a part was being challenged and overthrown his views quite naturally shift and deepen. The conversion to Catholicism is plainly part of the same process and presumably reinforced Dryden's already strongly moral outlook. Given his consistent belief that literature should instruct as well as please, preferably by good example, morality can fittingly become one of his major critical principles. I have had relatively little to say about this development, partly because Dryden tends not to concentrate on it himself. The change appears principally in his demands for poetic justice [27] and in occasional objections to the "immoral, low, or filthy." [28]

If my account of Dryden's principles and opinions is at all accurate, we may well enquire where his reputation for blithe inconsistency came from. I find two sources—one general and one particular. The occasional nature of Dryden's criticism, its studied casualness, and his preoccupation with technical matters of construction tend to obscure the real seriousness of his view of literature and his belief

---

expressions therefore are a modest clothing of our thoughts, as breeches and petticoats are of our bodies" (I, 223).

27. If "the encouragement of virtue and discouragement of vice" are the proper end of tragedy, the poet must show "the rewards of one, and punishments of the other; at least by rendering virtue always amiable, though it be shown unfortunate; and vice detestable, tho' it be shown triumphant" ("Heads of an Answer to Rymer," I, 213).

28. See "A Parallel of Poetry and Painting," II, 187; Preface to *Sylvæ*, II, 27–28.

in its essentially moral function. Amid the welter of details and particularities critics lose sight of substantive issues, and so apparent contradictions in details have loomed large. But the reason that they were not long ago explained is specific and rather sobering: early disparagement of Dryden's character has to this day affected appraisals of his work. The charge of inconsistency (often coupled with the claim that his work falls into several discrete periods) is, I suspect, largely a corollary and remnant of nineteenth-century disapproval of Dryden's conversions—from Cromwell to Charles and from Anglican to Catholic. The reputation for instability (or worse) that this gave him was carried over from biography and lies behind the assumption that he was too open to influence and quite ready to adapt himself as self-interest demanded.[29]

The view of Dryden as a critic which this perspective yielded remains subtly influential. The "periods" construct was given its clearest expression (at monograph length) by Wm. E. Bohn, who honestly admitted that the criticism "refuses to arrange itself under any simple principle of development."[30] Nonetheless, Bohn went ahead to establish five periods in Dryden's career, drawing heavily on biographical information which now seems seriously dated. First, to 1666: Dryden is feeling his way, "appreciating" a variety of approaches to literature, including the

29. Early critics do not seem to have wondered why Dryden remained so stubbornly Catholic during the 1690s when his reconversion (which was urged on him by friends) would have been welcomed and rewarded. Only post-Bredvold has his Catholicism been fully accepted by critics, and even now some of the odium of earlier condemnations still clings to him.

30. Wm. E. Bohn, "The Development of John Dryden's Literary Criticism," *PMLA*, 22 (1907), 58.

Elizabethan. Second, to 1675: as a court favorite he is influenced by fad and neoclassicism, and so turns against the Elizabethans. Third, to 1679: allegedly falling out of favor and fashion, Dryden is said to turn against the court, and in the process of rebelling against its standards revives his love of the Elizabethans.[31] Fourth, to 1689: he is recalled to favor to defend the court; critically, this is said to be a "rationalistic" period. Fifth, to 1700: permanently out of favor, Dryden becomes "independent" and returns to the free appreciation of the first and third periods, with the Elizabethans' stock rising again in consequence.

I see a number of serious objections to this interpretation. It leans heavily on extrinsic biographical speculation, and Bohn does not always succeed in establishing its relevance. In addition, owing to the scrappy and occasional nature of Dryden's criticism, we cannot assume that we possess anything like a full and balanced record of his opinions at any time. For the 1680s in particular we have only tantalizing scraps of information, and to postulate any general reading on them is misleading. Only *on drama during the 1670s* do we have enough data to feel confident of knowing what Dryden was thinking and how his views were changing. Consequently I am especially suspicious of Bohn's fourth period: from the evidence from which he deduces rationalism I derive only the observation that Dryden's concept of imitation in drama had become more literal. To take up a more specific point, I would say that Bohn's whole second period is postulated on a misread-

31. Bohn calls "The Grounds of Criticism in Tragedy" "transitional" since Dryden does support the Elizabethans (period three) but also exhibits Rymer's influence in stressing "rationalism" (period four).

ing of the "Defence of the Epilogue" (1672). Dryden's criticisms of the Elizabethans there led Bohn (and many others) to assume that he was actively anti-Elizabethan during the heroic drama period. But a careful reading of that essay, as Hoyt Trowbridge has shown, proves that the "Defence" is not anti-Elizabethan at all and represents no downward revaluation of the Elizabethans after *Of Dramatic Poesy*.[32] If these objections are as substantial as I believe them, they pretty well demolish Bohn's second and fourth periods, and with them his theory. The entire allegation of inconsistency rests principally on the idea that Dryden's opinion of Shakespeare varied wildly; but actually we possess no evidence that this was the case,[33] and neither do we have any reason to suppose that it might have been.

All in all, in both opinions and principles Dryden as a critic was vastly less erratic than his reputation suggests. In the explanatory mode his aims change very little. As he states in the "Apology for Heroic Poetry,"

they wholly mistake the nature of criticism who think its business is principally to find fault. Criticism, as it was first instituted by Aristotle, was meant a standard of judging well; the chiefest part of which is to observe those excellencies which should delight a reasonable reader [I, 196–197].

These "excellencies" consist, of course, of skillful imitation of appropriate nature; Dryden judges both the aptness of the imitation and the suitability of the chosen subject. Decorum as a general principle applies to both: the sub-

32. See Hoyt Trowbridge, "Dryden's 'Essay on the Dramatic Poetry of the Last Age'," *PQ*, 22 (1943), 240–250.

33. Bohn just *assumes* that the Elizabethans must have been out of Dryden's favor during the "rationalistic" 1680s.

ject must be moral (or at least yield a negative lesson), and the imitation must be fitting in order to be effective. Dryden never changes his mind on these points. His inconsistencies are almost all the result of a change in his concept of what was appropriate in dramatic representation. I suspect that his ill-fated application of the heroic ideal to drama was the combined result of the economic necessity of writing plays, a predisposition toward the heroic, and an unfortunate desire to outdo the Elizabethans. We should be struck, though, not by Dryden's abandonment of his experiment (which shows that he could learn from experience, even when the lesson went against his grain), but by the astonishing consistency of his assessments of other writers. Throughout his career he venerated the Elizabethans and felt quite clear on their relative strengths and merits—striking testimony to his critical acumen, considering that within this time he was writing some very different sorts of plays himself.

I suspect that one reason for this stability of opinion is Dryden's sturdy belief in the existence of objective critical standards: "If nature be to be imitated, then there is a rule for imitating nature rightly," he says in the "Defence of *An Essay*" (I, 122).[34] Dryden is, as Emerson Marks claims, a critical "absolutist," for as Hoyt Trowbridge shows, he believes in, looks for, and works from what he regards as unchanging standards.[35] Dryden believes that

34. Near the end of his career he makes the same point. Poetry and painting, "as they are arts . . . must have rules, which may direct them to their common end" ("A Parallel of Poetry and Painting," II, 191); "some rules of imitation are necessary to obtain the end; for without rules there can be no art" (II, 194).

35. See Emerson R. Marks, *Relativist and Absolutist: The Early Neoclassical Debate in England* (New Brunswick, 1955), pp. 37–

literature is the product of imitation heightened for effectiveness. This conviction is for Dryden not a tired cliché but a vital principle, and one which left him constantly torn between the desire to raise and exalt, and the demand for accuracy inherent in any mimetic literary theory. In view of his faith in objective standards, his persistent stress on imaginative imitation may seem surprising, since it would seem to allow considerable scope for what Trowbridge calls "individual preference and opinion." Is there a fundamental contradiction in Dryden's theory here? I think not, for his views on individuality in imitation seem analogous to those on local tradition: the foundations must remain unchanged, but the "superstructures" can be developed independently. In this way Dryden can reconcile his firm belief in the unchanging nature and function of literature with a theory of imitation which always allows scope for the writer's individual imagination. Even in the 1690s (when he was very cautious about imaginative imitation) he is able to devote much of his critical attention to the implicit character of the writers he discusses, for he can assume that each man's imitations reflect his way of looking at things. Thus he can maintain clear critical standards while remaining free of the fatal inflexibility which dogged his more literal-minded contemporaries—and in Dryden's persistent affirmation of individuality we can see the key to his success as a critic.

48; Hoyt Trowbridge, "The Place of Rules in Dryden's Criticism," *MP*, 44 (1946), 84–96.

Index

Page numbers set in italic indicate discussions of single essays.

[232]

[235]

Dryden's Criticism

Designed by R. E. Rosenbaum
Composed by Vail-Ballou Press, Inc.,
in 11 pt. Linotype Janson, 3 points leaded,
with display lines in Caslon Openface and Caslon 3371.
Printed letterpress from type by Vail-Ballou Press
on Warren's No. 66 Text, 60 lb. basis,
with the Cornell University Press watermark.
Bound by Vail-Ballou Press
in Holliston Roxite B bookcloth
and stamped in Swift's genuine gold foil.

[236]